THE

PUBLICATIONS

OF THE

Lincoln Record Society

FOUNDED IN THE YEAR

1910

VOLUME 80

ISSN 0267-2634
FOR THE YEAR ENDING 31 August 1989

PROBATE INVENTORIES OF LINCOLN CITIZENS

1661–1714

EDITED BY

J. A. JOHNSTON

The Lincoln Record Society

The Boydell Press

First published 1991

A Lincoln Record Society Publication
Published by The Boydell Press
an imprint of Boydell & Brewer Ltd
PO Box 9, Woodbridge, Suffolk IP12 3DF
and of Boydell & Brewer Inc.
PO Box 41026, Rochester, NY 14604, USA

ISBN 0 901503 53 3

British Library Cataloguing-in-Publication Data
Probate inventories of Lincoln citizens 1661–1714. – (The publications of the Lincoln Record Society founded in the year 1910)
I. Johnston, J. A. II. Series
942.0609425
ISBN 0-901503-53-3

The paper used in this publication meets the minimum requirements of American National Standard for Information Sciences – Permanence of Paper for Printed Library Materials, ANSI Z39.48–1984

Printed and bound in Great Britain by
Woolnough Bookbinding Ltd, Irthlingborough, Northants

PREFACE

My debt to the staff of Lincolnshire Archive Office, both those on the front desk and those in the back rooms, is immense. Help and advice from Lincoln Record Society and Honorary Editor, Mrs. D.M. Owen, has been unstinting. The errors are mine.

J. A. Johnston

CONTENTS

TABLES AND ILLUSTRATIONS

Tables

Plates & Figures

EDITORIAL METHOD

The inventories are printed in chronological order according to the date of appraisal. Each has been given a serial number and reference in the Introduction to a printed inventory is made by this number in heavy type within brackets.

All dates are given in New Style.

Each inventory is headed with the deceased's name, date of appraisal, document reference and parish of residence where this is given. The status or occupation of the deceased is included in this summary but where this information is derived from another source or from the internal evidence of the inventory it is placed within brackets.

The words 'imprimis' and 'item' at the beginning of inventory entries have been omitted as have 'praised at' and 'valued at' as conclusions to an entry. 'Summa totalis' and its variants are also omitted as are sub-totals of valuations by room or page in the text of some inventories.

The original spelling and punctuation are retained throughout but abbreviations have been expanded and converted to modern equivalents. 'ff' has been transcribed as 'F'. In the transcriptions the money values are retained in their original form of pounds sterling, shillings and pence but in the text of the Introduction decimal values are used.

Brackets are used to indicate loss of text, thus (....) and to enclose supplied words. Brackets are also used to indicate the true total at the end of an inventory where this can be calculated and the appraisers' total is faulty.

Specialist vocabulary or obsolete words which occur only once in the collection are defined at the end of the inventory. The Glossary at the end of the volume gives the more commonly used archaic words.

The place of publication of books is London unless otherwise stated.

INTRODUCTION

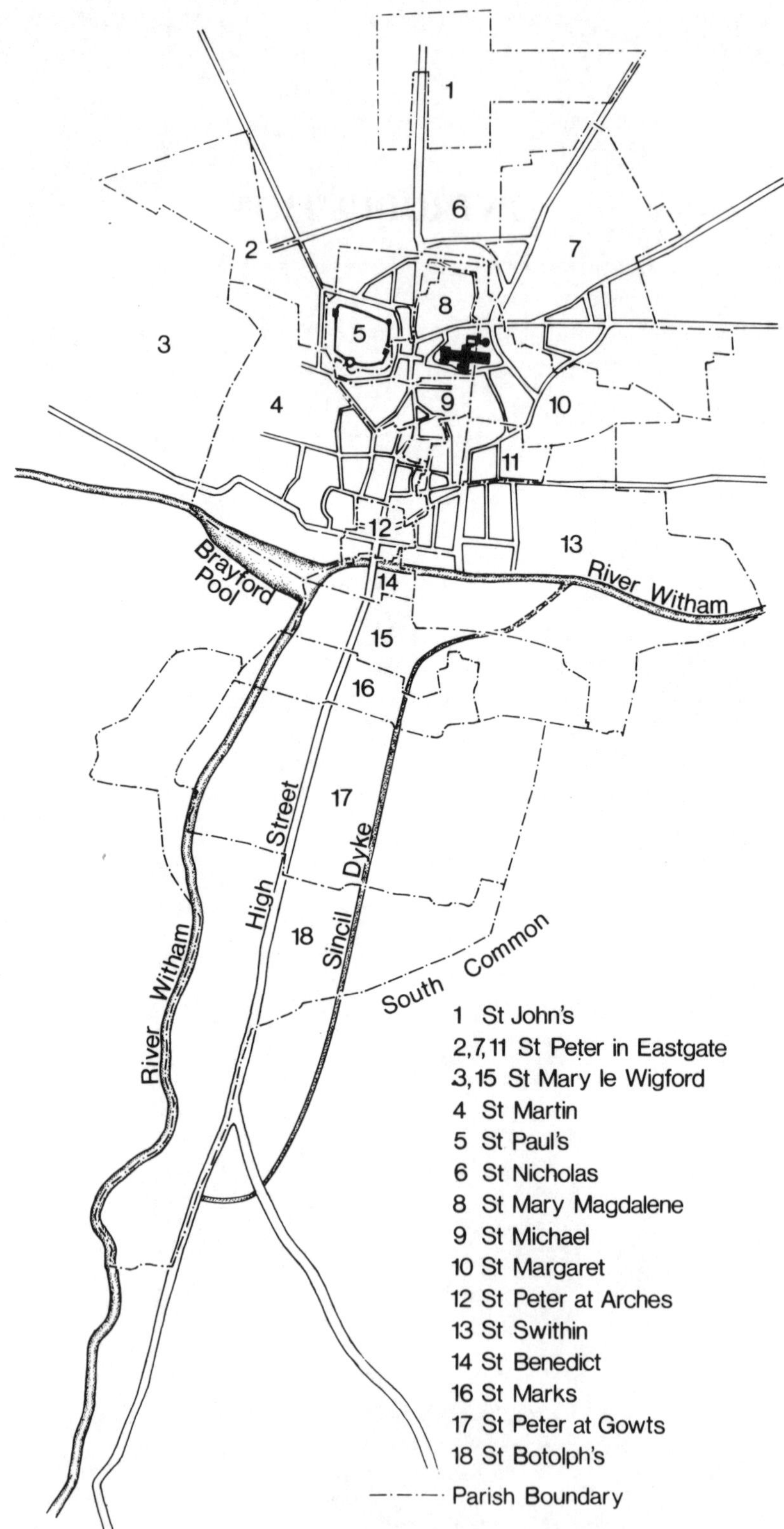

FIGURE I. Parish boundaries of Lincoln 1661

I

The inventories

The sixty inventories printed in this volume have been selected from the 590 that survive for thirteen parishes of the City and County of Lincoln between 1661 and 1714. These parishes were those in which urban occupations and residences rather than agricultural predominated. In the northern and uphill section of the city were the two parishes of St. Paul in the Bail and St. Mary Magdalene. They were within the Roman and medieval walls of the upper city and had the Castle and Cathedral within their boundaries. St. Peter in Eastgate spread beyond the walls to north, west and east. By 1714 this parish and St. Margaret, also to the east, were partly overbuilt by city residences and shops. St. Michael on the Mount was situated immediately to the south of the Cathedral and Bishop's Palace. St. Martin and St. Swithin, both of them much bigger parishes, covered the hillside down to the River Witham except for areas adjacent to the main street. St. Peter at Arches and St. Benedict provided the commercial centre of the city. St. Mary Wigford, St. Mark, St. Peter at Gowts and St. Botolph completed the southerly run of parishes along the single north-south main street which was the city's backbone. (See Figure I and Plate I.)

Probate inventories were drawn up to protect the heirs to an estate and to facilitate the distribution of bequests. Appraisers recorded and valued the household goods of the deceased, usually within two or three days of burial. A number of legal technicalities governed the process of making an inventory and its subsequent storage. If the deceased had left a will it was necessary to produce an inventory in an ecclesiastical court for the will to be proved before the estate could be allocated to heirs. Most of the Lincoln inventories were proved in the Bishop of Lincoln's Consistory Court and are now available for study as the PROB. INV series in Lincolnshire Archive Office. Some areas of Lincolnshire, and in particular the two city parishes of St. Margaret and St. Mary Magdalene, were under the probate jurisdiction of the Dean and Chapter of Lincoln Cathedral. Inhabitants of these parishes had their wills proved in the peculiar court of the Dean and these inventories now form part of the Dean and Chapter's documents in the Archive Office with Di as their classification. Ten probate inventories are still to be found with the wills proved in the Dean's Court. They remain with the D. & C. Wills series of documents and in Table I have been included as part of the INV series. During the 1690s, the distinction between the Bishop's and Dean's probate court ends and the two series merge in the Archive Office PROB. INV classification.

Those who died without making a will had their estates managed by administrators to whom the Consistory Court had granted letters of administration. This process too required an inventory of the deceased's goods and these are stored in the Archive Office in the L.C.C. Admon. series. One inventory is to be found in the collections of accounts provided by the administrators of those dying intestate.[1] This inventory is included with the L.C.C. Admon. group of inventories in all the analyses which follow.

A minority of Lincoln wills was proved in the prerogative court of the Archbishop of Canterbury. The very wealthy and those who had lands in more than one county are generally thought to have used this superior court. Only seven Lincoln people used this process in the period though none of them seems to have had an estate of the magnitude or complexity to warrant using the Archbishop's court. These inventories are to be found in the Public Record Office as part of the Prob. 4 and Prob. 5 series.

Nationally the three decades following the Restoration of 1660 provided large numbers of inventories but Lincoln's 590 is an exceptionally large number. Ipswich has 222 for the years 1583–1715 and Lichfield 140 between 1660 and 1680.[2] After 1700 there was at Lincoln, and generally throughout the country, a decline in the numbers of inventories. The inventories are a prolific source of information about the city and its inhabitants but before any attempt can be made to analyse them two major caveats need to be made. Firstly it is necessary to assess their distribution amongst the parishes and over the decades between 1661 and 1714. Secondly it is necessary to be aware of their inherent deficiencies as evidence for life in the city in this period.

There is an adequate coverage of inventories for the entire period. In Table I the incidence of the inventories over the years can be assessed. The bulk of them occur between 1661 and 1690 and the beginning of the decline in numbers is perceptible in the latter years of the period. 1673 was the best represented year with twenty-four inventories but no year had none. Undoubtedly these inventories are the survivors of a greater number but it is difficult to assess what proportion they represent of the original total. The inventories for 1671 and 1688/9 required much skilled repair work before they could be made available to readers. One so rescued is the sole inventory for a bookseller in the period (**11**). Without this inventory Lincoln would have appeared to have had no bookseller although other sources identify two in the period.[3] Inventories were of less permanent value than wills and demands for storage over the years together with the hazards of damp, carelessness and loss make it likely that there has been a substantial erosion of the original number. 555 Lincoln wills exist for the period but only 40% of them can be matched with their inventory. Of the 345 probate inventories in the INV series 30% cannot be joined to the will that would have accompanied them to the Consistory Court. On this basis it is likely that some hundreds of inventories have been lost from the original number. It is obvious too from an analysis of the apprentice enrolments that the inventories record only a proportion of the business men working in the city. Between 1661 and 1714 these enrolments show that 407 men and women engaged apprentices and only 80 of them (19.7%) are recorded as leaving inventories.[4] Some of the groups leaving inventories would not have needed apprentices; innkeepers and

[1] Lincolnshire Archives Office (subsequently L.A.O.) Ad. Ac 45/2.

[2] M. Reed 'Economic Structure and Change in seventeenth century Ipswich' in P Clark (ed.) *County towns in pre-industrial England* (Leicester, 1981) p. 103; D.G. Vaisey (ed.) *Probate Inventories of Lichfield and District 1568–1680* Staffordshire Record Society Fourth Series Vol. 5 (Stafford, 1969).

[3] Sir J. W. F. Hill *Tudor and Stuart Lincoln* (Cambridge, 1956) p. 215

[4] L.A.O. L1/5/2.

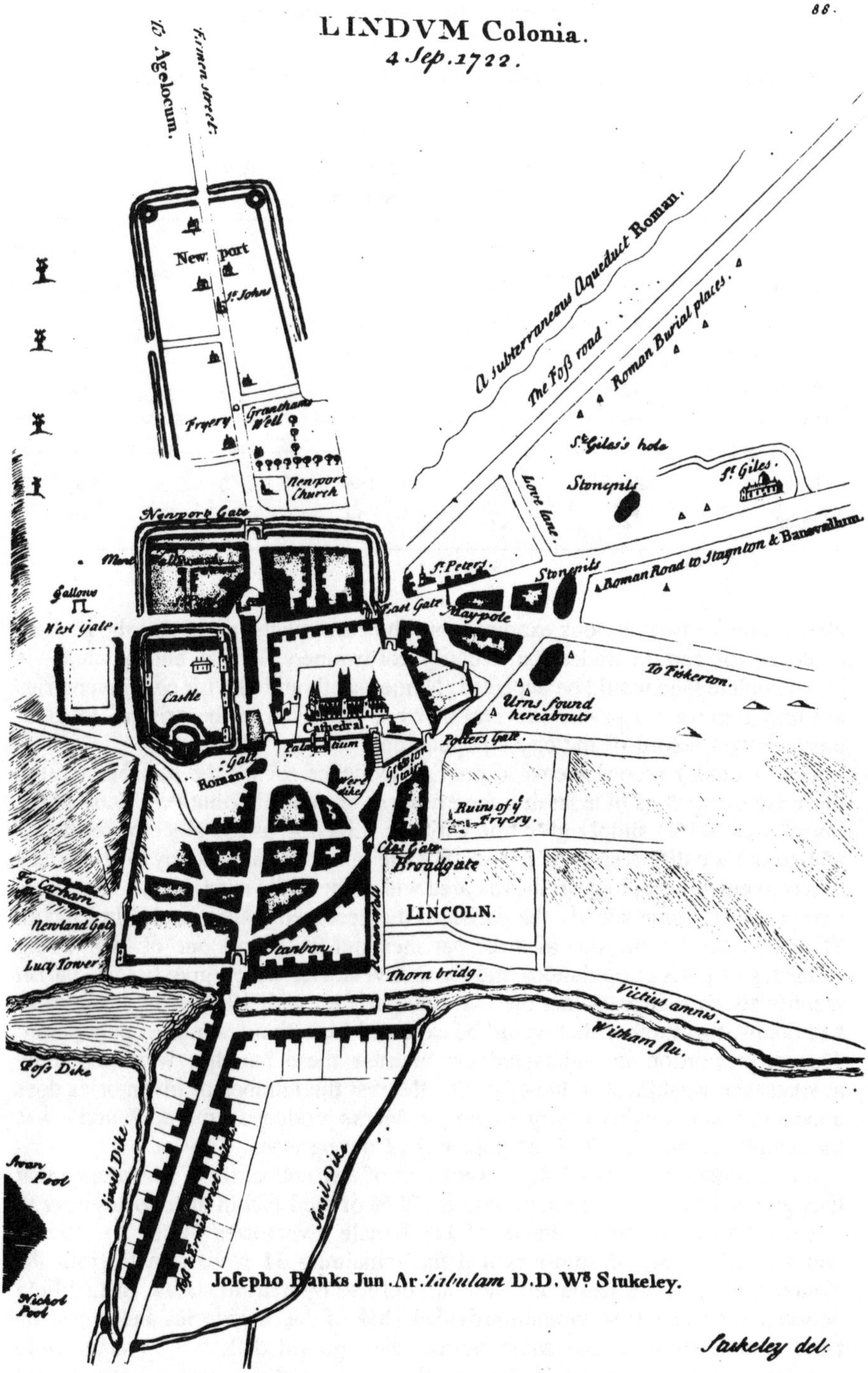

LINDVM Colonia.
4 Sep. 1722.

Josepho Banks Jun. Ar. *Tabulam* D.D. W^s Stukeley.

Stukeley del.

PLATE I. Map of Lincoln 1722
(By permission of Lincolnshire Library Service)

TABLE I. Inventory distribution by decade, archive deposit and sex

	INV.	D. & C. Di	L.C.C. Admon.	P.R.O.	Total
1661–70	69	27	27	1	124
1671–80	92	34	52	2	180
1681–90	62	18	25	3	108
1690–1700	53	3	13	1	70
1701–1710	52	–	32	–	84
1711–1714	17	–	7	–	24
Totals	345	82	156	7	590
Women	72	17	24	2	115

clergymen are two obvious examples but the enrolments imply that the probate evidence for certain trades, particularly cordwainers, bakers and butchers, is less complete than would be expected. Numerous though the Lincoln inventories are they represent a partial survival of what was even in the original form an unsystematic record of the city's population.

The inventory record seems to provide evidence for all the parishes though there are difficulties in assessing the evenness of their distribution. Many of the inventories (43%) simply give 'the City' or 'Lincoln' as the place of residence and do not identify a specific parish. For the uphill parishes many give the Bail as a convenient term to describe the area within the walls even though it contains two parishes. Some specify the parish of the deceased inadequately. In Lincoln St. Peters can be any one of three parishes and St. Marys one of two. Using estimates of parish populations and those inventories which give precise parish identifications it appears that the two Bail parishes with 40% of the inventories had double the number that would be expected from their estimated population. This disproportion is understandable because these parishes were reputedly amongst the wealthiest in the city. For the rest the number of inventories does appear to relate roughly to population. St. Marks produced a mere 3% and it was the poorest as well as the least populous of the parishes.

It is a generally acknowledged weakness of any collection of inventories that they give poor representation of women. 20% of the Lincoln inventories refer to women. Out of the total number of 115 female inventories 71 (61%) were of widows, 13 (11%) of spinsters and the remaining 31 were female from the evidence of christian name but were not defined by marital status. In Lichfield between 1661 and 1680 women provided 18% of the inventories and in nearby rural Lincolnshire in the same period they provided 12%.[5] Women were certainly under-represented in the Lincoln sequence of inventories but not to an exceptional extent.

[5] Vaisey *op.cit.* pp. 7–8

Inventories also under-represent the poor. When the deceased was poor and there was unlikely to be dispute over the settlement of the estate the legal process of probate was not required. The unfairness of consuming much of the value of a poor man's estate in the cost of probate was recognised in a note scribbled on one of the labourer inventories. The note suggested that probate be waived as the final charges would *cum to as much as is thought will be gotten*.[6] However Lincoln's inventory coverage of the poor is exceptionally good because there are 156 inventories of people who died intestate and many of these were poor. In the 1680s 31% of the L.C.C. Admons were for estates valued at less than £5.00 and 51% were at less than £20.00. Inevitably a process of selection which looks for inventories which are revealing and rich in detail involves a bias towards wealthier examples. The mean of all 590 inventories is £187.00 and for the printed selection is £257.50 although this does include examples of the lowest valuations. In this period a Lincolnshire labourer could expect to earn between 3p and 4p a day. A personal estate valued at £600 could be interpreted as a sign of gentility and a prosperous tradesman's estate would be in the range between £100 and £500. None of the Lincoln inventories show wealth of the level attained by the great merchants of London and the major cities. Only 10% died with estates valued at more than £500 and of these only 3% had estates valued at more than £1,000.

In addition to the kinds of bias already discussed the inventories present a range of problems to historians seeking to use them as evidence of a past society. Inevitably they seek to use them for purposes far removed from their original function. These problems have been often and cogently described.[7] The ones that are of particular relevance as a cautionary background to this collection can be summarised. The totals of valuations given at the end of each inventory do not give an accurate picture of the deceased's wealth. Real estate, such as land and property, were not valued and debts can be omitted. Both wills and administrator's accounts need to be consulted to gain confidence about the financial standing of the inventory's subject. The appraisers were fallible humans, their troubles with addition prove that, and uncertainties about goods in the deceased's usage but not his possession or what belonged to a widow from her marriage settlement or was credited to her by custom, a neglect of rooms or assets, carelessness or lack of expertise in the processes of listing and valuation are all factors than can reduce the value of inventories for the historian. But, as all such cautionary paragraphs conclude, they do provide a major historical resource which excites both the quantifying historian and those who find instruction and pleasure in the unique and sometimes eccentric record of a singular individual.

6 L.A.O. L.C.C. Admon. 1663/19.

7 J. S. Moore 'Probate Inventories – Problems and Prospects' in P. Riden (ed.) *Probate Records and the Local Community* (Gloucester, 1985) pp. 12–16.

II

Lincoln City 1661–1714

The city in which the subjects of these inventories had lived was a monument to past greatness and recent troubles. The past greatness was medieval. The Cathedral, the Castle, a Guildhall and two imposing early merchant houses remain as symbols of the power and wealth that came from the city's medieval status as a staple town and the centre of a vast diocese. Then came protracted economic decline as Lincoln's profits in the textile trade faded. The Civil War, particularly events between 1642 and 1646, had added to the desolation. By 1661 it was a market town existing in the ruins of a city. Visitors between 1661 and 1714 were very conscious of its decayed grandeur. In 1712 Defoe noted that the very hog stys were built from the relics of churches.[1] De la Pryme commented on both the decay and the fact that it was essentially a city of one main street.[2]

Stukeley's map of 1722 (Plate 1) although inaccurate in detail justifies his description. The main north-south road passed between Cathedral and Castle in the upper city and continued down the slope of the ridge with some side streets joining it until it passed through the lower south gate and across the Witham. South of this the skin of housing on either side of the road seems little more than one habitation deep. To the east of the Cathedral can be seen the houses where many of the ecclesiastical officers and the wealthy lived.

The number of people who inhabited the city and the changes in number between 1661 and 1714 can give a better measure of the city's status than either map or visitors' impressions. It seems likely that the population of the thirteen Lincoln parishes increased from about 3,500 in 1661 to about 4,500 in 1714. The evidence on which estimates such as these is based never engenders over confidence. (See Table II and Appendix I). For the period before the Civil War there are the Protestation Returns of 1641–2 in which male inhabitants recorded their loyalty to the Church of England, King and Parliament. There are the Hearth Tax Return of 1662 and the Compton Census of 1676 which purport to count the number of households with hearths eligible for taxation and the numbers of Anglicans and non-conformists old enough to take communion. There are for 1706, 1715–18 and 1721 three surveys instituted by the bishop which give numbers of families. The conversion of these diverse units to absolute population figures is complicated by omissions, evasions and awareness of the obvious practical difficulties that must have attended these administrative events.

The interpretation of these counts which implies growth of population can be verified by study of the parish registers and bishop's transcripts of the thirteen parishes. Here again omissions and the destruction of some evidence hinders precision but there is clearly growth in the city's population. Five of the parishes provide sufficiently consistent registration of baptisms and burials to justify

[1] D. Defoe *A Tour Through England and Wales* Vol. II (London, 1927) pp. 91–93.

[2] Abraham de la Pryme *Diary* Surtees Society Vol. LIV (Durham, 1869) p. 19.

TABLE II. Population 1642–1721

Parish	Acres	1642 Protestation	1662 Hearth Tax	1676 Compton Census	1706 Bishop's Survey	1715/18 Bishop's Survey	1721 Bishop's Survey
		(males over 18 years)		(Communi- cants & Non-Con- formists over 16 yrs)	(Families)	(Families)	(Families)
St. Pauls	27	69	–	168	30	61	60
St. Mary Magdalen	28	113	–	308	100	110	107
St. Michael	15	72	31	173	25	99	80
St. Peters in Eastgate	380	60	17	134	26	42	
St. Martin	96	153	61	372	80	174	160
St. Margaret	96	74	23	–	32	35	32
St. Swithin	154	163	67	325	150	168	
St. Peter at Arches	8	74	58	224	60		
St. Benedict	9	79	50	188	60	50	69
St. Mary Wigford	612	77	33	141	40	45	48
St. Mark	32	45	24	73	30	23	24
St. Peter Gowts	149	76	42	161	60	43	
St. Botolph	188	76	45	114	26	50	
Total	1794	1131	451	2381	719	900	580

aggregation.[3] For these parishes the increase in baptisms and burials between the two periods 1621–40 and 1701–20 is respectively 43% and 33%. The evidence from three other parishes is valuable in that it confirms that the major increase is in the years following 1680 and is particularly strong from the beginning of the eighteenth century.

The combination of the various attempts to count the city's population with the evidence from parish registers and bishops' transcripts gives a demographic dimension to the city's topography. St. Benedict and St. Peter at Arches were the two most densely populated parishes and St. Martin, St. Mary Magdalene and

[3] D. E. C. Eversley 'Exploitation of anglican parish registers by aggregative analysis' in E. A. Wrigley (ed.) *An Introduction to English Historical Demography* (London, 1966). The five parishes are St. Benedict, St. Mary Wigford, St. Martin, St. Michael and St. Swithin.

St. Swithin the most populous. South of the River Witham the density of population decreased with distance from the river. The Hearth Tax of 1662 identifies the number of households with one, two or more hearths and this enables another kind of analysis. St. Margarets was the parish with the highest proportion of large houses. Eight of its taxed twenty-three houses had more than six hearths and the parish's mean hearth rating was 6.96. There were only twenty two other houses of this size in the rest of Lincoln. St. Peter Arches with three houses of this size had a mean hearth rating of 3.55 and was the next most impressive parish by this measure but only marginally different from four other parishes with a mean about 3.00 – St. Benedict, St. Mary Wigford, St. Peter Eastgate and St. Peter Gowts. St. Marks had the lowest mean of 2.66. The urban topography of Lincoln was exceptional. The normal urban pattern was that of a concentric hierarchy, as in York and Exeter, with the houses of the wealthiest concentrated near minster or cathedral and the middling and lower classes of houses radiating in bands from this centre. Lincoln's pattern was bi-focal and linear. Near the Cathedral and eastwards from it was the concentration of prestigious houses recorded by both the Hearth Tax and Defoe.[4] Associated with them in the Bail were many shops. To the south in St. Peter Arches and St. Benedict was the concentration of commercial and artisan dwellings. Lincoln's elite, in terms of housing, was a small one, 8% of its houses were taxed for six or more hearths, York had 15%.[5]

The establishment of an approximate figure for Lincoln's population defines its place in the national hierarchy of towns. Lincoln did not enjoy the conjunction of advantages which created a large population. It had neither the specialist industry nor the long distance trades that gave regional capitals such as York, Bristol, Exeter, Hull and Newcastle populations of between 8,000 and 10,000. By comparison with the flourishing textile towns of East Anglia such as Ipswich, Bury St. Edmunds and Great Yarmouth it was small. It was on a level with the Winchesters and Lichfields of the time.[6] Its relatively lowly status is shown in a variety of ways. In terms of Land Tax and Hearth Tax paid to central government it appears as one of the smaller cities. There was no custom built residence for judges and in 1695 when William III visited the city he was entertained in a house in Pottergate. The Bishop's Palace was in ruins and most bishops based their activities at Buckden in Huntingdonshire. Surprisingly few Lincoln wills, only seven, were proved in the prerogative court of the Archbishop of Canterbury. There was no library, social club or newspaper.

Yet its condition improved between 1661 and 1714 like most other county towns. Like them it benefitted from the greater efficiency of transportation and the greater purchasing power available in decades of improving wages. Lincoln's traditional and complex system of municipal government was more than a relic of a great past. It did provide an administrative structure that could support trade and commerce and the records of the Quarter Sessions contain evidence to show that this was done. The re-opening of the Fossdyke canal which provided reliable water transport between Lincoln and the River Trent

[4] Defoe *op.cit.* p. 92.

[5] D. Hibberd 'Data-Linkage and the Hearth Tax : the case of seventeenth century York' in N. Alldridge (ed.) *The Hearth Tax: Problems and Possibilities* (Hull, 1983) p. 62.

[6] A. Rosen 'Winchester in transition 1580–1700' in Clark *op.cit.*; Vaisey *op.cit.*

was successfully achieved within the period.[7] It is clear too that in physical terms the city was recovering from the troubled times of Civil War and Interregum. Damaged churches were rebuilt, many private buildings were modernised, often with frontages, chimney stacks and wings made of brick.[8] Lincoln's roles as shire and diocesan centre ensured that the city and its facilities were known to the agents of secular and ecclesiastical administration whether they were justices of the peace or churchwardens. It provided for the gentry the political and legal contacts necessary for their status in society and as well a range of services which included inns, horse racing, cock fighting, barbers, upholsterers and specialist shops.

There are a number of ways of measuring Lincoln's hinterland. One is by plotting on a map the references in inventories and wills to places beyond the city boundaries. Such references are usually to debts, land owned or the residences of people to whom a bequest is made. This indicates the social and economic influence of the city. There are 495 such references in the inventories and wills. Nearly a third of them, 32%, were to places within ten miles of the city, an area which takes in 79 Lincolnshire and 6 Nottinghamshire parishes. Of those remaining, 44% refer to other Lincolnshire parishes and 24% to places outside the county. Nottinghamshire has 6% of these references, London 5% and Yorkshire 4%. The references within Lincolnshire tend to cluster along the ridge north of Lincoln and the heathland south of it. There are very few references to the Wolds and none to the south west corner of the county around Stamford. The concentration of references to the immediate ten mile radius from the city is characteristic of a market town but the diffusion of such a large proportion of them to the county at large indicates the city's influence as a county capital.

This influence can be assessed in another way by plotting the birth places of brides and grooms who married in city churches. 1182 such marriages were recorded, 42% by people born within ten miles of the city. Outside this circle the distribution of birthplaces throughout Lincolnshire is interestingly diffuse. There were few groupings of four or five parishes anywhere in the county which did not have a bride or groom born in that cluster of parishes married in one of the city churches between 1661 and 1714. Many of them had been born in the smaller market towns. Two arcs of smaller towns were Lincoln's satellites. The nearer arc of towns, Sleaford, Horncastle and Gainsborough were just beyond the ten mile radius. Further away were Grantham, Boston, Spilsby, Alford, Louth, Caistor and Brigg. They provided stepping stones for servants and artisans who wished to move from rural to urban life. The social hinterland of Lincoln as indicated by these marriages illustrates a county influence much wider than that of other early modern market towns. The distinctive county nature of this dispersed influence is shown by the relatively few marriages by brides or grooms in city churches who had been born outside the county. This combination of evidence from inventories, wills and city marriages gives Lincoln a social centrality to an

[7] Hill *op.cit.* pp. 126–8; L.A.O. L1/4/8.

[8] Hill *op.cit.* p. 202; S. Jones, K. Major and J. Varley *The Survey of Ancient Houses in Lincoln* Vol. I Priorygate to Pottergate (Nottingham 1984) pp. 21, 30, 32–3, 41.

area much greater than the ten mile radius generally associated with the ordinary market town.[9]

The underlying basis of this influence was agriculture. Lincolnshire participated in the agricultural growth of this period and although like other regions it experienced bad years there were only two, 1686 and 1711, in which Lincoln's cereal prices were above the national average. The county benefitted from the improved transport, including coastal shipping, that was a feature of the late seventeenth century. The rise of wages of some 5% and the 12% increase in purchasing power of those wages indirectly provided much of the wealth recorded in Lincoln's inventories.[10] There is no dramatic evidence of agricultural innovation within the county during the period but in a multitude of small ways Lincolnshire's agricultural productivity became more flexible and more profitable. Enclosures, the consolidation of estates and better buildings express the general advance. On Cliff, Heath, Wolds, to the west of the Cliff and in the central vale the mixed farming economy based on barley and animal husbandry was generally successful. The mixed farming cushioned the farmers from the impact of bad harvests or animal diseases. In marshlands and fens the 'lusty' long stapled wool of Lincolnshire sheep was in demand by the clothiers of East Anglia and the West Riding. The fens contained the finest pasture land in England. Their capacity to fatten animals for the London market gave satirists in Anne's reign the phrase *fat as a Lincolnshire heifer* for their descriptions of fat women.[11] The fenland too was bounteous in its provision of fish, fowl and agricultural bye products such as tallow, quills, fighting cocks, well bred horses and coleseed.

Despite these advantages of influential status and its position as county capital of a region experiencing some agricultural development Lincoln's own development seems no more than modest. It suffered from its position as the capital of a peninsula and being sited half way along the neck of that peninsula. The markets for the agricultural produce and the main routeways for its export did not bring as much profit to Lincoln as might have been expected. Two of the main ports which facilitated and benefitted from this trade, Hull and King's Lynn, were outside the county. The other major port, Boston, looked southwards and not towards the county town. The estuary of the Humber led to the great waterway of the Trent and beside the Trent the main roadway was the Great North Road. These skirted the county. Gainsborough, Grantham and Stamford benefitted from their traffic but the currents of trade eddied some fourteen miles or more west of Lincoln. Drove roads led through the county to the fenlands but their benefit to the city is hard to measure. In 1688 a herd of 107 cattle en route from Beverley to Smithfield passed through Lincoln. The city benefitted by the sale of five trusses of hay and wages for watching the herd and guiding it through Lincoln. The record of £0.56 income to Lincoln's citizens is a

[9] A. Everett 'The Marketing of Agricultural Produce' in J. Thirsk (ed.) *The Agrarian History of England and Wales 1500–1640* Vol. IV (Cambridge, 1967) pp. 498–500; A. D. Dyer *City of Worcester in the Sixteenth Century* (Leicester, 1973) p.68; M. Reed 'Economic Structure and Change in seventeenth century Ipswich' in Clark *op.cit.* p. 99.

[10] R. J. Bowden 'Agricultural prices, wages, farm profits and rents' in J. Thirsk (ed.) *The Agrarian History of England and Wales 1640–1750* Vol V.II (Cambridge, 1985) pp. 3, 61.

[11] Ned Ward *The London Spy* (London, 1927) p. 193 cf. pp.209–10.

minor indication of the profits trade could bring.[12] A more significant one is the inventory of a Lincoln based farmer (**14**) which shows his agricultural operations involving the fens and the London market. Such profits were certainly reduced by Lincoln's geographic position. Many of the markets that attracted Lincolnshire farmers were outside the county. Lincolnshire sheep were sold at Rotherham and Doncaster, its horses at Market Harborough, its cereals at Barnsley and Halifax as well as in the markets and fairs of Lincoln and the county.[13] The economic framework of the city between 1661 and 1714 was benign but it was not so advantageous to the citizens as to sustain dramatic change.

III

Occupations and professions

In the preamble to 197 of the Lincoln inventories an occupation or profession is assigned to the deceased. This is not a satisfactory basis from which to describe the commercial activity of the city. The appraisors who drew up the inventories were not apparently very interested in ascribing occupations. Status in the community mattered at least as much as a man's job. That a man was an alderman or gentleman or had in his lifetime earned the appellation of 'Mr' provided a more fitting description than identifying him as a timber merchant or chandler. Moreover there were serious practical problems in giving a single occupational title. Town life gave the opportunity for a diversity of jobs and this must have been one of the great attractions of town life. The gardener (**38**) who possessed two looms as well as his own stock of seeds and plants is a lowly example of this prudent diversification. The apprentice enrolments illustrate how widely certain kinds of trade were connected. They generally link fishmonger and chandler, fellmonger and glover, plumber and glazier. They also illustrate how a man's occupation could change in the eyes of the public, for example Francis Newell was variously described as blacksmith and whitesmith within the space of a few years.[1] Complexities such as this make Lincoln's apparent tally of 63 occupations and professions from inventory evidence a poor indication of reality. It compares poorly with the record of other contemporary towns, York and Bristol with over 200, Winchester with about 100 and Norwich with 80.[2]

In fact by identifying occupation from evidence contained within the inventories themselves and by using occupations ascribed to inventory leavers from other sources, particularly letters of administration it appears that the Lincoln inventories record 81 occupations. (Table III, column iii.) This figure

[12] D. M. Woodward 'Cattle droving in the seventeenth century : a Yorkshire example' in W. H. Chaloner (ed.)*Trade and Transport: Essays in honour of T. S. Willan* (Manchester, 1977) pp. 49,52.
[13] Everett *op.cit.* pp. 499, 501, 509, 538; D. Hey *Packmen, Carriers and Packhorse Roads* (Leicester, 1980) pp. 149, 172, 175, 226.
[1] L.A.O. L1/5/2–3. ff. 8, 18.
[2] J. Patten 'English Towns 1500–1700' (Folkestone,1978) pp. 166–7.

agrees closely with the 77 occupations recorded by the 555 Lincoln will makers of the period. Testators were likely to have a clearer, though sometimes more exalted, view of their own line of business than appraisers.

However it is clear that both inventories and wills under-represent the diversity of occupation in the city. The last column of Table III lists the occupations derived from other sources and identifies a total of 166 Lincoln occupations. Most came from parish registers which sporadically record the occupation of fathers, bridegrooms and those buried. Apprentice enrolments, letters of administration, leases and municipal records have provided others. This information adds considerably to the picture that is obtained simply from the occupation declared in the inventory preambles. Moreover it reveals a number of business interests that the reticence of appraisers partly conceals.

TABLE III. Occupations and Status 1661–1714

Column (i) records the occupations and status of the probate inventories. The median value of the appraised wealth of some occupational groups is given in brackets. This is based on the numbers in column (iii).

Column (ii) gives the total of each occupational or status group recorded by the appraisers on the inventories.

Column (iii) adds to the totals of column (ii) those whose occupations can be deduced from the goods in inventories and those whose occupation is recorded in a letter of administration. The final total is more than the number of inventories because some record both occupation and status and some show evidence of more than one occupation.

Column (iv) records occupations given in other Lincoln sources – administration accounts, apprentice enrolments, parish registers, witnesses to inventories and wills.

Occupations

(i)	(ii)	(iii)	(iv)
Aledraper	1	1	
Alehousekeeper	1	10	
Apothecary	2	2	Apparitor
			Attorney
Baker (£58.07)	13	21	Bailiff
Barber	5	10	
			Basket maker
Beerbrewer	1	1	Bellfounder
Blacksmith (£149.52)	5	8	
Boatwright	1	2	
Bodicemaker	1	1	
Bookseller		1	Bookbinder
Brewer (£196.53)		24	Brazier
			Bricklayer
Brickmaker	1	3	
Bridlecutter	1	1	
Bridlemaker	3	3	
Bridleman	1	1	
Butcher (£111.80)	10	12	

(i)	(ii)	(iii)	(iv)
Carpenter (£53.75)	6	9	
Carrier	2	3	
Chairmaker	1	1	
Chandler (£171.64)	3	6	Chancellor
Chapman	1	2	
Clerk (£207.80)	13	13	City Clerk
			Clogmaker
			Coachman
			Coalporter
Confectioner		3	
Cooper		2	Cook
Cordwainer (£36.60)	9	14	Coroner
			Costermonger
Currier		1	Cutler
Dancing Master	1	1	
			Dishturner
			Doctor of Laws
Draper		1	
Druggist		1	
Dyer (£62.13)	2	3	Duckdecoyman
Earthernware retailer		1	Excise Man
Farmer		19	Farrier
			Fellmonger
			Feltmaker
Fisherman	1	2	Fiddler
Freemason	1	1	Fishmonger
Fruiterer	1	3	Fuel seller
			Furrier
Gardener (£20.75)	2	9	Gaoler
			Gingerbread Maker
Glazier	4	5	
Glover (£39.06)	2	4	
Goldsmith	1	2	
			Grazier
Grocer		1	
Haberdasher	1	5	
Haberdasher of Hats	1	3	Hatmaker
Harness sellers		6	
			Heelmaker
			Hempdresser
			Horsebraker
			Hosier
Innholder (£183.81)	10	17	Instrument maker
			Ironmonger
Joiner (£28.16)	4	4	
			Justice of Peace
			Lawyer
			Leatherhanger

(i)	(ii)	(iii)	(iv)
Leather trader		1	Limestone burner
Linendraper	1	4	
Maltster (£423.98)	3	17	
			Mariner
Mercer (£467.36)	9	12	Mason
Merchant	2	2	
			Merchant Taylor
Miller (£24.25)	4	5	Milliner
Minister	1	1	
Musician	1	3	
			Notary
Organist		2	
Painter		1	
			Painter stainer
Parchment maker	1	1	Periwigmaker
Pewterer (£78.00)	4	6	
Physician	5	6	
Plumber	1	1	Pipemaker
			Porter
			Postmaster
			Proctor
			Rabbit seller
			Rake maker
			Ribbonweaver
			Roper
			Roughmason
Saddler	1	3	
Schoolmaster		1	Scribe
			Scrivener
Seamstress		1	
Servant	1	1	
			Shearman
			Sheriff
Shepherd	1	1	Shoemaker
			Sievemaker
			Silk Dyer
			Silversmith
			Skinner
Soldier	1	1	Steward of Choiristers
Surgeon (£15.55)	3	4	
			Sword bearer
			Sword cutler
Tailor (£32.91)	14	14	
Tallow chandler	1	1	
Tanner (£253.00)	9	18	
Tapster	1	1	Thatcher
			Tile maker
Timber merchant		2	Tobacco pipe maker
			Trenchermaker

(i)	(ii)	(iii)	(iv)
			Trunk maker
			Turner
			Turnkey
Upholsterer (£204.78)	3	4	
			Verger
Victualer	3	3	
Vintner	1	1	
			Waggoner
Watchmaker	1	1	
Waterman	4	5	
Weaver	1	2	
Wheelwright	1	1	
Whipmaker		1	
Whitesmith	2	2	Wine cooper
			Woodseller
Wooldraper (£231.00)	5	8	Woolcomber
			Woollencardmaker
			Woolwinder
			Worsted weaver

Totals (ii) 63 occupations from 197 inventories giving occupation
(iii) 81 occupations from 379 inventories
(iv) 85 occupations
= 166 occupations

Status

Gentleman	45
Alderman/Mr	38
Yeoman	15
Husbandman	1
Labourer	11
Man	173
Woman	30
Spinster	13
Wife	1
Widow	71
Total	398
Total Occupations and Status	595

There seems to have been an almost total disinclination to acknowledge the importance of barley and the products made from it. The inventories identify one alehousekeeper and wills and letters of administration add two alehousekeepers to the list. This must be a formidable misrepresentation of the scores of alehousekeepers who would have supplied Lincoln's citizens with ale and beer. One beer brewer is named in the inventories but at least twenty four of them record brewing on a scale that is beyond the needs of even a late seventeenth century household. There is a similar understatement about malting and the keeping of inns and lodging houses. The manufacture and trade in malt was one of the most profitable and widespread of urban occupations.

Also the city seems from inventory evidence to have been singularly, perhaps blessedly, free of administrators and civic officials. There is no recognition of the bailiffs, coroners, gaolers, excise officials and scribes who inevitably provided support for complex and perennial legal and administrative processes. The existence of lawyers, notaries and scrivenors who worked for corporation, church and gentry is not visible, or perhaps disguised at the higher levels by honorific terms.

Moreover there is as one would expect serious under-representation of the labour force which worked for the entire range of commercial enterprises. The parish register for St. Paul records occupations between 1700 and 1705 and 37% of the men listed are described as labourers. In the same years St. Peter Gowts register records occupations and 23% of these were labourers. The inventory sequence has 2% labourers.[3] The single servant in the inventories must have been one of a numerous group. The apparent absence of journeymen and apprentices can be partially explained. As young men they would not often be involved in documentation linked to mortality but probably some of the lodgers or craftsmen with goods valued at less than £5.00 were representatives of this group. Only the bad luck of dying in Lincoln meant that some of the transients, like a soldier or a dancing master, provided inventories. These two must stand as representatives of other groups such as actors and drovers who contributed in their particular ways to the economic and social life of the city.

The most surprising omission in the catalogue of occupations by all the sources of evidence is the practically complete avoidance of any direct reference to farming. Farms came right up to the city walls and indeed the great South and West Commons made arable farming and animal husbandry an integral part of the city's life. There is an almost total absence of the terms yeoman or husbandman which were used so frequently by appraisers in rural areas. Many of the inventories show the importance of direct participation in farming to Lincoln citizens. Indeed some would, apart from their attribution to the city, defy differentiation from those of a rural yeoman.

IV

Selection and organisation of the printed inventories

Roughly one in ten of the Lincoln inventories between 1661 and 1714 are printed in this volume. Selection poses obvious and serious problems. There is no generally accepted classification of the occupations, professions and services of an early modern city. There have been practically as many ways of organising

[3] L.A.O. St. Paul Par. Doc. 1; St. Peter Gowts Par. Doc. 1.

inventory evidence for the study of urban life as there have been studies. The apparently convenient division of the inventories into those describing manufacturing, distributive and retailing trades is invalidated by the overlapping functions of individuals. Each city requires a particular approach if a selection of evidence is justly to reflect its economic and social status in a given period.[1]

Lincoln was the commercial, administrative and social centre of a county. The varying extent to which it acted as a centre for these functions and the validity with which probate inventories mirror them has already been considered. The inventories show most clearly Lincoln's roles as a marketing, commercial and social centre. The occupations of the majority of the population were based on agricultural produce. It is therefore appropriate to divide the majority of Lincoln's inventories into three groups which relate directly to this agricultural basis. Most business activity in Lincoln sprang directly or indirectly from cereals, hides or textiles. In addition to the occupations derived from these products mineral resources, mainly from out of the county, provided work for a fourth and smaller group. The service occupations and professions form a fifth group which expresses particularly the social contribution the city made to the region. The merits of this simple division are that it recognises the agricultural basis of the city's wealth and provides a convenient framework for a selection of inventories to represent the city. It will also be necessary to consider a sixth group, the largest numerically, who were not distinguished by any occupation or profession. This group consists of the men identified by status titles and including many who are simply named on the inventories with neither title or occupation and a majority of the women who left inventories.

Inventories have been selected that as far as possible contain detailed evidence for the implements and stock that were characteristic of an occupation. The process of selection provides scope to illustrate such extremes of poverty and wealth as the evidence allows and for examples of males and females in all the social groupings. It follows that the selection contains evidence for the entire range of households and their furniture and fittings. In the process of description of each of the groups which follows and particularly for the first four groups to be considered the starting point will be the occupation's nearness to the raw product whether it be cereal, hide, fleece or mineral. There is in general terms a progression from this starting point towards more sophisticated and skilled occupations. The sense of hierarchy in such treatment is inevitably complicated by the variation of wealth and commercial activity displayed by individuals. The system of grouping leads to some incongruities. Those who dealt with wood, whether carpenters or timber merchants, have been included in the first group as have the fishermen. Some illogicality must attend any attempt to systematise the occupational structure of Lincoln between 1661–1714. The selection very properly includes certain individuals who defy categorisation today as successfully as they did in their own time.

The inventories themselves are printed in chronological order. Generally wherever there are four or more inventories relating to a particular occupation or profession at least one is printed. Table IV lists the selection of printed inventories.

[1] J. Patten 'Urban Occupations in pre-industrial England' *Transactions of the Institute of British Geographers* N.S. Vol. 2. No. 3 (1977) pp. 301–310.

TABLE IV. The printed inventories

	Name	Status or Occupation	Appraised wealth (in £ sterling)	Date of appraisal	Reference (all L.A.O.)
1.	Glen, Joh	Barber	133.79	25. 5.1662	L.C.C.Admon.1661/74
2.	Clarke, Charles	Blacksmith	63.12	14. 1.1664	Inv.162/61
3.	Sewell, Katerne	Widow (Dyer)	219.74	9. 8.1664	Inv.164/90
4.	Marshall, Benjamin	Mercer	1203.77	18. 1.1665	L.C.C.Admon.1667/131
5.	Lewis, Thomas	Labourer	12.72	9. 1.1667	Inv.166/43
6.	Featley, John	Dr.of Divinity (Precentor)	207.80	21. 3.1667	Di 38/2/10
7.	Towndrow, John	Mr. (Baker)	58.07	26.11.1668	Inv.168/76
8.	Norton, William	Maltster	452.91	17. 3.1670	Inv.172/264
9.	Younglove, Francis	(Harness Seller)	77.28	25. 4.1670	Inv.172/327
10.	Hazelteine, Richard	(Labourer)	5.46	(....) 1670	Inv.172/321
11.	Williams, Eden	(Bookseller & printer)	153.71	11.12.1671	Inv.173/387
12.	Shoosmith, George	Glazier	38.85	8. 4.1672	Inv.175/201
13.	Dawsons, John	(Farmer)	159.42	24. 4.1672	Inv.175/234
14.	Kent, William	Gent. (Malster, Farmer)	951.23	(....) 1672	Inv.175/29
15.	Nickinson, Mary	Widow	106.44	29. 5.1673	Inv.174/21
16.	Peacock, Sissie	–	25.61	31.12.1673	L.C.C.Admon.1673/85
17.	White, Thomas	(Wool merchant)	244.49	3. 2.1674	Inv.174/228
18.	Bate, Elizabeth	–	10.73	28. 2.1674	L.C.C.Admon.1673/7
19.	Atkinson, John	Tanner	80.88	(..) 6.1675	L.C.C.Admon.1675/5
20.	Wood, Jefre	(Labourer)	4.06	(....) 1675	L.C.C.Admon.1675/111
21.	Atkinson, William	Tailor	30.64	11. 1.1676	Inv.177/144
22.	Langforth, John	Whitesmith	72.01	7.10.1676	Inv.179/222
23.	Wignall, John	(Brick & tile maker)	317.15	19.12.1677	Inv.219A/183
24.	Fawkes, Edward	Alderman, Upholsterer	141.61	29. 3.1679	L.C.C.Admon.1679/79
25.	Mitchell, Henery	(Haberdasher)	379.33	14. 4.1679	Di 39/1/134
26.	Pearson, Robert	Waterman	46.33	28. 8.1679	Inv.180/236
27.	Watson, Abigaile	Widow (Saddle maker)	288.04	1. 9.1679	Inv.180/242

28.	Wanleste, Henry	–	23.11	6. 9.1679	Inv.180/248
29.	Browne, William	Goldsmith (Brewer)	643.55	21. 1.1680	Inv.180/252
30.	Corbet, Henry	Dr. of Physic	893.92	9.11.1680	Di 37/3/112
31.	Biron, George	(Farmer)	108.17	23. 5.1681	Inv.182/33
32.	Leach, John	Gent. (Grocer, Brewer)	299.50	7. 1.1682	Inv.182A/230
33.	Peart, William	Gent. (Coffee House Proprietor)	157.76	21. 3.1682	Di 39/2/53
34.	Ellis, Richard	(Whipmaker)	13.95	24. 5.1682	Di 38/1/86
35.	Winne, Richard	Alderman (Pewterer)	59.22	12. 3.1683	L.C.C.Admon.1683/127
36.	Eure, Thomas	Gent. (Farmer)	947.57	19. 6.1684	Inv.185A/194
37.	Evison, William	Gent. (Timber Merchant)	381.00	16. 5.1685	Inv.186/237
38.	Burtons, Robert	Gardener (Weaver)	87.31	9. 7.1688	Inv.188/70
39.	Hill, Thomas	(Confectioner)	53.35	16. 7.1688	Inv.187/13
40.	Wood, Roger	Glover	20.63	29. 8.1688	Inv.188/163
41.	Fleare, Edmund	Bodice maker	146.59	6.10.1688	Inv.188/99
42.	Houghton, William	–	485.16	13. 1.1695	Inv.191/16
43.	Drake, Michael	Clerk	38.30	31. 3.1696	Inv.192/368
44.	Dring, John	Joiner	174.62	4.12.1696	Inv.192/362
45.	Douce, Robert	Gent. (Innholder)	493.13	15. 6.1698	Inv.193/394
46.	Littleover, Elizabeth	–	9.55	10.11.1699	Inv.194/102
47.	Feris, Thomas	Glover (Tanner, Brewer)	393.52	15. 4.1700	Inv.194/289
48.	Manby, Elizabeth	–	861.38	7. 5.1701	Inv.195/20
49.	Green, Richard	(Brewer)	670.80	14. 6.1701	Inv.195/245
50.	Wright, George	Chandler	356.71	3&4.8.1702	L.C.C.Admon.1702/1
51.	Norris, John	(Steward of Choristers)	80.14	12. 9.1702	D. & C. Wills 27/8
52.	Osburne, James	(Linen Draper)	864.80	9.10.1702	L.C.C.Admon.1702/50
53.	Hanson, Godfrey	Miller	53.40	2.10.1703	Inv.197/44
54.	Pell, William	Victualer	80.85	6. 7.1706	L.C.C.Admon.1706/92
55.	Hobman, John	(Butcher)	38.53	2. 1.1707	Inv.200/34
56.	Faux, William	Alderman (Maltster, Mercer)	1000.50	10. 5.1708	L.C.C.Admon.1708/52
57.	Warriner, William	Cordwainer	36.55	(....) 1712	Inv.203/381
58.	Newcomen, Charles	Woollen Draper	468.52	(....) 1713	L.C.C.Admon.1714/65
59.	Gryme, Elizabeth	Widow	19.82	28. 6.1714	L.C.C.Admon.1714/37
60.	Lees, Margaret	–	1.63	20. 7.1714	Inv.204/153

V

Farmers, gardeners, millers, bakers, confectioners, maltsters, brewers; joiners, timber merchants; fishermen

None of the inventories is attributed to a farmer and only fifteen are of yeomen. At this period farmers and yeomen in the rural parishes near Lincoln had on average 64 sheep, 14 fattening cattle, 9 dairy beasts, 5 calves, 2 oxen and 6 horses. Estimates of cereal output depend upon the chance of detailed and seasonally apt inventories so no average size can be given to the acreages of their farms though most would have practised mixed farming. The mean value of their estates was £149.00. Husbandmen had about half the number in their herds and far fewer sheep, oxen and horses. Their estates had a mean value of £61.00.[1] On these criteria nineteen of the Lincoln citizens who left inventories would have been designated as farmers or yeomen by rural inventory appraisers.

The inventories of four farmers are printed. Dawsons (**13**) of St. Peter Eastgate is indistinguishable in his house, its furnishings and his agricultural stock from his peers in rural parishes. His farming economy with its balance between the fattening of cattle and a sizeable flock of sheep and his cereal production of barley and fodder crops is a typical example of good farming practice in the area. In varying ways the other farmers in the sample illustrate common divergences from this basic pattern. Thomas Eure (**36**) was a more prosperous landowner and indeed lived in some comfort in his Lincoln house using the profits of his lands in Coleby to support his lifestyle. Like Dawsons he preferred barley and fodder crops in his cereal production but horse breeding takes the place of fattening cattle in his farming strategy. Eure too can be taken as a representative of seven other absentee landlords whose inventories show that they possessed land in the nearby parishes of Boultham, Branston, Nettleham and Riseholme or further afield in Spittlegate and Nettleton. Including them in the list of Lincoln's farmers brings their total to twenty six. Kent's inventory (**14**) is the best and most interesting example of a man with scattered agricultural interests. He is identified as a gentleman and included in this volume as much for his role as a maltster as a farmer. The range of his agricultural interests was wide. As a citizen of Lincoln he pastured two beasts on the city commons but they were a small fraction of his wealth in animals. He had flocks or herds at Newbell, Scampton and Skegness.[2] The animals at Skegness were described as being at pasture, on what were the richest fattening lands in the county. His inventory recorded the posthumous sale of some of his animals at London. This is the clearest inventory evidence of a Lincoln man participating in the growing supply of food to London and proof that some at least of the marketing profits of agriculture contributed to Lincoln's well being.

Three other inventories illustrate the variety of agricultural practice. Biron (**31**), like Kent, but on a much humbler scale, was primarily concerned with

[1] J. A. Johnston '17th Century Agricultural Practice in Six Lincolnshire Parishes' *Lincolnshire History and Archaeology* Vol. 18, 1983 p. 12.

[2] Newbell is Newball a hamlet in the parish of Stainton by Langworth.

animal husbandry. The emphasis in his inventory was for bye products such as tallow, skins and cheese. His inventory is one of the very few in which food, flitches, a chine of bacon and neat's tongue were valued. These could have been for sale rather than domestic consumption. White (**17**) specialised in just one aspect of Lincolnshire's agriculture and should probably be best described as a wool merchant rather than a farmer. Katerne Sewell (**3**) is included principally because she was the pre-eminent dyer of the period, but she also maintained arable and animal husbandry within the City boundaries in conjunction with her main business.

None of the yeomen inventories, bar one, exhibit much evidence of agricultural activity and on this evidence their titles seem to be more honorific than indicating farming. The one exception provided horses and hay. His horses and waggons were given the very high valuation of £100.00.[3]

This consideration of the farmers and yeomen who lived in the city must underemphasise the farmyard aspects which would certainly make the most vivid impression on any visitor from the present day who could return to see, or smell, the city as it was between 1661 and 1714. Discounting the herds and flocks in transit through the streets and the omnipresent horses many of the inhabitants kept farm animals. 15% of the inventories included one or more pigs and 11% had at least one cow in their valuations. One bridleman had seventeen pigs and at the other extreme one man was credited with a half share in a sow and a pig.[4]

Economically akin to the farmers but operating at a much humbler level was a small group of agricultural specialists. The appraisers identified two gardeners and one fruiterer but the evidence in other inventories identifies another nine. There seems to have been no practical distinction between the two titles. There were almost certainly more than this number who provided fruit, vegetables and plants for the city. The evidence for their occupation would be slight in inventories drawn up in the winter. They provided apples, artichokes, berries, carrots, cherries, herbs, liquorice, onions, pears, peas and seeds in small quantities. Both fruits and vegetables were valued, irrespective of season or species, at a shilling a strike. Grafts, prickings, roots and stocks were available in their gardens and orchards. There was no indication of flowers or flower seeds although a number of houses contained flowerpots. The median value of their estates, £20.75, gives them a lowly economic standing. Skill in this occupation must however have provided an admirable secondary means of earning. The inventory of Burtons (**38**) shows he worked both as a weaver and as a supplier of fruits, vegetables and herbs. Another of the gardeners made pattens, two were widows and three men of labourer level, all with the surname Wise, must represent a continuing family interest in this occupation.

There are four inventories of millers and a fifth, styled a yeoman, can be added because of his horsemill valued at £2.00. The number of millers was small considering the production of bread and malt that took place. The 1722 map (Plate 1) however makes it clear that the rank of windmills which served the city was sited along the ridge and thus the majority were in parishes to the north of the city itself. Leased assets were not normally included in inventory valuations

[3] L.A.O. Inv. 190/132.
[4] L.A.O. Inv. 167/66; L.C.C. Admon. 1678/98.

but the Lincoln custom was to include them whether for land or structures such as mills. The inventory of Hanson (**53**) gave a value for the lease he held from the Corporation. Its value was more than half his appraised estate. He, like the other Lincoln millers, had a status in society roughly on a level with that of a rural husbandman.

Millers such as Hanson would have competed for the trade of the twenty one Lincoln bakers. This is a surprisingly large number. In the same period Newcastle, one of the largest towns in the country had no more than four or five, Lichfield had three and the Telford area two.[5] It was a trade much under the scrutiny of magistrates who were determined to prevent popular unrest arising from expensive or poor quality bread. The opportunities for becoming rich in the trade were considered poor and the best routeway to wealth was considered to lie in the falsification of the tallies whereby the debts of the poorer customers were recorded. The median value of baker estates was £58.07 but this figure lies between the extremes of £4.02 and £306.80. In this trade as in most of the others there was always a small group whose estates were valued at or about £4.00. Usually, as with four of the bakers, it is only the occupation given by the appraisers that makes occupational identification possible. Frequently such tradesmen were living in one room and these inventories probably represent either journeymen or retired traders. Their presence inevitably reduces a median or mean. The trade of baking must have provided opportunities for any man ready or able to diversify his trade. Four of the more prosperous bakers enhanced their profits by brewing, malting and keeping an alehouse.

Towndrow (**7**) was a baker of middling fortune and his house and equipment exemplify most of the characteristics of the trade. There was a corn chamber which received his purchases of wheat and rye. After this had been ground by a miller it was stored in the meal chamber and later sifted before baking. One of the surest signs of a baker's establishment is the clutter of sieving implements that appraisers valued – bolting mills, screeles, sieves, searges and temses. This process gave either good quality whitish flour, 'temst' or the browner and more nutritious bran. Yeast or malt or hops and water were added and the mixture kneaded to a dough using meal troughs, moulding tubs and moulding tables. All of these were valued by the appraisers but they ignored the ovens as an integral part of the bakery. The wooden fuel, kids, which was needed to heat the ovens, was another characteristic of baker inventories. The size of a bake and of stock must have varied between the bakeries but at the death of one of Towndrow's rivals the appraisers valued ninety dozen penny loaves of rye and twenty dozen penny temst loaves.[6]

In the wealthier towns the best bakers were also confectioners or where there was sufficient demand specialists provided biscuits, exotic pastries and sweetmeats. It is somewhat of a surprise to find three artisans in Lincoln who made at least part of their living by producing biscuits, gingerbread and liquorice sweetmeats. The demand for biscuits at the more prestigious funerals would

[5] J. Ellis 'A dynamic society : social relations in Newcastle-upon-Tyne 1660–1760' in P. Clark (ed.) *The Transformation of English Provincial Towns* (London, 1984) p. 219; Vaisey op.cit. p. 6; B. Trinder and J. Cox *Yeomen and Colliers in Telford* (Chichester, 1980) pp. 64–5.

[6] L.A.O. L.C.C. Admon. 1674/132.

have provided cconsistent trade. Thomas Hill's inventory (**39**) represents this trio.

The demands made by bakers and confectioners on the cereal production would have been far less than the quantities required by the city maltsters. There were seventeen of them although the inventories name only three. They were generally wealthy. The median of their estates is £423.98 placing them closely second to the mercers whose median of £467.36 made them the wealthiest occupational group in the city. The fact that so few of the maltsters were identified by appraisers is partly a result of business success which gave them status. Eight of them were styled 'gentlemen', four were 'Mr' and two were aldermen. The indentification of thirteen of them as maltsters is proved by their possession of Kiln house, furnace, fuel and the minor equipment needed for malting. Six of the inventories record debts due to men who simply traded in the commodity without apparently involving themselves in its manufacture. The twentieth maltster is so identified at the top of an inventory that is too fragmentary to give more information. Six farmers, two bakers, a mercer and one wealthy shopkeeper added to their profits by making malt. Given capital and space, time and skill, it was a profitable pursuit. The maltsters had £1,388.00 owing to them from the sale of malt and they had in stock at the time of their deaths 2,166 quarters of malt worth on average £1.00 a quarter. This quantity would have made 311,904 gallons of strong beer. Lincolnshire malt was highly regarded by brewers, in Holland, as well as England. It also seems to have been a convenient short term investment for those with ready money. This seems the best way to explain the very many dispersed quantities too large for normal family requirements and in houses with no brewing equipment.

Three maltsters inventories are printed. One of them William Kent (**14**) was both farmer and maltster and Faux (**56**) was primarily a mercer. The third is that of Norton (**8**). He was described as a maltster on his inventory and it gives the best evidence of the malting process. The malt was usually made from barley but oats, rye, pease and beans were also used. The barley was steeped in water for some sixty hours, then, when judged soft enough to bruise, it was piled in heaps and left to sprout. When this happened the piles were spread out and turned every five or six hours until dry. Then it was dried under a slow, constant fire of smokeless fuel, either charcoal or kids. It could then be stored in a dry place and await sale to traders or brewers.

The inventories name only one brewer. Interestingly he is described as a beer brewer and the inventory gives no indication whatsoever of his trade even though the implements of brewing were a very common feature of many households. 58% of those with estates worth more than £100 had brewing equipment as did 53% of those with estates in the range £50–£99 and 9% of those with goods worth less than £50. The range of investment in such brewing equipment was from the woman who in 1679 had brewing materials worth £1.50 in an estate valued at £4.88 to Alderman John Kent who possessed a copper, coolers, implements and three great vats worth £160 in an estate of £2756.43.[7] There is no difficulty in assigning the title of brewer to Kent but to decide how many of the other inventories belonged to men or women who brewed commercially is difficult. Ordinary household consumption was, by twentieth

[7] L.A.O. Inv. 177/153.

century standards, heavy. The sailors of Pepys's navy expected a gallon a day. It has been assumed that wherever the value of brewing equipment, beer or ale and casks was more than £10.00 that this is evidence of brewing for sale and profit. On this criterion twenty five inventories record brewers. It was a trade conveniently practised by anyone accruing profit in another business. Two bakers, a butcher, a chandler, a chapman, three farmers, a glover, a goldsmith, a leather trader, two mercers and five maltsters were brewers. In addition seven innkeepers and six alehouse keepers had more than £10 of brewing equipment and certainly added to the public availability of both ale and beer. Profits could be considerable. It was a pervasive trade and the inventory evidence for it must be partial.

Four of the printed inventories give evidence of brewing at a level where commercial motives predominated. They are the inventories of the goldsmith Browne (**29**), Leach (**32**) a gentleman and grocer, Feris (**47**) a tanner and glover and Green (**49**) who seems to have concentrated solely on brewing. Leach managed two breweries but Green's inventory gives the best list of the main equipment used. The mill was used to grind the malt before it was boiled in a water filled copper. The furnaces were not valued. The first brew or wort was drawn off into containers called underbecks. Every one of the brewers had an assemblage of tubs and soes in which the beverage was fermented and stored.

Lincoln's brewing trade as revealed by the inventories was very much that of a provincial town. The development of brewing towards bulk production was already well advanced in London and the big cities but only John Kent's capital investment suggests that this was happening in Lincoln. Ale deteriorates rapidly and where there is a limited demand a number of small producers most easily satisfies the market. Moreover ale is mentioned seventy one times in the inventories and beer twenty times. Beer was still a drink associated with urban life and more expensive than ale. Lincoln's addiction to ale has a provincial flavour to it. Even if one accepts that the term ale can encompass both ale and beer the terms do seem to be used in some of the inventories with precision and indicate the city's preference for ale. It was probably good ale, when the Fossdyke came into use, much Lincoln ale was shipped westwards.

All the occupations so far considered have derived their work from arable farming. Another natural 'crop' provided work for twenty one of the citizens, all of whom gained a living by working wood. The county was then more extensively wooded than it is now. These local supplies, together with imports mainly from the Baltic, provided the working materials for nine carpenters and four joiners. Little distinguished their inventories in terms of wealth or product. Their stock in trade consisted of chairs, window frames, wainscot and coffins, particularly the last. Ladders, gunstocks, benches and beds were also valued as their products. One woodworker with a stock of hoops and staves should perhaps be identified as a cooper and a second cooper can be assumed as an employee in the workshop of one of the timber merchants. There was one wheelwright. Their tools were valued at between £3 and £5 and their stocks of wood rarely amounted to as much as this. The median estate valuation of all these woodworkers at £53.75 places them at normal artisan level, the level seen in all inventory collections containing urban carpenters.

There are a number of interesting features in their inventories. One stocked a second shop at Sleaford with chair frames, a chest of drawers and the inevitable coffins.[8] The appraisers of another of the carpenters distinguished between his workshop and his shop and described the latter as a toy shop. It is a remarkably early example of a specialism recognising the needs of children. London had no toy shop at this time.[9] The Lincoln toy maker was probably before his time, he was one of the poorest of the woodworkers.[10] The inventory of John Dring (**44**) is printed. The description of his tools is exceptional both in its detail and the value given to them. He had a saw-pit, a stock of wood that included pear, elm, oak and walnut. His house contained veneered tables and chests of drawers in walnut. It would be surprising if some of those items were not for sale.

Two gentlemen can be included in this group because their livelihood was certainly based on wood and the inventory of one of them, Evison (**37**) is printed. Both were timber merchants. They supplied the carpenters and builders though Evison's business incorporated workshops employing carpenters and coopers. He was a wealthy man with such prestigious accoutrements of status as a rapier and a coffee pot which make the waistcoat and coat he had left in pawn the more incongruous.

Four of the inventories give a reminder that Lincoln was a river city. There are two boatwrights one with boards and wood for boat building valued at £30.89 as well as small boats, pitch, tar and nets. His operations will have overlapped with the two fishermen who can be identified in the inventories. One of them, Ruxton, owned nets and boats for fishing worth £5 and leases worth £100 for his fishing rights between High Bridge and Thornbridge and Brayford.[11]

VI

Butchers, tanners, glovers, cordwainers, sellers of horse and animal gear, minor leather workers

The main animal products which provided work for Lincoln were meat, hides and fleeces. The inventories provide little evidence for the sale of sheep, cattle and horses in the markets or fairs of the city but from these sales in the city and elsewhere came the raw materials for a number of important trades. The trades which derived from meat, tallow and skins can be considered first. Trade and work in leather alone probably involved some 10–20% of the nation's work force and the inventory record for Lincoln shows it was an important branch of the city's trade.[1]

Butchers were the first agents whereby animals became the raw material for a craft or trade. There were twelve butcher inventories in the period. They had a high rate of recognition by appraisers all but two of them being given their trade

8 L.A.O. L.C.C. Admon. 1673/108.

9 J. H. Plumb 'The New World of Children' in N. McKendrick (et al. eds.) *The Birth of a Consumer Society* (London, 1982) p. 288 fn. 10.

10 L.A.O. Inv. 194/292.

11 L.A.O. Inv. 203/395; Catalogue of City Leases 10a, 24.

1 L. A. Clarkson 'The Leather Crafts in Tudor and Stuart England' *The Agricultural History Review* Vol. 14, 1968 p. 29.

title. These two can be identified as butchers, one because he possessed a slaughter house and the other is identified on a letter of administration. The readiness of appraisers to give these men a title was fortunate because there is usually very little amongst their possessions to define their trade. Their specialist equipment was rarely valued at more than £2.00. When itemised it consisted of cambrills, sets, block and ropes, scale, beam and weights. The main requisites of their trade were described as the ability to judge the weight and health of an animal, skill in cutting and dressing the meat, and courage and strength.[2] Lincoln butchers seem to have possessed such qualities for the median level of their estates at £111.80 denotes a comfortable existence. One profitable bye product of their trade was the knowledge they acquired of the countryside and the farmers who supplied them. This encouraged diversification. Two of them were farmers in their own right. Two died owning large quantities of wool, another much corn. Two were maltsters and one was comfortably supported by a collection of mortgages and bonds worth £710.00. The printed inventory of Hobman (**55**) is of one of the poorer butchers.

Eighteen tanners appear in the inventories. Twelve of these were engaged in tanning the heavier hides of cattle, calf and horse. One was tanning, or more accurately dressing, the lighter skins of sheep, calves, goats and dogs. Three, somewhat surprisingly, as it was unusual, appear to have been working in both modes. For two there is insufficient detail in their inventories to make an allocation to either branch of the trade possible.

John Atkinson's inventory (**19**) is the chosen example of the heavy tanning process which produced leather for shoes, saddles and upholstery. It is an extraordinary inventory for the clear picture it gives of a tanner's yard in the late seventeenth century. His work was based on fifteen vats or tubs. These containers were probably clay lined pits lined with barrel staves in which the hides were immersed. These hides, either procured from local slaughter houses or imported from London, had had the hair and fat removed from them by a process of scraping and soaking in a solution of lime. They were softened by the application of bird or dog droppings and then soaked in solutions of bark and water for six to twenty four months. This lengthy process meant that tanners needed to make a considerable investment with no expectation of a quick return. The Lincoln tanners with leather in process had an average outlay of £111 in hides, one of them being credited with hides worth £340. Atkinson's hides were valued at £61.38. Assuming each of his pits could have held 15–25 hides he could have tanned 375 hides at a time. He was working at less than full capacity and with all but three of his pits in use was engaged in tanning 127 hides. He was perhaps being cautious. Tanning was a risky business. It involved critical decisions at the transfer of hides from tub to tub, each of which had to contain carefully judged strengths of bark solution. A mistake could ruin an entire consignment. The presence of both lime and bark in the inventory shows Atkinson was a producer of heavy leather. The 'crust' leather he produced would have been made supple by a currier.

The treatment of lighter skins, particularly for gloves, but also for fashionable items such as fans can be seen in the inventory of Feris (**47**). The dressing of these skins was quicker and cheaper and was achieved by soaking them in oil and

[2] R. Campbell *The London Tradesman* (Newton Abbot, 1969 edn., 1st pub. 1747) p. 281.

then applying a paste of alum mixed with salt, flour and egg yolks. The process took weeks rather than months. Feris appears to have trebled the value of his skins by dressing them. The three tanners who both tanned heavy leather and dressed lighter skins were described as bridlecutter, bridlemaker and bridleman. Their participation in both processes must spring from their need for the two kinds of leather for horse harnesses, the heavy variety for saddles and the lighter for strapping.

The biggest group of craftsmen to make use of leather was the cordwainers. There are fourteen cordwainer inventories and with a median value to their estates of £36.60 they were the poorest of the craft groups. Their tools were inexpensive; their lasts, trees, seats and hammers were seldom valued at more than £1.00. Their investment in leather was usually higher and for a majority of them it represented more than half the value of their estates. Their stocks of finished shoes were large for a craft which is usually supposed to have made shoes to order. Warriner (**57**) whose inventory is printed had 124 pairs of shoes in stock and his fellow cordwainers for whom a count is possible had 47, 79, 104, 238 and 375 pairs. They cost on average around £0.10 a pair. There is some accuracy in describing Warriner's co-workers as 'fellows'. One of the cordwainer's inventories has the only Lincoln reference to a craft guild where in the inventory of Yates in 1665 there is reference to his debt of £0.66 to 'the Company'.[3]

There are only four glover inventories. Three describe unpretentious craftsmen and the inventory of Roger Wood (**40**) illustrates their level in his household goods and his equipment. Feris (**47**) has already been mentioned as a tanner and brewer. He specialised in the manufacture of the lighter skins used for gloves but his stock included pairs of breeches at £0.15 each. Lincoln's mercers stocked large quantities of gloves and their competition must have been a serious obstacle to the maintenance of the craft in the city.

The historical record does not do justice to the horse. Its importance to every shopkeeper who dealt in bulky goods, to carriers and innkeepers is obvious. It provided the most highly regarded means of personal transport and possession of a good horse conferred social prestige. The network of horse dealers and horse breakers, none of whom leaves an inventory, must have enjoyed a place in common conversation and repute much like that of present day car dealers. 25% of the Lincoln inventories included the valuation for a horse or horses. 11% had more than one horse and nine of this group stabled more than five horses. Although the Lincoln record contains no inventory of a horse dealer it is an exceptional record because it includes a substantial group whose working life was devoted to the horse trade. There were ten of them and they were appraised under a variety of title, bridlecutter, bridlemaker, bridleman, saddler and six others who can be joined with them because they all provided harness in the myriad forms that the beast, even then, required. Some of them did little more than sell garth web but as a group the median value of their estates at £277.00 is evidence of the demand for their products and the profits available to a competent tradesman or tradeswoman. Such competence seems to have been a family trait of the Watsons for there were six of that surname in the group. The inventory of Abigaile Watson (**27**) is a compendium of horse gear including the

[3] L.A.O. L.C.C. Admon. 1665/117.

utilitarian basics of bridles, stirrups and buckles as well as the garnishings of Spanish silk and gold thread that made both horse and rider impressive. Her workshop was equipped to make saddles and all the equine accessories in leather. There is no evidence that she possessed her own tanning facilities but two of the tanners were Watsons. Three of the group cured their own leather as their inventories listed cisterns for train oil.

It is convenient to include at this point a comment on three inventories of shop keepers whose trade defies easy categorisation. These are linked because each of them sold basic agricultural necessities many of which were associated with the harnessing of animals. The stock was less glamourous and less dominated by leather than the previously considered harness makers and saddlers but there is an overlap in stock although this trio is more concerned with the harnessing of cattle and oxen. They provided yokes and collars, some saddles, pads and pommels as well as rope, sacks, sacking and haircloth. Younglove's inventory (**9**) shows their range of provision which concentrates on the unexotic ordinary day to day needs of farmers. His stock of rope can serve to make one negative point that none of the Lincoln inventories comes from a ropier. These three shops must have been as well frequented as any in the city but none such appear in other printed collections of urban inventories.

The occupational groups so far described whose work was based on leather must account for only a proportion of the leather workers. There were the labourers with varying skills who assisted the tanners in moving hides from tub to tub and the employees in the saddlers' workshops and apprentices to cordwainers and glovers. There were also the specialists who appear in the inventories as single examples. The widow with an estate of £34.50 who had train oil and lamp black worth £5.00 and working tools worth £1.00 must have been a currier.[4] She would have used the oil and lamp black to make supple and waterproof the leather required by a number of craftsmen. Another specialist was the parchment maker.[5] Ellis (**34**), a whip maker, can stand as representative of this cluster of craftsmen associated with leather. The detail of his working tools and materials for his highly specialised craft justify his inclusion.

Animals provided more than meat and skins and their tallow was the basic resource of the six chandlers who left inventories. All of them possessed candle houses with the tallow, moulds, candle rods and troughs valued at between £5 and £60. This value depended largely on the amount of rendered tallow they had in stock at death. Two of them were aldermen and as a group they were wealthy. The poorest of them had an estate of £54.36 and he was the only one with an estate worth less than £100. The median value of their estates was £172.00 and the richest of them, Dawson, had an estate valued at £896.73.

Although candles were very rarely appraised except as shop stock they must have been one of the most widely spread and common purchases of the time. Nationally they cost about four shillings for a dozen pounds and few households would not have purchased some during the year. Daylight and rushlight were cheaper but candles were a convenient indulgence to the poor and a humble luxury to those who were somewhat richer. Their sale provided the basic security of the chandler's trade. Their shops were within the experience of the

[4] L.A.O. Inv. 204/26.
[5] L.A.O. L.C.C. Admon. 1681/36.

entire population and their success was based on the sale, in small quantities, of these and other everyday necessities. As the purchasing power of the population increased in the late seventeenth century and foreign products became cheaper chandlers found a growing sale for goods that were new and had recently been luxuries. A contemporary Lancaster shopkeeper whose diary records the commercial shifts of the period records how tobacco sales came to account for a third of his business.[6] Chandlers had the customers and seem to have had the skills to profit from incorporating new items in their stock.

The Lincoln chandlers exemplify this trend. All of them, and particularly the first in the series, Lambe in 1663, provided the basic necessities with small stocks of candles, copperas, ginger, nails, salt, soap, tar and tobacco.[7] They all sold a variety of household necessities, earthenware, glue, pots, pitch, rosin and trenchers and cleaning equipment such as blue, sand, starch, washballs and wood in the form of firdales and latts. They stocked bellows, besoms, bottles, brushes, candlesticks, cork, glasses, handsaws, lanthorns, rubstones, thread, smoothing irons, wool cards and wormseed. Increasingly their customers were tempted by and able to indulge in purchases of an even wider range of stock. The choice of ribbons increased as did the stock of dyes which now included the brighter and cheaper colonial products like logwood and redwood. Other colonial products such as currants, spices, sugar and tobacco became normal items in a chandler's shop. These lists do insufficient justice to the infinite variety of their provision. Buttons, dog collars, fishing lines, gunpowder, horn books, pencils, spectacles and writing paper can serve as symbols of their omnium gatherum.

There is from the inventory evidence no system in the organisation of these items within a shop. The impression is of an expanding trade in the poor man's emphorium which overlapped, if it did not rival, the shops of mercer, grocer and eventually haberdasher. The Lincoln chandlers moulded their stock to their own judgements of what would be profitable. Malton in 1712 matched any other shopkeeper in the city with his variety of dyestuffs, raisins, sugar and tobacco.[8] The range and nature of the debts credited to Dawson, £315.67 in 1698, show that he was acting as a wholesale agent for other chandlers.[9] Howrobin's stock in 1688 had an emphasis on brandy and strong waters, an early instance of exploiting a trade that was to bring eighteenth century chandlers great profit.[10] By 1700 the chandlers' shops in Lincoln had become very akin to the infinitely stocked village shop of the late nineteenth century. Wright's inventory (**50**) illustrates many of these points.

Wright's inventory and those of four others of the Lincoln chandlers reinforce the analogy with the village shop because all five of them had branches in nearby villages. The site of Wright's country shop is unrecorded but the others were in Harmston, Saxilby, Scothern and Washingborough, all within six miles of the city. Their stocks were not great but they replicate in miniature the range from necessities to minor luxuries which were on sale in the city shops. Wright's

6 J. D. Marshall (ed.) *Autobiography of William Stout of Lancaster 1665–1752* (Manchester, 1967) p. 161.
7 L.A.O. Inv. 161/24.
8 L.A.O. L.C.C. Admon. 1712/64.
9 L.A.O. Inv. 193/422.
10 L.A.O. Inv. 187/82.

stock in the country shop was valued at £6.20. Dawson's shop in Washingborough was the most lavishly provided of the country shops with a stock worth £15.00. Stout of Lancaster provided £10.00 worth of stock when he set someone up in a similar shop and the style of business in such a shop is splendidly and vividly described in the diary of Roger Lowe who, as a journeyman, managed such a shop in Ashton-in-Makerfield.[11]

VII

Wool merchants, weavers, dyers, tailors, bodice makers, upholsterers, woollen drapers, linen drapers, mercers

By 1661 Lincoln's role in the textile industry was largely indirect. It played some part in the transmission of wool to the major centres of cloth production in the West Riding and Norfolk and provided a growing market for the finished products. These products, whether woollen or linen, provided much business and many occupations.

White's inventory (**17**) illustrates the direct participation that arose from providing the wool that the manufacturing centres outside the county required. Spinning wheels were valued in 11% of the women's inventories in the city but although one widow owned two linen wheels and had 72 yards of unbleached hemp and linen cloth the impression is that spinning was less common than it was in rural parishes.[1] Only two of the city inventories recorded looms for weaving and for only one of these was the occupation of weaver specified. His loom and goods were valued at £10.00 in an estate of £34.07.[2]

Much of the cloth that came into Lincoln would have needed dyeing as the next stage in the process that led to a customer buying it. There seems to have been trade enough to support one major dyer in each generation. The earliest of the three dyers, Katerne Sewell (**3**), a widow, had when she died in 1664 an estate valued at £219.70. This surpasses the other two dyers who left estates worth £62.13 and £38.19 and surpasses both their inventories in the detail it gives of her business. One reason for the smaller estates of the two later dyers could have been the greater availability of the cheap colonial dyes available at the chandlers and mercers. Katerne Sewell owned a dye house with its copper, cistern, vats and fuel supply. She had a press house in which the newly dyed cloth was given its gloss. She had the shears, tenters, buckets and tubs required by her trade and she stocked a comprehensive range of dyes. Her working equipment was valued at £31.50 and her dyes at £66.25. There were quantities of the traditional English dyes, fustick to give a yellow or olive colour, copperas for greens and blues and madder for yellow. There was woad in such quantity,

[11] Marshall *op.cit.* p. 165; W. L. Sachse *The Diary of Roger Lowe of Ashton-in-Makerfield, Lancashire 1663–74* (London, 1938).

[1] L.A.O. L.C.C. Admon. 1677/6.

[2] L.A.O. Inv. 169/213.

two tuns of it, valued at £35.00 that she must have supplied dyers outside the county. There were also the more exotic colouring agents from the East and West Indies, redwood, logwood, argell, indigo and brasill. Her range of stock was as good as any recorded in a provincial town of the period and her prices much the same as those recorded at Lichfield and Wellington in the same period.[3] Her prices were much less than dyers in less accessible areas such as Slaithwaite.[4] She also managed a farm with an emphasis on the production of hay.

There are inventories for fourteen tailors. Everyone of them is so identified by the appraisors. Such identification is very necessary for there is usually no evidence in the inventories that would enable attribution to a trade. The tailor's inventory which is printed, William Atkinson's (**21**), is selected principally because there is such evidence for his tools valued at £0.40. Moreover with an estate valued at £30.64 he is a good representative of a group the median value of whose estates was £32.91. Their comparative poverty is matched by other groups of urban tailors. None of them had stocks of cloth though one, Reynolds in 1676, had two cloaks that were probably for sale. Their number indicates a steady demand for their services to make up clothes from cloth provided by customers. The risks of under-employment are implied by the hints their inventories give of reinforcing their income through the presence of bee hives, stills, lodgers and fowling pieces.

A small additional group of cloth workers can be associated with the tailors. They were specialists who provided, mainly for women, particular kinds of garments or skilled services. One such specialist was Edmund Fleare (**41**) who produced the complicated bodices required by the fashion of the times. He had 315 in stock, for children as well as women. The stalwart linens, both tickings and basings, which provided the basic quilted padding of the garment and the slivers of whalebone which were slotted into this to create an upper foundation garment were listed and valued by the appraisors. Little of these garments would have been seen because ribbons and needlework were the affectation of the time. English women were renowned for their needlework and milliners and seamstresses were available in many towns to provide fashionable garnishings. None was appraised with these titles in Lincoln but the evidence of their trade could easily be subsumed in generalised valuations. One widow's inventory did contain a collection of pins, threads and silk laces and four shirts valued at £0.50. These could indicate that her skills at needlework were employed on a commercial basis.

The inventories of four upholsterers are significant evidence that Lincoln was catering for the richer elements of county society. Upholsterers had adapted very skillfully to the changing fashions of late seventeenth century customers for furniture and furnishings. At aristocratic level their influence on the development of interior decorations was marked. They were becoming the fashioners of fashion. Their influence is more difficult to detect in the inventories of non-aristocratic households. Direct descriptions of matching furniture and fashionable ensembles of textiles and colour did not come often or easily to the

[3] Vaisey *op.cit.* p. 282; Trinder and Cox *op.cit.* p. 251.

[4] P. C. D. Brears (ed.) Yorkshire Probate Inventories 1542–1689 *Yorkshire Archaeological Record Series* Vol. CXXXIV (Kendal, 1972) p. 137.

appraisers of more humble households. Hints at the ways in which the lessons of the best upholsterers were being copied are discernable on occasion in the rather flat descriptions of the Lincoln appraisers. When they record the bedsteads and chairs in the same colour or when they name a room from its predominating colour or, when, as they do in Featley's inventory (**6**), they describe four chairs and four stools as 'suitable to the bed' they are almost certainly reflecting upholsterer influence. The textile embellishments of a room had been a mark of status from the Middle Ages. The range of colours and materials at the disposal of late seventeenth century upholsterers provided them with endless permutations in the matching of window and bed curtains, seat coverings, cushions, carpets for tables and cupboards and for wall hangings, though these last were becoming less common.[5] The impact of such a lavishly decorated room is difficult for the present day reader to visualise. Appraisers' language does not help. They saw rooms in terms of shillings and pence. They cannot record for us the impression made by an expensively furnished and lavishly upholstered room with a range of looking glasses reflecting and reinforcing the impact of luxury, both in daylight and even more impressively when the evening candles and looking glasses combined in a display of fashionable grandeur.

The materials stocked by the Lincoln upholsterers show they were capable of leading provincial fashion. The stocks of three of them were valued at £74.00, £74.10 and £317.10. The fourth inventory is a widow of one of these.[6] She appears to have managed the business for twenty one years but at her death in 1702 her entire estate was worth only £37.40 although upholstery materials were included in it. All of them stocked the variety of fabrics necessary for webbing, lining and show, the decorating studs and nails that fastened fabrics to the frames of furniture and set off the colours of the various coverings of textiles, carpet, sheepskin and leather. Those with the money to follow their taste or that of the upholsterers could have transformed the simple bed and chair frames listed in the upholsterer inventories into personal and ostentatious demonstrations of affluence and status. The number of inventories implies there was a trade for one or two upholsterers in Lincoln and the inventory of the earliest, Alderman Edward Fawkes from 1679 (**24**) is printed. His trade and that of the others focused the work of many craftsmen in textiles, wood and leather.

A characteristic of all the occupational groups so far associated with textiles is that they all contributed towards the production of articles to be sold. The remaining groups who drew their wealth from textiles are all retailers of finished products. Thirteen of them were drapers, eight specialising in woollen and four in linen cloth and one whose inventory does not define the kind of textile he stocked. To them can be added seven haberdashers, three of whom specialised in providing hats, and twelve mercers. Together they form a large and wealthy concentration of merchants whose activity did much to identify Lincoln as a retailing and wholesale centre.

The eight woollen drapers were wealthy men with a median value to their estates of £231.00. There is little evidence from their inventories that the dominance of woollen clothing was being challenged by the lighter cloths which

[5] P. Thornton *Seventeen Century Interior Decoration in England, France and Holland* (Over Wallop, Hampshire, 1981) pp. 97–105.
[6] L.A.O. L.C.C. Admon. 1679/79; 1702/100; Inv. 182/91; 199/1.

were becoming as popular. Their capital investment in cloth was considerable, on average each had a stock worth £264.72, 44% of their estates. Five of the inventories were detailed enough to show that these five had on average some 1041 yards of woollen cloth for sale. Richard Cracroft who died in 1687 left 1,455 yards of cloth valued at £592.67.[7] Their stock was all in woollens with no intrusion of the new draperies. It consisted of broadcloths, kerseys, wool cloths with a fuzzy nap known as cottons, flannels and bays. Two of the inventories simply divide the stock into these five categories. Most however stocked friezes as well. These were coarse woollens very similar to bays and can be seen as an extension of this category. In all these inventories broadcloth was the most strongly stocked and the most expensive. Kerseys were the next most popular with the other kinds of woollen cloth forming a very small proportion of the trading stock. Prices do not vary significantly throughout the period with cottons at about £0.03 a yard, kerseys from £0.10 to £0.23 and good quality broadcloth valued at £0.75. The balance of stocks varies a little. Storey's inventory of 1672 had more kersey than the others and Beck's wares in 1695 were apparently more lavishly coloured but this could be simply a result of one set of appraisers using the colours as a distinguishing feature in a shop full of textiles. The later inventories had a greater variety of named woollens than their predecessors. Newcomen's inventory (**58**) of 1713 is an illustration of this. He demonstrates a tendency to stock more of the cheaper and lighter woollens and to give them names as exotic as those describing the rival, lighter and cheaper stuffs that were coming from Norfolk. His stock could be a response to the growing competition he and other woollen drapers were facing from the mercers who were increasing their stocks of the newer and more fashionable materials. If so the livery, philamontes, rash, serge, swanskins and cyniment of the early eighteenth century woollen drapers of Lincoln was the only indication that the traditional dominance of wool for clothing was being threatened.

The inventories of the four linen drapers are very different from those who traded in woollen cloth. Their inventories display very great variations in wealth and their stocks are much more diverse. Moreover all four occur between 1702 and 1713 without any representation from the earlier forty two years. This, and the very wide range of commodities they sold, could be one consequence of Lincoln's growing population and commercial influence in the region. One of them, Mr. Edward Fane, had linen valued at £593.15 and provided night gowns, tobacco, books and packthread.[8] The inventory printed is that of James Osburne (**52**) whose estate was valued at £864.80 and although like Fane his stock was founded on linens much of it was of kinds normally stocked by mercers or haberdashers. Linen drapers do not appear to have been as conservative as the woollen drapers in the adaptation of their stock to meet changing trends. His inventory lists 334 items of cloth which in all were some 10,000 yards in length. His linens ranged from the coarser kinds of Dowlas, Fustian, Osenbridge and Ticking to the lighter, fine materials such as Kenting. The bulk of his stock was in the canvas like, heavy and serviceable linens. In addition he stocked the lighter and more fashionable textiles such as allamode, muslins and stuffs and some of the coarser woollens like Scotch cloth. On the evidence of two bills of

[7] L.A.O. Di 37/3/125.

[8] L.A.O. L.C.C. Admon. 1703/58.

sale his trade as a wholesaler extended beyond the city and he was a supplier of bibles, caps, japan callico and flowered muslin to other drapers.

Appraisers and executors identified one haberdasher and one haberdasher of hats but a study of the haberdasher's inventory shows that his sole commercial concern was the selling of hats and on similar evidence a third can be added to the Lincoln total. The most informative of the three inventories is unfortunately much damaged but this hatter, Leachman, had a stock of 991 hats in 1688.[9] Many of them were cheaply valued, such as straw hats at £0.80 a dozen or the 'chip' hats for girls. The presence of rabbit skins in his inventory suggest that his 'beavers' were made from this cheaper and more readily available material. His men's hats at £0.13 each and his nineteen French hats show that he catered for wealthier customers.

There are four retailers who can properly be described as haberdashers although none was so identified by appraisers. All of them had a stock that mainly consisted of dress accessories and small ware such as thread, pins and paper. One of the inventories is uninformative in that these items were shortly described and their combined value given as a lump sum. Another was the inventory of a barber but the description of his equipment for trimming and wigs was curtly completed and was followed by a catalogue of caps, handkerchiefs, head rolls, hoods, ribbons, sashes, scarves and sleeves.[10] Another, describing a widow's estate, had a similar list and included gloves, hosiery and a variety of ready to wear clothes which was unusual for the period when the making up of clothes was often a household task or the business of a tailor.[11] She had mantles and loose gowns for men and women, shirts, petticoats of sarsenet and flannel for sale. It is also noteworthy that she had 134 children's petticoats and 79 coats in stock. Such provision of specifically juvenile clothing is also uncommon for the period. Several of the good debts listed in her inventory were due from maid servants. The printed inventory of Henery Mitchell (**25**) gives the fullest listing of accessories and fashionable devices that were in demand even in a provincial city. Some of his items of stock remain comprehensible to the present day reader but a glossary is necessary to appreciate the purpose of the busks, ear knots, bossoms, cornatts, patches and stomachers that were fashionable in the late 1670s.

The distinction between the inventories of haberdashers and the poorer mercers can be a fine one. The poorest five of the twelve Lincoln mercers could, without occupational identification by appraisers, be allocated to haberdashers or even the poorer chandlers. The seven wealthier mercer inventories however reveal the comprehensive range of this trade. By 1661 provincial mercers had developed this business far beyond the silk wares that had originally formed their basic stock. The main Lincoln mercers sold six categories of merchandise. Three of the inventories did no more than record the value of the goods in these categories without any detail. Their mercery ware consisted of light cloths including some silk. Silk wares remained a distinct category and consisted of silk ribbons, silver and gold lace. Their stock of linen draperies was often large and included the entire range from light textiles for clothing to the coarser domestic

[9] L.A.O. Inv. 188/143.
[10] L.A.O. Di 39/1/72.
[11] Public Record Office (subsequently P.R.O.) Prob. 4/3619.

linens. Their hosiery section was predominantly of gloves and stockings. Haberdashery included not only dress accessories but also ready made clothing and an enormous clutter of miscellaneous items. Their grocery stocks were comprehensive. If chandlers' shops can be seen as ancestors of the small corner shop then the mercers were the ancestors of the department store. Apothecaries, linen drapers, chandlers, glovers, haberdashers and grocers must have felt the impact of their competition. Although none of them stocked broad cloth their stocks of the new draperies would have affected even the woollen drapers. The Lincoln mercers themselves faced competition within the county for some of the smaller towns and villages had very well stocked mercer shops. A Folkingham mercer of 1670 with a stock of £784.85 rivalled the wealthiest of the Lincoln mercers and at Winteringham in 1702 a mercer's stock must have met the needs of the local population for both day to day and many more luxurious items.[12]

Every one of the seven wealthiest Lincoln mercers had made an investment of over £200 in their stock, the mean value of the seven was £400.60. The stock of the poorer five had a mean value of £13.10. The stock of the seven was balanced between the major categories of merchandise in ways that must have reflected their location and customers and their skill in matching stock to present needs and developing trends. One had 43% of his stock value in grocery, another had 60% in mercery ware. The detail of their shops can best be seen in two inventories, that of Benjamin Marshall (**4**) and William Faux (**56**).

Marshall's stock was worth £649.53 and was divided between mercery making up 29% of the total value, silks 15%, linen 25%, haberdashery 13% and grocery 18%. His mercery and linen draperies made up more than 3,000 yards of cloth. The only mercery material in his stock valued at less than a shilling a yard was black cypress, a light often diaphanous lawn much used at funerals. His major lines of cloth were of sempeternums, serges and tammies. These were durable cloths and relatively cheap and light in comparison with the traditional woollen broadcloths. He stocked only small quantities of the more expensive materials like sarsenet. His stocks of linen, hosiery and haberdashery were large and these and the groceries are desribed in detail. The description 'old fashioned' is used twice in the inventory, a telling indication of the rapidly developing commercial world of the late seventeenth century, as is his selection of children's ware.[13] Marshall's inventory contains two other examples of the new commercial techniques of the period. It was a contemporary trick of the times to invent new and attractive names for cloths in the belief that such well chosen titles would increase the sales of stock that had begun to languish.[14] Two of the cloths in his inventory, callacine and tamelettoe seem to be examples of such practice. They are not cited or described in any other source. His debts show his buying and selling hinterland in which Hull, London and Norwich figure as sources of supply. Some of his creditors came from as far afield as Coventry and Bangor. The total of his debts significantly reduces the impression of wealth given by the inventory, although their extent can be interpreted as a

[12] L.A.O. Inv. 172/202; D. Neave (ed.) *Winteringham 1650–1760* (Winteringham W.E.A., 1984) pp. 130–1.

[13] N. McKendrick 'The Consumer Revolution of Eighteenth Century England' in McKendrick *op.cit.* p. 15.

[14] P. Corfield 'A provincial capital in the late seventeenth century : The case of Norwich' in P. Clark and P. Slack (eds.) *Crisis and Order in English Towns 1500–1700* (London, 1972) p. 281.

measure of his credit worthiness. Finally his inventory is one of the few that records funeral expenses in detail. Amongst other things it illustrates the commercial importance of funeral rites in supporting the trade of mercers like Marshall himself.

Faux's inventory of 1708 is forty three years after Marshall's. His stock was valued at £154.85 and was less evenly balanced. Mercery made up 69% of its value, silk 6%, hosiery 4%, haberdashery 12% and grocery 9%. Twenty-one kinds of cloth were listed in his mercery wares against the twenty-seven in Marshall's but again they made up more than 3,000 yards of material. Only eight of the named materials appear in both inventories, callimencoe, camblett, drugget, sagathee, serge, shalloon stuff and tabbie. Where comparison is possible Faux's prices were cheaper. Price comparisons must always be tentative as there is no reliable way of assessing the changing quality of a cloth even though the name may be unchanged but certainly Faux's range of cloth was very different from Marshall's. More than a third of his stock was valued at a shilling a yard or less. His major lines were Norwich stuffs and light weight mixtures of wool, silk and linen like anthorite and cantaloon. It was not an eccentricity of locals or customers that explains Faux's emphasis on such stuffs. He is reflecting and encouraging the growing market for these lighter cloths.[15] One of his competitors, a mercer of the Bail, also died in 1708 and his stock revealed the same emphasis.[16] The great growth of English overseas trade is also reflected in the two inventories. Where comparison is possible Faux's prices for cinnamon, ginger, indigo and mace are cheaper as they are for the more prosaic items like prunes and stoneblue. Both Faux and Marshall sold sugar and tobacco in quantity but the complexities of quality that Marshall had make pricing comparisons impossible. Both of them stocked sugar and tobacco of the poorest quality thus making sales possible to the widest range of customers. Faux added to his profits by acting as a maltster. His balance of assets seems sounder than Marshall's with money invested in house, tenements and gardens but £200 of his debts were regarded as irrecoverable. Both of them were amongst the wealthiest business men of the city. Mercers were in fact the wealthiest occupational group in the city on inventory evidence and one indication of their status and influence is in one being identified as 'Mr' and four of the others being aldermen.

VIII

Brick and tile makers, blacksmiths, whitesmiths, pewterers, plumbers, glaziers and goldsmiths

Lincolnshire had no major mining industry in the late seventeenth century. Thus the occupations in the Lincoln inventories to do with mineral resources are largely those involved with the processing of imported minerals. Coal was the

[15] *Ibid.* pp. 280–2.
[16] L.A.O. Inv. 202/170.

bulkiest of these imports but none of the inventories reveals a merchant who specialised in its distribution. The coal, and the iron from the Derbyshire mines and forges, would have reached Lincoln via the Trent and the value of the Fossdyke for this kind of commodity is well revealed by the tolls levied on these products.[1] Within Lincolnshire itself quarrying for stone, clay for bricks and limestone for lime manufacture would have been widespread but in this period such activities took place outside the city boundaries.

There is an inventory for one freemason who would have found himself in competiton with past generations of stone masons dating back to Roman times. A patchwork of stone cut in many different periods is still a distinctive characteristic of the buildings and walls of Lincoln. Brick had become an acceptable alternative to stone and in the decades after the Civil War was much in demand. Inventories show three people engaged in the manufacture of bricks and tiles. Wignall's inventory (**23**) is the most informative of them. His brick prices at ten shillings for a thousand bricks were cheaper than the contemporary Lichfield prices.[2]

Specialists who processed metals provided the majority of the mineral derived occupations. The eight blacksmiths formed the biggest group. Their trade was a basic one for the times as a reading of any contemporary account book, for example that of Sarah Fell of Furness will show.[3] The shoeing of horses, the manufacture of simple iron devices and the constant need to repair such in an economy where mass produced spare parts were unknown gave a reliable and skilled workman consistent occupation. Clarke's inventory (**2**) illustrates the unpretentious artisan level of the trade. His more successful rivals, like Saul in 1702, left more highly developed businesses. In Saul's workshop there were six anvils, two tons of iron ware, 12,000 nails and 300 lbs of rushes – the cylindrical metal sleeves that take the axle pole of a wheel.[4] Four of the smiths had developed a second source of income as alehouse or lodging house keepers. One of them named Blith with £20.00 in ale and casks, £9.00 in brewing equipment and a house with 65 seats in chair, bench or settle form appears to have been the most successful in developing this second line of business.[5] The generally accepted distinction between black and white smiths was the former's ability to forge iron. Increasingly the whitesmith was seen as specialising in the construction or repair of the more complex iron mechanisms. The Lincoln inventories support this distinction. There were two whitesmiths and a third, called a watchmaker, can be linked to them. Langforth's inventory (**22**) shows a range of tools and evidence of a business in which the repair of jacks and gun mechanisms was important. The watchmarker's inventory had two watches and a clock valued at £3.00 and four watch movements at £4.00. He also possessed the equipment for a distinguished leisure life or even a part-time occupation with two pair of virginals, a cittern and a viol.[6]

[1] P. Riden (ed.) *George Sitwell's Letterbook* 1662–66 Derbyshire Record Society Vol X (Oxford, 1985) pp. 41, 145–6; L.A.O. L1/4/8.

[2] Vaisey *op.cit.* p. 122.

[3] N. Penny (ed.) *The Household Account Book of Sarah Fell of Swarthmoor Hall* (Cambridge, 1920) pp. 163, 177.

[4] L.A.O. Inv. 196/121.

[5] L.A.O. L.C.C. Admon 1705/6.

[6] L.A.O. L.C.C. Admon. 1686/16.

Pewter was a far more widely used metal then than it is now and the presence of the inventories of six pewterers is an indication of this popularity. Two of them were manufacturing a range of pewter vessels as their equipment in the form of moulds reveals, for one of them earning a valuation of over £100.00. The other four pewterers all had workshops but their purpose seems to have been mainly for the repair of pewter and other metal vessels. The inventory of Winne (**35**) gives the most detailed listing of stock. One plumber, five glaziers and two goldsmiths complete the list of Lincoln tradesmen whose living was based on working with metal. The inventory of the glazier Shoosmith (**12**) and a goldsmith Browne (**29**) are printed. Shoosmith's inventory lists the normal range of equipment used by these craftsmen but exceptionally does include a value for the diamonds he used when cutting glass. Browne's stock of gold was not remarkable but the seventy seats and fourteen beds in his house and his investment in brewing equipment and malt suggest that service activities as an alehouse and lodging house keeper were important to him.

IX

The professions and their ancillaries; clergy, Stewards of the Choristers, musicians; physicians, surgeons

As an administrative centre for both secular and ecclesiastical government Lincoln was naturally the working base for representatives of several professions. Only two groups of such professional men are made visible by the inventories, those to do with the church and with medicine. The existence of other professional groups, such as lawyers, is not apparent from their evidence.

On inventory evidence the largest professional group in the city consisted of clergy. They are represented in fourteen inventories. Six of these reflect the importance of the cathedral in the religious life of the city. Two of them were precentors, Thomas Laney and Dr. John Featley. The latter's inventory is printed (**6**). There are five inventories of city parish priests and one of a Minister of the Gospel, John Abdy, a puritan preacher. The second clerical inventory is that of Michael Drake (**43**) who was clerk of St. Swithins and a presbyterian sympathiser as well as being the poorest clergyman in the inventories. The livings of the remaining two clergymen cannot be identified.

Generally the Anglican clergy in the inventories were well endowed. The median value of their assessed wealth was £207.80 and four of them had estates valued at more than £500. Their furnishings bespoke their status and comfort. All but three of them possessed libraries and some of these were of considerable value, the most expensive being assessed as worth £85. As a group they were exceptionally well equipped with plate, musical instruments, watches, clocks and wearing apparel, much of the last was identified as ecclesiastical vestments. Their furnishings were lavish with Spanish tables seeming to be a particular fashion of the Minster Yard houses. Featley's inventory (**6**) displays all these characteristics.

Two other occupations can be linked to the cathedral establishment. Inventories exist for three musicians, all of whom had lived in Dean and Chapter properties and in one of them the deceased had owned two surplices. Between them they mustered a range of instruments, citterns, cornets, harpsicalls, spinets, violins and viols. One possessed forty music books. The other occupation for which there is evidence in two inventories is that of Steward of the Choristers. The first of these, of John Blundifield, is unfortunately in a damaged state but in what remains there is a valuation of the furnishings in the 'Chamber above the School'. He and his successor both lived in the Choristers' House, now 10 Minster Yard. The inventory of the second Steward, John Norris in printed (**51**). The house in which they lived is illustrated as Plate II.[1]

The inventories provide evidence that Lincoln was important enough to sustain the whole range of medical services available in the period. The most esteemed and most expensive treatment came from physicians who specialised in the cure of internal illnesses by prescribing medicines. In the mid-eighteenth century Campbell in his 'London Tradesman' considered that the necessary attributes of a physician were books, a Latin Diploma, a grave face, a sword and a long wig.[2] Lincoln had six physician's inventories and they all possessed books. Two of them were described as Doctors of Physic and their estates, valued at £893.92 and £499.93, imply that they had skills as well as some of the attributes Campbell described. One of them owned one of the three coaches valued in the Lincoln inventories. The inventory of the richer, Dr. Corbet (**30**), is printed. It reveals more about the degree of comfort that success in his profession could secure than about his modes of treatment. The remaining four physicians were poor. Their combined estates were valued at only £55.00 and as two of them were obviously lodgers they could have been itinerants.

The four surgeons recorded were even poorer with combined estates valued at £48.79. All four inventories provided some evidence for their task of remedying physical ailments in the form of boxes of instruments, plaisters, pots and gallipots. The houses of all four were indistinguishable from the lowest levels of inventory society. Three of the inventories were of people who specialised in the provision of medicines, two of them described as apothecaries. None of the inventories provides detail on the types of medicine. A widow, Mary Cracroft, can be associated with the two apothecaries. Her inventory simply describes her as a widow but it records drugs, comfits, pots and glasses.[3] In the vocabulary of the time she could best be described as a druggist. These thirteen people would not have been alone in providing medical care in Lincoln. The inventories do not make visible the ancillaries who must have helped, the midwives, nurses and purveyors of herbal and folk medicine. The one barber-surgeon who apparently continued the traditional diversity of role in his occupation title will be considered with the barbers.

[1] Jones, Major and Varley (eds.) *op.cit.* p. 49; L.A.O. Inv. 190/355; see below p. 120–1.
[2] Campbell *op.cit.* p. 41.
[3] L.A.O. Di 37/3/124.

PLATE II. 10 Minster Yard
(By kind permission of Lincoln Civic Trust)

X

Services: inn, alehouse and coffee house keepers; barbers, chapmen and watermen; bookseller and miscellaneous

Just as the professionals and their ancillaries provided service for the citizens of Lincoln and its hinterland so did a range of less skilled business men. The most numerous and public of these were the keepers of the inns, alehouses and lodging houses of the city.

One symbol of urban status was the presence of inns. The fourteen miles that separated Lincoln from the Great North Road were sufficient to deprive the city of inns as munificent and vast as those in the towns along the road at Newark, Grantham and Stamford. There were however two or three which could have satisfied the most demanding of guests. The most prestigious Lincoln inn was the Angel in the Bail. The earlier of the two inventories that describe it is printed (**45**). It must have fulfilled all the necessary functions of a major inn though an inventory will give evidence of only a few of them. It had thirty three rooms offering accommodation, with the best, the Little Cross, having furnishings valued at £14.00. Its cellars contained a good quantity of ale, beer and wines, including Canary the most expensive and fashionable drink of the time. Its bowling green and cockpit are evidence of the social life that would have centred upon such an inn but the inventory can give no indication of the entertainments that would have taken place. Some rooms, for example the Mitre with its elegant furnishings, can indicate the meetings that would have been held for horse and land sales, electioneering and legal business. The rooms too must have provided the setting for discreet marketing in all manner of agricultural produce.[1]

Douce's inventory for the Angel in 1698 was one of seventeen inventories describing inns. His successor in 1704 had managed the establishment with few changes to its layout since Douce's death except that a stable of coach horses worth £50 had been added.[2] The Angel's nearest rival seems to have been the Reindeer. One of its rooms with furniture and furnishings valued at £28.00 was the most expensively equipped room in any of the Lincoln inns. The inventories of the Angel, the Reindeer and five other inns have the distinctive characteristics of a first rate establishment. All have carefully chosen names for their main rooms. Many of these names provided the names of public houses in the next two centuries, the Lion, the Bull, the Half Moon, Rose and Crown and Fleur de Lys. They all had guest rooms in which appraisers saw furnishings worth more that £10.00. Most had a heavy investment in pewter and linen, most had seating for a hundred or more. All but two had their own brewhouse but only in three was a stock of wine valued. All these inventories were valued at more than £200. Two of the innholders were described as gentlemen.

[1] A. Everitt 'The English Urban Inn 1560–1760' in *Landscape and Community in England* (London, 1985) pp. 165–6, 169–184.

[2] L.A.O. Inv. 198/2.

Another five inventories were about men described as innholders but these were the owners of inferior establishments. To these can be added the inventories of a yeoman and one undesignated man both of whom had rooms which were given titles and were probably available for hire. These were all unpretentious households with from six to ten rooms available for accommodation. One or two of these rooms were as comfortably furnished as the average in the principal inns but the descriptions of furniture and linen and the valuations given to them show that they catered for poorer travellers. One, with two rooms described as the 'Troupers' and 'Ostry' must have operated at a level scarcely distinguishable from that of an alehousekeeper. This and probably some of the others might have provided the kind of discomfort that made even such a hardened contemporary as Ned Ward write his critical and pungent description of a night's lodging at a poor inn.[3] All of them had brewing equipment and several already had the bell, bar and slate that were to accompany English drinking for many years to come. Generally throughout England lesser inns and alehouses were becoming both more respectable and more lavishly appointed. There is no evidence in the Lincoln inventories that the facilities of these lesser inns were improving. Indeed their attachment to ale rather than beer and their minimal stocks of wine would have made them seem provincial to travellers from London.[4] Only one of them provided spirits.

The identification of alehousekeepers from the inventories is very difficult. There appear to be five in the Lincoln record, an aledraper, an alehousekeeper and three victuallers. The last were still synonymous with alehousekeepers as the development whereby their provision of food eventually distinguished them was not yet far advanced. The inventory of one of them, Pell (**54**), is printed. Lincoln would certainly have had more alehouses than this. Estimates of the proportions of alehouses in towns vary between one in six and one in thirty two houses[5] and from the inventory evidence for maltsters, brewers and inns Lincoln was not an unnaturally abstemious city. The inventories of the five alehousekeepers identified by the Lincoln appraisers contained little that would define them as providers of ale and lodgings. They lived in unexceptional houses with seating for no more than twenty. Two did possess more than £10.00 of ale and all but one had brewing equipment. Another ten alehousekeepers can be identified with some confidence by taking such evidence as exceptional quantities of casks or ale, chairs and settles, quart and pint pots, jugs and chamber pots as indicators. Two of them were widows, one a baker and four were blacksmiths. The median value of their estates was £92.99 and these would have been the successful exponents of what was a risky business.

Peart's inventory (**33**) is most appropriately mentioned in connection with innkeepers and alehousekeepers. He had on his premises a stock of ale, meads, beer and cider in quantities that makes personal indulgence unlikely. He also had tobacco, honey and the necessary equipment for making and dispensing coffee. This unique combination of refreshments, for Lincoln, can best be explained by identifying his house as the only coffee house the city seems to have possessed. Such resorts were common enough in London and major provincial towns by

[3] Ned Ward *op.cit.* pp. 40–1.

[4] P. Mathias *The Brewing Industry in England 1700–1830* (Cambridge, 1959) p. xvii.

[5] P. Clark *The English Alehouse* (London, 1983) p. 44; Hey *op.cit.* p. 208.

1680. Ned Ward's account of London in the reign of Queen Anne makes it clear that not all of them were non-alcoholic and elegant centres of social interchange.[6] Peart's hall was probably Lincoln's response to the fashion of the times. He was identified as a gentleman and there would have been customers enough in the city to justify this alternative to inn or alehouse.

Barbers' shops provided another recognised recreational centre in seventeenth century towns. There are ten Lincoln inventories for barbers and only one of them was specifically described as a barber-surgeon and would have run an establishment in which leisure and recreation were not the obvious function of the shop. Traditionally the barber-surgeon had fulfilled the tasks of dentistry, simple first aid, bleeding and shaving. Only Simpkin in 1662 seems to have kept up this tradition and his inventory contains valuations for a store of drugs and 'blood' vessels.[7] The medical aspects of the barber's trade were declining nationally. The increasing emphasis on the non-medical side of the business is exemplified by Glen's inventory for 1662 (**1**). His shop had accommodation for some six customers and the equipment for heating shaving water together with the basins, towels and smocks but no provision of medical materials. His wife continued the business with some success for eight years after his death.[8] Neither of them made provision for the maintenance and manufacture of wigs, a branch of the barber's business which was to flourish in the later decades of the century. Every Lincoln barber after 1677 had the blocks and powdering tubs which the new fashion demanded. The custom of barbers providing music for their customers remained in two of the Lincoln barber's shops with citterns available. One of the few songs of the time that we would recognise today is *Come lasses and lads take leave of your Dads* which first became popular in the 1670s.[9] An even more common feature of barbers' shops was the availability of spirits, usually gin or brandy, which were more commonly available at barbers than at inns or alehouses. Four of the barbers had their own still and strong water measures in the shop. Mrs. Glen's successful maintenance of her late husband's business seems to have involved the development of this aspect of the trade.

There are inventories for two chapmen, three carriers and five watermen. They must afford minority representation for unrecorded porters, ostlers, drovers and others who moved produce and products in and out of Lincoln. The chapmen would have distributed small wares and news in Lincoln's hinterland. One of them was a widow whose pack was valued at £7.65, some three quarters of the value of her estate.[10] The other, although styled chapman, had an inventory that contained nothing to confirm this occupation but his market benches were valued, a reminder that he and many of the shopkeepers already described would have competed for custom from their stalls at the markets and fairs held in the city. One of the two carriers had five horses and with an estate worth £89.78 was the wealthier of the two. Pearson's inventory (**26**) represents the five watermen. The coal, turf and agricultural produce valued in it illustrate

[6] Ned Ward *op.cit.* pp. 10–13, 23–7.
[7] L.A.O. Inv. 161/391.
[8] L.A.O. Inv. 172/330.
[9] N. Ault (ed.) *Seventeenth Century Lyrics* (London, 1950) pp. 381–3.
[10] L.A.O. Inv. 186/23.

the importance of the River Witham and Fossdyke for the transportation of bulky goods to the city.

The remaining occupations that can be identified by a title or by the internal evidence of the inventories form a very miscellaneous group. There was the inventory of Sam Crosthwaite, a dancing master, who appears to have been a lodger and probably moved from centre to centre giving lessons. The bulk of his estate was in his purse and apparel valued at £13.13. The remainder consisted of trunks and such objects as a sword, violin, bible, three music books and a pair of silver shoe buckles.[11] There was one inventory of a soldier, a transient also, who came to his death in Lincolnshire and left a cottage at Navenby to his heirs.[12] There was a painter with his colours, brushes and grinding stone but with no indication of his subject matter whether it was landscapes, coach doors or coats of arms.[13] Two of the deceased were identified as merchants but with no indication of the nature of their activities. One possessed £577.46 in bills and bonds but neither lived in particular luxury.[14] There remain two inventories in this miscellaneous group that are worth consideration and printing.

The first is of a bookseller Eden Williams (**11**). Not only is he the single example of a bookseller in the Lincoln record but the range and value of his stock is a useful indicator of Lincoln's status. Wealthy mercers and chandlers could and did run businesses from small towns and villages. None of these in seventeenth century Lincolnshire had a bookseller. Moreover it is an inventory with good detail marred by only two annoying defects. Its vertical sides are much damaged and the beginnings of the descriptions of some items and some valuations have been lost. It would too have been so much more valuable if the appraisers had possessed the time and skill to list the authors and titles of the books. There could have been a first folio Shakespeare in his secondhand stock.

His secular stock of folios and smaller books numbered 1,991. The folio books were valued at £0.13 each. Sizes of books in this period were not yet standardised but all sizes were related to the folding of one large sheet of printing paper. A folio book was one for which such a sheet had been folded once to give two leaves or four pages. Folding a similarly sized sheet twice gave eight pages and a quarto book, three folds gave sixteen pages and an octavo book. Smaller books were defined by the 'mo' abbreviation. This is written in the inventories as 'o', like a degree sign. The number signifies the number of leaves made by folding twelve, sixteen or twenty four times to give double this number of book pages from the original large basic sheet of printing paper.[15] Each book would have been in sheet form. The purchaser would have bargained with Williams, or a bookbinder elsewhere, for the labour intensive, often highly individual and expensive addition of binding the sheets in book form. The shop stock included the more ephemeral stitched or folded publications of ballads and political pamphlets. As would be expected of any bookseller of the time, but especially one in a cathedral city, there was a big stock of bibles, testaments, prayer books and grammars. Normally these were already bound and were therefore more

[11] P.R.O. Prob. 5/1408.
[12] L.A.O. Inv. 197/219.
[13] L.A.O. Inv. 202/59.
[14] L.A.O. Inv. 175/226; 175/408.
[15] P. Gaskell *A New Introduction to Bibliography* (Oxford, 1972) p. 81.

expensive. His great shop, where the books were concentrated, also had for sale the bound paper writing books that every user of parochial records can recognise. These were the books bought by parish clerks, churchwardens and overseers of the poor in which to enter their registers and accounts.

The little shop was the main stationery department. It contained a variety of good writing papers. By this time most of the paper used was produced in England but if the descriptions are to be believed Williams had a clientele prepared to pay for expensive Dutch and Venetian paper. The parchment and vellum required for the more important documents, leases and marriage settlements, were available from London, Grantham and Lincoln. Presumably the Lincoln parchment maker who left an inventory was one of Williams' suppliers. Here too were stocked the trappings of literacy, wax, lead pencils and the standishes to hold them. The third department of Williams' business was sited across the street where he had two hand presses although no type, which was expensive, was valued with them. There was also a plough press which was used in the binding of books and shows that this was another service available from him.

The last individual inventory to be discussed makes better than any other the point that the complexity of urban life offered opportunity. It is the inventory of Houghton (**42**) who leased the buildings and 6.75 acres enclosed by the Castle walls. He lived well on his estate with comfortable furnishings, including a dining room, books and a clock. Some of his buildings were required for legal usage but he disregarded this responsibility to the extent of storing wheat and cheese in the Grand Jury Room.

His possessions show how he used his buildings and lands for a variety of purposes. He exploited his prime uphill site to provide lodging accommodation for his twenty two beds must record commercial use. His stabling, some of it new, his smithing equipment and his six good horses, together with his brewing capacity indicate that the Castle had become the centre for a number of occupations. He seems also to have acted as a seventeenth century equivalent of a builder's merchant and the inner bailey of the medieval castle was his yard. There were coals in a coalhouse, lime in the sally port, wood in the yards, bricks at the door and wood, leather and coopery ware at the gates. His fourteen pigs had good foraging and provided brawn and bacon for sale. The multiplicity of the occupations he facilitated makes it impossible to define his role in a single word. It has been a feature of many of the inventories already discussed that diversification of occupation was a characteristic of urban life and makes precise categorisation and assessment of the occupations a difficult task. Houghton's inventory expresses this problem powerfully.

XI

Social groups: gentlemen, aldermen, yeomen, labourers, men; widows, spinsters, women

Only a minority of the probate inventories identified an occupation or profession in their preambles. The majority either described the deceased in terms of social group or for women in terms of marital status or did no more than identify sex by virtue of a christian name. (see Table III). On the evidence of other sources or from the internal evidence of the inventories themselves many of these were seen as in fact following a trade. Despite this erosion a majority of the inventories record people in ways that give no evidence for the work that had provided the appraised estate. The hierarchy of social groups from gentleman to labourer for males and of widow and spinster for females is one that was nationally applicable and used by appraisers throughout the country in both urban and rural contexts.

Forty five of the Lincoln inventories were attributed to gentlemen. Six of these inventories are printed by virtue of the gentleman's business as farmer and maltster (**14**), grocer and brewer (**32**), coffee house proprietor (**33**), farmer (**36**), timber merchant (**37**) and innholder (**45**). Certainly many others were involved in business or professional activity. Three were maltsters. One was described as having a 'practice' and, with fees owing to him of more than a hundred pounds, he was either a lawyer or a physician.[1] Eight of them would have been identified as substantial farmers in any set of rural inventories. Others were tanners and millers. Only two of them were gentlemen in the technical and heraldic sense of the word. The others, as was normal for the period, had acquired the title, which their appraisers recognised, by their social, economic or financial stature. The value of their estates and the contents of their households do not provide any distinguishing feature of their status. The mean value of their estates, on inventory valuation, was £456 with the median at £262. The mean of their investment in leases, bills and bonds was £347 and of their purse and apparel was £56. At the same time the title embraced one who lived in the Close whose estate was valued at £3.17.[2] He can be contrasted to another gentleman lodger whose estate included £1,000 in purse and apparel, £1,500 in mortgages and merely £1 in purse and apparel.[3] The lodgings and houses of these gentlemen were scattered throughout the city but once allowance has been made for the twelve simply described as living in the city with no precise parish of habitation they did concentrate uphill with thirteen dying in the parishes of St. Mary Magdalen, St. Paul and St. Peter Eastgate.

Thirty eight of the inventories were attributed to men described as aldermen or 'Mr'. The inventories of four of them are printed as a baker (**7**), alderman and upholsterer (**24**), alderman and pewterer (**35**) and alderman and mercer and maltster (**56**). Others of them followed the trade of brewer, chandler, maltster, mercer and tanner. Business as a chandler with its opportunities for contact with

[1] P.R.O. Prob. 4/11,111.
[2] L.A.O. Di. 38/2/12.
[3] L.A.O. L.C.C. Admon. 1678/84.

large numbers of the citizenry seems to have been a good political base. Information from the inventories does not provide them with any particular distinguishing feature. The mean value of their estates was £456 and the median £198. Their investment had a mean of £257 and their purse and apparel £12.

Fifteen men were described as yeomen by the appraisers. Again on inventory evidence there is nothing to distinguish them from others except their title. None of them had an identifiable occupation, with the exception of the miller, and none of their inventories is printed. The mean value of their assessed estate was £258 with the median at £96. One of them had an estate worth £1,690 but was not recognised with a title more exalted than yeoman. The mean of their investments was £192 though this drops to £63 if the wealthiest of them is excluded. The mean of their purse and apparel was £20. By rural standards most of them were poor. In the last three decades of the period only three yeomen were so designated and this at a time when the title was being more commonly applied in the nearby countryside. As a title it seems to be on the way to being abandoned in the city context. Unpretentious though this group appears in financial terms, and their households and furnishings confirm the modest life style they achieved as a group, they are in the conditions of their time worthy of a distinguishing title when their circumstances are compared with the financial status of their inferiors, the labourers.

Eleven labourers were so designated in the inventories and to this small group can be added the husbandmen and the single shepherd. The mean of their estate was £17.65, the median £12.12. The mean of their purse and apparel was £4.4. None of them had bonds, leases or mortgages. The inventory of one of them Thomas Lewis (**5**) is printed though two others (**10**, **20**) that are printed are obviously from representatives of the same social group. Lewis lived in a small but adequately appointed house. He had three cows which must have contributed to his comparative affluence and a small selection of personal tools, scythe, spade and hatchet. Affluence is an appropriate word to describe his status amongst his peer group. The majority of the labourers did not reach the level of probate documentation, and seven of the eleven labourers had estates valued at less than £10.00.

The largest group of inventories comes from undistinguished men, undistinguished in the sense that their appraisers gave them neither occupational nor social definition. 75 of these 173 undistinguished men can be allocated an occupation, and the remaining 98 had estates whose mean value was £64 and purse and apparel at £5. 82% had assets worth less than £100 and 29% goods valued at less than £10. Henry Wanleste (**28**) can represent the group. His household and status was on a level with the whipmaker, tailor and waterman already described (**34**, **21**, **26**). He was one of a group of artisans, journeymen, retired business men who had most of them attained a modest level of comfort and security. 13% of them appear to have been lodgers in that they owned no beds or furniture. If occupations could be assigned to them with accuracy they would add something to the diversity of Lincoln's business life in the period but it is unlikely that such identification would significantly change its basic outline. They represent the husbandmen of urban society.

This generalisation requires some amendment. It was a diverse group by the very fact of its lack of definition and Houghton's inventory (**42**) is a representative of the wealthy minority in this group who were not defined by a title or occupation. Six had estates worth more than £200, one of them with more than £500 of appraised goods. Their business activities are often hinted at in the inventories. The wealthiest with an estate of £657.18 had unspecified shop wares worth £353.66.[4] Seven of them had shops, two had so much fuel in the shape of faggots, kids and coal that they probably acted as fuel merchants. Another owned seventy seven stone of hemp and another so many bowls that he could have been either a dish turner or retailer.

In terms of wealth the inventories of the seventy one widows represent an even greater range spanning the entire range between abject poverty and the rich. Although 23% had estates worth less than £10 there were 37% with more than £100. The median value of these widow estates at £124 is a statistical and oblique reference to the wills of the period in which the husband's determination to provide as well as he can for his widow is a characteristic feature. Widow Nickinson's inventory (**15**) is an example of such security and the comfortable life style sometimes achieved, Elizabeth Gryme's (**59**) of a far more precarious existence which apparently ended in a rented room. Six others were lodgers too. At least twenty two of them worked after the death of their husbands. The inventories of the dyer Katerne Sewell (**3**) and the saddler Abigaile Watson (**27**) argue a high degree of business competence on the part of some at least of these widows. The inventories show that widows continued their husbands' business as baker, barber, goldsmith, haberdasher, innholder, mercer, tanner and upholsterer. Only one of them, the mercer, was so described on her inventory. Other occupations followed by widows were those of alehousekeeper (three of them), brewer, bridleseller, carrier, currier, druggist, fruiterer, milliner, seamstress and spinster. As a group they are distinguished, perhaps not surprisingly, by a rather high average valuation for purse and apparel at £22.36. Bonds, even of a few pound's value, and a few fragments of silver are common amongst their possessions.

Thirty women were simply named on their inventories with neither the usual addition of widow or spinster. Like widows they as a group represent the extremes of poverty and wealth. This range is represented by Margaret Lees (**60**) whose level of creature comfort as expressed by her possessions must have been matched by many, male and female, who left no inventories. At the other extreme Elizabeth Manby (**48**) enjoyed wealth, security and a luxurious house. The inventories of Elizabth Bate (**18**) and Sissie Peacock (**16**) are good examples of the level of furnishings that most of the women, whether widow or not, were able to enjoy. Bate was a lodger and Peacock with her range of animals, including what was in effect a dairy herd, could have attained security and a livelihood from them. Only one wife is represented in the Lincoln inventories. Such a small representation is usual. Probate record of a wife's personal possessions was allowed in law only in exceptional circumstances. This, like most others, follows from an earlier agreement made at marriage.[5]

The appraisers' use of the word spinster makes it practically synonymous with servant. Twelve of the thirteen Lincoln spinsters were lodgers and no furniture was valued in their inventories. The assets of one of them were listed as just her

4 L.A.O. Di. 37/2/1.
5 L.A.O. L.C.C. Admon. 1670/98.

wages £4.00 and £0.50 for personal possessions.[6] Four of them had savings in the form of bonds of small value, two of them had small items of silver. Littleover's inventory (**46**) is typical of these serving girl inventories. Her savings took the form of the sheep she had at what was probably her home parish of Benniworth.[7] Her assessed wealth was £9.55. The one exceptional member of this group, almost certainly an older woman and not a servant was the most prolific money lender amongst the Lincoln inventory leavers.[8]

XII

Houses and their furnishings

The inventories provide a mass of information about the houses of Lincoln citizens and the ways in which they furnished them. The evidence provided is however uneven and partial. Some inventories do little more than name a room and give a value for the furniture in it with no attempt to differentiate the various items. Such generalised descriptions become more common in the eighteenth century but involve no more than a small minority of the Lincoln inventories before 1714.

More importantly it is very difficult to be sure that an inventory describes an entire house. Appraisers were required to list and value goods and chattels. An empty room was of no concern to them. Moreover they were fallible humans and could entirely miss a room. One of the few houses still standing in Lincoln that can be positively linked to two probate inventories is No. 10 Minster Yard. (See Plate II). It would be impossible on the evidence of the first inventory accurately to draw up a plan of the house because through neglect, or because it was empty, the appraisers did not name two of the rooms.[1] Omissions for these reasons seem to be rare. The reading of many inventories leaves a strong impression that appraisers were conscientious and then as now even if a room was unused it was a convenient dumping ground for miscellaneous items of furniture and these most appraisers would have noted and valued. A greater cause for concern is visible in several of the Lincoln inventories. They include appraisals of the chamber above the shop but nothing in the shop is appraised, presumably because it had been rented to someone else. The inventories provide no way of checking how much of a building was rented and occupied by someone other than the owner or tenant whose inventory was being compiled. The goods of sub-tenants were not the concern of the inventory appraisers. Furniture in some rooms could be on loan or hire or could have been given away before the death of the householder. There are examples in the Lincoln inventories of rooms in which only half the furniture is appraised because it had already been given away and of furniture dispersed in other households which belonged to the

[6] L.A.O. L.C.C. Admon. 1675/108.

[7] A. Kussmaul *Servants in husbandry in early modern England* Cambridge, (1981) p. 39.

[8] P.R.O. Prob. 4/1305.

[1] Jones, Major and Varley (eds.) *op.cit.* p. 49. See above p. liii.

deceased(**9**). Multiple occupancy of a building was a characteristic of seventeenth century urban life. In Chester in 1664/5 a hundred households lived in forty-six houses.[2] Unfurnished rented rooms or even sequences of unfurnished rooms leased to a sub-tenant would not be the concern of appraisers. Uncertainties such as these make confident visualisation of the plan of a house from inventory evidence an impossibility although tentative generalisations based upon recurring patterns of room sequence are possible.

It is however possible to analyse both the functions of rooms and their furnishings from inventory evidence. The furniture and furnishings the deceased had been able to amass to grace his life was the business of the appraisers whether the deceased had ended his life in a hired room as a sub-tenant or as the sole occupier of a house. The reservations expressed in the previous paragraph need to be remembered but the mass of inventory evidence is relevant for attempts to appreciate the style of life and degree of comfort which the subjects of the inventories had experienced.

Such analysis is not facilitated by organising interpretation within the framework of occupational or social groupings or by relating furnishing expenditure to the totals of assessed wealth. Some wealthy people, then as now, chose to live in unostentatious surroundings, if not squalor. It is useful at this stage to consider houses and furnishings on the basis of the appraised value of a household's furniture and furnishings. The great majority of the inventories, 510 of them, are written in sufficient detail for the value of furniture and furnishings in each case to be calculated. This sub-total ignores purse and apparel, bonds, mortgages, leases, stock in shop, agricultural produce including animals and yard material. Plate has been included in the valuation of household goods. Although it was regarded as practically the equivalent of ready money, and is indeed included with the purse and apparel sections of some inventories, it was also widely regarded as the most impressive item of household display. The thirty inventories in which there is no evaluation of furniture are excluded as are a number of others where it is difficult to distinguish personal from commercial possessions, for example in the inventories of innkeepers or the joiner's inventory (**44**) where his furniture includes items that could have been for sale. The distribution and range of valuations of household goods is expressed in Table V.

18% of those inventories possessed household goods worth less than £6 at their death, 49% had furnishings worth between £6 and £35. The remaining 33% had household possessions worth from £36 to more than £200. The Doctor of Physic's household (**30**) was the most munificently furnished in all the inventories. It is a difficult but necessary exercise to fit descriptive words to this statistical skeleton. Houses in which the value of the furnishings was less than £5 could only have attained adequate standards of comfort though in any consideration of these relatively mean households the majority whose wealth did not lead to the composition of a probate inventory needs to be remembered. A labourers' wages were between 3p and 4p a day in a period when regular full time employment was uncommon.[3] At this level of earning there was small scope for comfortable furnishing. Comfort does seem to have been achieved by

[2] N. Alldridge, 'Hearth and Home : a three dimensional survey' in Alldridge *op.cit.* p. 91.
[3] L.A.O. Sutterton 19/3 Rates of Wages . . . 1676; Court Papers 69/4/32.

TABLE V. The range and distribution of valuations in household goods

Value	Number of Inventories	Percentage of Inventories in each financial category
£		
1– 5	91	18
6– 15	112	22
16– 35	138	27
36– 50	64	13
51– 75	47	9
76–100	27	5
101–150	20	4
151–200	8	2
201+	3	1

those who could afford furnishings which their appraisers were eventually to value at between £6 and £35. Into this band of expenditure came those who were successful enough or who cared enough about appearances to expend more than a fifth of their wealth on furnishing their dwelling place. The remaining third of those leaving inventories demonstrated furnishings that must have correlated with a range of description from modest luxury to ostentatious affluence.

The appearance of luxury or exceptional comfort did not matter to them all. Some had furnishings apparently ill-adjusted to their wealth. There was the draper with an estate valued at £864.14 whose furnishings were worth a mere £15.22 (**52**). There were two households with a luxurious and similar level of furnishings valued by their appraisers at £88 and £82 but whose estates were worth £1,194.13 and £131.30 respectively.[4] Their attitudes to home life must have been very different. The weight of evidence from the inventories is that concern for comfort and ostentation was slight. Security mattered more and security resided in investment and good debts. 27% of those leaving inventories had leases, 26% had good debts, bonds or mortgages worth from £1 to £50, 7% had such investments worth from £51 to £100 and 15% had investments worth more than £100. Both gentlemen and yeomen had 76% of their estates in good securities, aldermen had 43%, the clergy 42%. The major shopkeepers' estates show the same primacy of concern, drapers had 47% of their appraised estate in stock, mercers 44%, tanners 38% and chandlers 32%. The evidence from wills in the shape of real estate for these groups would certainly reinforce the impression that security through investment mattered more to all but a minority than the comfort and show that came from expensively furnished rooms.[5]

The uses to which rooms were put gives further evidence of how different social groups and individuals allocated varying importance to the issues of

[4] L.A.O. Inv. 169/183; L.C.C. Admon. 1673/91.

[5] R. P. Garrard 'English Probate Inventories and the Significance of the Domestic Interior' in Ad Van Der Woude and A. Schuurman (eds.) *Probate Inventories*, A.A.G. Bijdragen 23 (Wageningen, 1980) pp. 56–8.

comfort and show. There are 402 of the inventories that can be effectively used for discussion of room function. In them the appraisers employed the common vocabulary of the time in giving titles to rooms and described the furniture in them in sufficient detail for the main uses of the room to be defined.[6]

The first of the elements that made up most dwellings was the room called the 'hall' or 'house'. The former was used 106 times, the latter 226 times. Three inventories cited both 'hall' and 'house', seven had a room described as 'hall or house', three had a 'hall, house or kitchen', one had a 'dwelling house'. Function varied in this room as widely as the titles. In some dwellings the 'hall' or 'house' was literally the living room in which were centred all the functions of cooking, sleeping and living (**20**). Those able to afford larger accommodation were able to remove the business of cooking and sleeping from this room and it became much more the living room in the modern sense in which the superior furniture, the better pewter, good chimney furniture in the form of ornate landirons, tongs and shovels were displayed. Appraisers were inclined to distinguish between 'hall' and 'house' partly on grounds of function and partly on social judgement. 'House' was generally applied to rooms in the more poorly furnished residences where the total valuation of the furnishing was less than £35 and in which at least two of the three functions of cooking, sleeping and living were concentrated. Some of these could well have been one room habitations though the possibility that appraisers in these inventories did not bother to distinguish separate rooms makes accurate numbering impossible. The presence of beds was one of the decisive factors that led appraisers to select the word 'hall' or 'house'. Only 9% of the halls had beds in them, 64% of the labourers' 'houses' contained beds.

A kitchen was described and named in 57% of the inventories in which room usage can be identified. It was a more common room in those houses where more than £35 had been valued for furnishings with 78% having such a room. 19% had both a kitchen where the food was prepared and an adjoining store room or buttery. Several other names were used to describe service rooms associated with the preparation or storage of food. A larder was named in seven inventories but with no indication that it was put to a specific use such as storing meat. Pantry occurred in thirteen inventories, scullery in nine, drinking room in two, without any distinctive use other than storage and food preparation being identifiable from the contents of any of these rooms. There were six wash-houses and one sink house, none of which need have been integral with the structure of the main building, but in them the presence of tubs, implies that they were in use for the business of washing clothes.

The usage of the description 'parlour' has similar characteristics. They were named in 196 of the inventories. Traditionally this had been the bedroom and in those modest households where the bed could be removed from the 'house' the custom still prevailed. In houses with furnishings valued at less than £35 there were beds in 72% of the parlours but in the more lavishly furnished households only 38% of the parlours had beds in them. The function of these bedless parlours was developing towards the drawing room/lounge of more modern times. Indeed two rooms were described in the inventories as withdrawing

[6] U. Priestley and P. J. Corfield 'Rooms and room use in Norwich housing, 1580–1730' *Post Medieval Archaeology* Vol. 16 (1982) pp. 103–119.

rooms. In the wealthier households hall and parlour are sometimes indistinguishable in terms of function as far as their furniture is concerned. In sixty-two of the inventories the process of development goes even further because they all have a second parlour, most frequently described as the 'little parlour'. All these developments echo in their humble context the process whereby the family, in the modern sense of parents and children, was allocated private spaces free from the intrusions of work or servants. The great aristocratic mansions expressed the same social trend in their sequences of rooms from public state rooms to the privacy of the cabinet or closet.[7]

In rural households of the period 'house' or 'hall' and parlour were on the ground floor. The presence of a shop on the ground floor of many urban households would have put pressure on ground floor space and have been one factor in what became a national trend towards having the principal bedroom on the first floor. In the Lincoln inventories these bedrooms are usually described as the 'best chamber' or the 'great chamber'. The appraisers seem to have used the word 'chamber' to describe a room on the first or second floor. They very frequently named a chamber in relationship to its position over the parlour, hall or shop downstairs. Despite this custom 'chamber', like the word 'room', cannot always be assumed to be above stairs. This is another uncertainty in any attempt to draw up house plans solely on the evidence from inventories. 'Street chambers' and 'middle chambers' are commonly described and this terminology does imply a building gable end on to the road. Some of the chambers were named by colour perhaps showing the influence of upholsterers. On this evidence red, green, yellow, blue, white and purple provided the basis of interior colour schemes, with red easily the most popular colour. Many of the chambers can be associated with functions of storage whether cereals and malt or shop goods, with work, or with bedrooms for servants. Where a house had a second floor, at what was often described as garret level, servants' bedrooms and storage dominated usage.

Other names for rooms are relatively uncommon. Twenty of the inventories name a dining room, all but one of them sited in wealthy households where more than £35 had been spent on furnishings. The best of these were obviously impressive rooms with sums of more than £20 invested in the table, chairs, cupboards and attendant furnishings (**30**). There were seventeen studies, most of them containing books, but the word itself was still in the process of definition and one called the 'study in the shop' was presumably what we would now call an office (**4**). One room was described as an office and appears to have fulfilled its modern function.[8] There were similar single examples of the use of dressing room, organ room and gun room. Six of the chambers looked out on to gardens and were described as 'garden chambers' by the appraisers but the view from most chambers that did not overlook a street would have been on to a yard with stables, sties, belfreys and lean-to structures and a farmyard like clutter. It needs to be remembered that room usage was not immutable. The function of a room could change in response to family need or the whim of an occupier. One buttery was certainly in use as a bedroom and one pantry was in effect a sitting room.[9]

[7] Thornton *op.cit.* pp. 10, 60.
[8] P.R.O. Prob. 4/1305.
[9] L.A.O. Inv. 219A/183; 173/377.

TABLE VI. Median value of certain classes of furnishing (in £ Sterling)

Total Assessed Value of Furnishing (number in sample)	Best Bedroom	Bed	Linen	Pewter	Brass	% of total Estate in furnishings
1– 5 (41)	1.1	0.8	0.5	0.4	0.5	30
6– 15 (57)	3.8	1.9	2.6	0.9	1.0	33
16– 35 (87)	7.4	3.5	4.7	2.1	1.6	19
36– 60 (51)	8.9	3.6	6.8	2.9	2.2	22
51– 75 (30)	10.0	5.1	5.5	2.6	2.3	19
76–100 (26)	12.6	6.6	18.4	6.6	5.1	16
101+ (30)	25.0	9.5	21.0	9.4	6.1	11

The inventories provide a mass of detailed evidence about the furniture and furnishings of Lincoln houses between 1661 and 1714. A starting point for consideration of this mass of evidence is given in Table VI. Here the median values of certain basic types of furniture and furnishings are related to the owners' overall expenditure on furnishing their house. Not every inventory gives sufficient detail to provide evidence for this Table but there are enough for each level of total expenditure to give significance to the medians. The use of medians is a useful guide to the identification of normal patterns of expenditure but it does mask the individual extremes that were displayed in particular houses.

Although some at each of the financial levels of expenditure in Table VI will have had higher priorities in spending money than on their own creature comforts the figures do give a picture of the norms and trends of purchasing furniture. Even the group who spent less than £6.00, generally the poorest, allocated their expenditure in ways that ensured a modicum of provision in every class illustrated in the Table. Indeed they spent 30% of their estate in securing what was in general terms a barely adequate standard of comfort. It would seem that those capable of or willing to spend between £6 – £15 achieved a level of modest comfort albeit with the outlay of a third of the value of their estate. Interestingly it is on the bedroom and the provision of linen where they particularly improved their level of possessions. Those who could afford between £16 – £35 had apparently satisfied normal aspirations in these classes of furnishing which now represented at 19% a significantly lower proportion of their estate. This group would have had reason to be contented with the interior of their homes because their level of provision was at a good average level. Their superiority over the 40% of Lincoln's population who owned less than £15 of furnishings would have been particularly apparent in the bedroom. The inventories of the remaining third of the population whose investment in furnishings was above £35 had houses whose furnishings exhibited varying degrees of luxury. There is within the £36 – £50 group with a 22% expenditure on furnishings some evidence of a determination to distance themselves from the average household. Having attained this superiority expenditure was probably channelled into other classes of furnishings. Once again expenditure of linen is a particularly interesting indicator of status in the furnishings of most lavishly furnished households.

Beds were frequently the most highly valued item of furniture in an inventory. They had for every social group no matter how humble the same importance as a symbol of status that they possessed in the houses of the great. It was a widely held aspiration to own an impressive and commanding bed. Appraisers recognised this and their descriptions of beds and their accoutrements often take up three or four lines in even a short inventory. Many of them were complex assemblages. The framework, or bedstead, would have had a net of cords across it to support some mats. On these mats would have rested a number of mattresses or 'beds'. Covering them were blankets, sheets, bolsters and pillows with a top covering in the form of a coverlet, quilt or rug. What gave the late seventeenth century bed an infinite capacity to express the standing of the owner was the very common practice of providing hangings to the bed. These provided shelter from draughts and privacy as well as demonstrating wealth and taste. Such beds had corner posts that supported a roof or tester. From this tester fabric borders, a valence, were draped and also hangings which could be drawn to enclose the bed. The colour and texture of these fabrics could be continued at mattress level by counterpoint and base valences. Buttons, loops and cups could add to the decorative impact of these beds. Chairs, carpets and curtains could carry a theme of fabric or pattern out into the bedroom itself.[10]

There are examples of such great beds in the Lincoln inventories. They are usually described as standing beds and several are valued at more than £10 (**4**, **33**). There was a gradation of less impressive structures. There were half headed beds whose testers merely reached half way down the bed. More common were the French or high beds which dispensed with the tester but retained valence and hangings which were suspended from rods or poles joining the four posts of the bed. Canopy beds simply had a cloth covering suspended from the ceiling. The lowliest bed form was a simple bedstead on wheels, a truckle bed. These were low enough to roll underneath the more superior beds. The filling of mattresses was well worth the appraisers' attention for financial reasons and they too indicate levels of comfort. The cheapest and least comfortable was the chaffe mattress stuffed with corn husks, then the flock mattress filled with coarse tufts of wool and the very common 'featherbed' which like Abigaile Watson's (**27**) was crammed with feathers, 8 stone 3lbs of them, worth £0.38 a stone. The best mattresses were filled with thistledown. Beds, then as now, took up much floor space and the inventories name a variety of folding beds described variously as

[10] Thornton *op.cit.* pp. 149–179.

fold up, turn up, press or settle. The last two condensed in the form of a cupboard or settle.

The bedrooms which were the settings for these beds varied as much as the beds themselves. At best the expensive fabrics of the bed itself were matched by upholstery and coverings around the room. It is impossible to judge the subtlety of these colour schemes from the bald descriptions of the appraisers but the impression forms that the colouring was robust. Nickinson's bed chamber with its red and yellow bed against green carpets and blankets implies that the luxuriance of materials and their colours mattered more than the delicacy of matching tones (**15**). These were the rooms that most closely expressed the individuality and status of the owner. They were far less private than today's bedrooms. They were reception rooms for friends as can be seen by the sometimes lavish provision of seating. Newcomen's (**58**) best bedroom with a bed valued at £8.00 is an example of such a quality bedroom. With the bed hangings drawn back Newcomen could have been pleasantly gratified by his surroundings which contained looking glasses, dressing boxes, cane chairs, an easy chair, a stove, pictures, toys, curtains and wall hangings. Window curtains and their supporting rods were sufficiently important and new in Lincoln to be carefully noted and valued by appraisers. The gradations of comfort and expenditure between the show bedroom and the lesser ones for servants was well illustrated in the inventories of Sewell and Eure (**3**, **36**). In many bedrooms two or more beds were common. In aristocratic mansions a closet adjoining the bedroom was becoming the most private room and the repository for the most valued possessions such as jewellery. Lincoln had such closets but most seem to have fulfilled the functions of a modern boxroom (**49**).

The printed inventories illustrate the kinds of bedroom provision made at various levels of wealth. There are the show piece assemblages of Marshall (**4**) and Featley (**6**), Towndrow (**7**) and Shoosmith (**12**) for the middle range and Burtons (**38**) and Hanson (**53**) at the lowliest level demonstrating with few resources that the furnishings of a bedroom were important. The value of the furnishings in these private bedrooms gives a standard by which to assess the comfort of inns and alehouses. The furnishings of the best room in the Reindeer in Mrs. Fisher's time were worth £28.00, identifying it as one of the most expensively furnished bedrooms in the city.[11]

Table VI shows that lavish provision of linen was a particular characteristic of a well furnished household. The variations in fabric available for sheets, pillowcases, napkins, towels and table cloths gave scope for the richest luxury and humble emulation by the less wealthy. For them there was at least a change of linens within their purchasing power in coarse hemp or flax derived textiles described as hempen, harden or huckaback. Pairs of sheets in these abrasive materials were valued at from £0.9 to £0.25. Linen sheets of varying qualities were valued from £0.25 to £1.00. The best quality Holland linen sheets, Diaper, Damask or Cambric were valued at £1 to £2. Burton's (**38**) stock of linens represents average provision and Browne (**29**) with his twenty dozen sheets of linen and two dozen pillow cases is a good example of lavish provision, Featley's inventory (**6**) shows luxury for the master and lesser quality provision

[11] See below p. lxxvii.

for servants. The appraisers of Watson (**27**) were particularly scrupulous in distinguishing the varieties of linen.

Brass was a common factor in nearly all the inventories. Its particular properties made it a suitable material for many utensils and implements, the majority of which were associated with the preparation and serving of food. It was durable and heaviness was one mark of its durability, pans weighing as much as ten pounds were valued (**58**). It was a poor conductor of heat and thus was of value in bowl or pan shape as a mobile hot plate which kept food ready for eating after it had been cooked on an open fire. This quality made it useful in the manufacture of warming pans and for skellets, the three legged saucepans that could be left on a trivet by the fire and when needed be safely transferred to the table. As a consequence most rooms where food was cooked had some or all of the range of brass chaffing dishes, kettles, ladles, pans, pots, skimmers and saucepans. Brass candlesticks were also very common. These utensils were also cheap with pot brass usually valued at 1p at pound and kettle brass at 3p. Appraisers' values were often half the price of shop ware. Many households possessed thirty to forty pounds and most of the bigger inns well over a hundred pounds. Appraisers needed scales for many of these valuations. Two inventories give good lists of the normal range of brass ware (**1**, **3**).

Implements made from other utensils were frequently present in the cooking rooms. Iron pots and candlesticks were commonly present. Tin dripping pans to collect the juice of meat on the spit were often itemised and their lack of weight was convenient. Copper cans were also present in many of the kitchens but the most common utensil was the wooden trencher and the hecks in which they were stored. Earthenware was valued in surprisingly few of the inventories.

In many of the richer households hot food would have been transferred from the kitchen brass ware to the pewter ware of the dining table. In a pewterer's shop three kinds of pewter were defined, ordinary or 'sad' ware which in shops was appraised at 3p per lb, 'hollow ware' which formed receptacle ware such as bowls at 4p a lb and the alloyed pewter with an addition of tin known as 'lay' ware at about the same price. Appraisers' valuations in private houses were little if at all below shop prices. Pewter ware includes, basins, cans, candlesticks, chamber pots, close stool pans, cups, dishes, flaggons, mustard pots, plates, pots, porringers and salts. Many households had some 50lbs of pewter ware. One of the inns had 715lbs (**45**). The inventories of Featley (**6**) and Watson (**27**) illustrate the variety and values of pewter implements.

Chimney furniture was as common a factor in the inventories as beds, linen, brass and pewter. It is less easy to treat this equipment as a single entity because it fulfiled two functions. One was where the hearth was the centre for cooking, the other was where the hearth was seen solely as a centre of heat and display. The range of implements was further complicated by the type of fuel in use, wood and coal fire requiring somewhat differing sets of tools. The wood fire used as a cooking station is generally easily recognised. There were iron bars, called variously andirons, endirons or fire dogs to raise the logs from the hearth and secure a draft of air that would keep them burning. When cooking was a function they would be used in conjunction with cob irons or land irons which supported spits in front of the fire. Bellows, tongs, a fire shovel and sometimes a fire fork were usually placed adjacent to the fire and their presence was usually the sign of a wood burning fire. The jack, a mechanical device that automatically turned the spits, with its array of pulleys, chains and weights, sometimes in association with a clock, was a sign of affluence. They were generally valued at between £1 and £2. Within the fireplace itself was the galleybalk from which hung the cauldron or kettle in which the bulk of a household's food was boiled. Racken or running hooks enabled the position of the cauldron above the fire to be adjusted. Racks to hold spits and trivets such as brandreths, credle irons and grid irons were also sited near the fire and usually appraised in company with the other chimney furniture. The baskets in which fuel was stored for ready use and the iron fire backs were infrequently listed. The latter must by now have been generally regarded as a fitting and would have been ignored by the appraisers. The coal fires were usually described as a range, stove or grate and can be identified by the presence of pokers and the absence of endirons. The use of grates, most of them iron cages some eighteen inches in height, increased during the period.

Fireplaces where cooking did not take place provided a social focus for a room as well as heat and an opportunity for display. Log fires were still regarded as socially more acceptable than coal in such rooms. The andirons in them were more decorative and often described by reference to their bosses and brass fitments (**33**). Some rooms had chimney pieces, a hood like over mantel projecting above the hearth, often with a shelf on which ornaments such as shells, toys and earthenware were displayed (**50**, **58**).

In ordinary homes the chair had lost its symbolic status as the seat of the greatest in the room though the presence in some halls of one chair distinguished from the others by its higher valuation and sometimes described as 'armed' or 'leather' shows that tradition still lingered, as it does today. The highest valued chairs in general use were those upholstered in turkey work, most of which by 1661 came from Norwich. These were valued at £0.40 – £0.45 a piece. The cane chairs which became fashionable in the early Restoration period were worth £0.20 – £0.25 each. The clergy round the Cathedral and inn keepers made great use of them. They were fashionable, light, unattractive to moths and easy to dust. Leather upholstered chairs were appraised at £0.15, wickerwork or wanded chairs at £0.1 and the rush bottomed or bass chairs at £0.05. These last were the most common kinds of chairs appraised in the inventories. By comparison there was one appraisal of a flowered satin armchair with a matching set of stools.[12] Settles and stools, especially the buffet stools for use at table, were numerous.

Tables, like chairs, were changing their form and few of the heavy old-fashioned tables supported by frames or trestles were recorded. Tables rarely caused appraisers to add descriptive words. They did acknowledge another favourite with the Cathedral clergy, the Spanish or folding table, and the increasingly common extending table with leaves known as a draw table. They also recorded the exceptional such as the veneered table in Dring's house (**44**) and the single tea table.[13]

The kinds of furniture so far described were common to practically every inventory, for all occupations and every social group, but one of the attractions of inventories which list an individual's lifetime of expenditure in furnishing is

[12] L.A.O. Inv. 194/175.
[13] L.A.O. Inv. 195/20.

the record they provide of exceptional possessions. There are certain categories of possessions that indicate social standing or the aspiration towards such standing. Some of the exceptional items of furniture can be seen as indicators of social change and greater material wealth.

One symbol of wealth was surprisingly well spread. Silver was appraised in 44% of the inventories. Often this meant no more than two or three silver spoons in an otherwise poorly furnished house but for the wealthier there was an expensive show of spoons, tankards and salts. Such collections were displays of affluence, often literally so, for the silver was arranged on a cupboard to impress visitors. Only 5% of the inventories had valuations of gold objects and nearly all of these recorded two or three gold rings. Many of these will have been bequests from dead friends and relatives. There was impressive consistency in the valuation of silver. In thirty-three inventories the weight of silver was given as well as its value. In all but three it was valued at £0.25 an ounce. At Lichfield in the same period the usual valuation was £0.23. Jewellery was appraised very rarely, in only four inventories, and bequests of this before death were probably common.

Coaches, clocks and watches, china, books and pictures were other symbols of distinction. Lincoln's status as a three coach town has already been mentioned. They with their harness were valued at £10, £13 and £20.[14] Forty-five clocks were appraised and eighteen watches, one of them an alarm watch. China was listed in seven inventories and coffee pots and mills in six. Books were valued in 139 inventories (44%) with the Bible identified in 32 of them. The only other books identified were four copies of the Book of Martyrs, two of the Book of Common Prayer and single copies of a Psalter, the Whole Duty of Man and Practical Piety. Pictures were present in 75 houses and maps in 9. Two of the maps were described as of London and of England. One of the pictures was of 'Kings and Queens' and five were landscapes.

The paucity of weapons in the inventories makes it difficult to accept that the Civil War had taken place so recently. There was one set of armour consisting of back, breast and head piece. There were 17 swords and 5 rapiers, one with a silver hilt. There were 15 pistols, most of them in pairs and usually cased. There were 14 'guns' and another 10 more innocuously described as birding or fowling pieces.

Evidence for leisure pursuits was almost as slight. One man owned cock pens, another an angle rod, another a hunting saddle. Two had fishing boats which in the context of their inventories must have been for recreation rather than earning a living. The love of music was more impressively recorded. In the period Lincoln could have mustered 2 bass voils, 3 citterns, a cornet, 2 dulcimers, 3 harpsicords, a lute, 2 organs, a sackbut, 2 spinnets, a triangle, 5 voils, a voil bandero, 8 violins and 10 virginals. Some of these were associated with an occupation. There was fragmentary evidence for the pleasures of gardening, flower pots, rollers, shears, watering pots and one of the gardens contained a summerhouse.

There were looking glasses valued in 210 of the inventories some of them valued at more than £110. Their value in terms of interior decoration was immense because of their capacity to reflect and reinforce the lights that came

[14] P.R.O. Prob. 4/11, 111; L.A.O. Inv. 219A/31; Di 37/3/112.

from fire and candles. Anyone who has worked on the probate inventories of south or west England will become aware that warming pans were very popular in Lincoln. They were valued in 165 inventories. Anyone who has lived in Lincoln will appreciate why they were so common in the pre-centrally heated city.

There were close stools in 68 inventories and chamber pots in 110. Many more of the latter would have been subsumed in bulk valuations for pewter or in the common phrase 'other implements'. There were two houses of office.[15] Only six inventories give evidence for wells and one house had its own conduit and piped water.

There are a few items which appear only one or twice in the inventories and some of these indicate how closely Lincoln was in touch with the fashions of the time. Punch bowls were first used in England in about 1692 and Lincoln had two. Sash windows were new in 1686 and one was recorded in a Lincoln inventory of 1698. One of the punch bowls and the sash window came from the Angel (**45**). Wallpaper as a covering for walls occurs in the earlier years of the Restoration period and Lincoln's only 'paper chamber' is recorded in 1693. The list of such items is unimpressive. Lincoln's appraisers would rarely have been puzzled by the sight of objects so fashionable and exotic as to be beyond their every day comprehension.

The appraisers' convention of valuing purse and apparel together is a frustration to historians interested in assessing the availability of ready money or details of costume. The assessment in the inventories is more generally in round sums of £1 or £5 or £10 for this first item than it is of any other. When clothing was separately valued it seems to be a record of something particularly exceptional, or new, or of items that were produced for sale. A cleric's wearing apparel and habits worth £30.00 or a sarsenet gown, a petticoat, a tabby waistcoat and two coats at £2.80 are examples of this unaccustomed detail in the valuation of clothing.[16]

Food was another item generally ignored by the appraisers. It seems often to have been recorded and valued when it was a commercial asset normally sold by the deceased. Flitches of bacon, tongue, sugar loaves and quantities of cheese are the most commonly named items of food. Salted meat was never valued although there was mention of a number of salting troughs.

The appraisers did social historians a great disservice. They did not record the minor bric a brac that would have given individuality to many rooms. Their convention of subsuming the trivia in phrases like 'things unseen and forgot' or 'husslements' is a deprivation. The single bird cage they identified has the merit of indicating what must be a major understatement not just of bird cages but of the presence of the cats and dogs which as pets added to the life of many houses. The litter of small knives, tinderboxes, broadsheets, charms, earthenware, pipes and spoons that they very understandably ignored in their desire to finish their listing leaves our mental reconstructions of these rooms more stark and lifeless than their owners would recognise.

Evidence that furniture was changing over the period or that standards of comfort were improving is not easily extracted from the inventories. There are

[15] L.A.O. Inv. 179/222; 185A/183 and perhaps (**4**).

[16] L.A.O. Di 39/1/8; L.C.C. Admon. 1678/7.

two approaches to the mass of evidence in the inventories that give general indications of the kind and rate of change between 1661 and 1714. The first is to see if there was an increase in the number of certain small items of furnishing that betoken the achievement of modest luxury. The second is to identify inventories of the same house which are separated in time.

Plate, looking glasses, the presence of a grate or jack and warming pans were common enough in the inventories to provide some measure of changes in their availability. The inventories of all the men not identified by an occupation or profession and all the women were taken as a basis for this analysis. Lodgers and servants were excluded from the sample as were those submitting inventories to the Dean and Chapter's Court to the Archbishop's Court or those who applied for letters of administration. There remain enough to provide a viable number for a comparison to be made of the incidence of these furnishings in the two periods of 1661–1680 and 1691–1710. This is summarised in Table VII.

From these figures it appears that for the men there were no significant changes in the proportion possessing plate or a warming pan but that looking glasses and warming pans became much more common. The big increase in grates means an increase in the use of coal for fuel. The disadvantage of this would have been the dirtier smoke caused by a coal fire but presumably the advantage of reliable and cheap supplies of coal offset this inconvenience. The women leaving inventories seem to have been more comfortably housed than the men, they possessed more proportionately of every item of furnishing. Like the men their incidence of plate and warming pans did not change significantly but like the men they were using more looking glasses and grates or jacks in the later decades of the period. This is evidence for change and for a modest improvement in the standards of household comfort.

TABLE VII. Incidence of certain furnishings 1661–1711 (in percentages)

	Plate	Looking glasses	Grate and/ or Jack	Warming pan	Number in sample
Men					
1661–80	31	18	9	30	44
1691–1711	27	33	30	30	30
Women					
1661–80	39	37	18	39	38
1691–1711	47	44	38	44	34

It seems unlikely that the inventories contain sufficiently detailed evidence to identify changes in furniture at the level of the ordinary household. The existence of new and fashionable types of furniture, such as Spanish tables, is visible but for most the basic furniture was stoutly made and very durable. It could and was expected to last for more than one generation and provided the basis for the improved furnishings of the next generation. It is likely that the most obvious outward signs of a general improvement in furnishing in the ordinary houses would have been in the soft furnishings, particularly those in the bedroom and about the bed. The lack of detail and specific valuations for many items of furniture makes assessment of change in these soft furnishings impossible to judge from inventories.

However some confirmation, or otherwise, of the durability of furniture can come from considering the inventories of the same houses in different years. Unless such houses are to be identified by study of an additional and complex range of other primary sources in addition to the inventories the only way of identifying such houses from inventory evidence alone is to begin by looking at houses which belonged to people of similar surname. Many complications prevent two inventories of different dates being confidently declared the same on inventory evidence alone. Appraisers gave their own names to the rooms they appraised. There are too many uncertainties attached to an attempt to match one appraiser's vocabulary of little chamber or matted room to another's identification of garden chamber and little parlour to be sure they are describing the same house. Moreover the problems caused by unfurnished rooms or those appraisers might have forgotten, changes of business and new building add to the difficulties of correlation. Correlation is made easy in exceptional buildings, for example inns where the custom of giving each room a distinctive name can help matching.

There were 101 surnames which appeared twice or more in the Lincoln inventories involving 302 inventories but the difficulties described above mean that only twenty two houses can confidently be identified as appearing more than once. All appeared twice except two which appeared three times.

In ten of the pairs of inventories the second records the establishment of a widow. One is of little value in the consideration of change as she died only a month after her husband. Their inventories were practically identical in format, items and valuations.[17] As the same appraisers produced both inventories such a close correlation is not surprising. The only major difference between the two was that the widow's inventory contained none of the crops and animals valued in her husband's inventory. The time between the remaining pairs of inventories varies from three to eighteen years. With one exception the furnishings, room functions and valuations were very similar. One of them indeed was an almost precise copy of her husband's inventory which had been made five years earlier except for the absence of one chair, and the recording of a garrat in the widow's inventory and goods in a warehouse. In all ten widows' inventories they still owned the same furniture which was appraised for the second time at generally identical prices. In one of these inventories two chambers containing furniture in the husband's time were not appraised in the widow's inventory.[18] One of the widows had added much to her stock of furniture, particularly beds and curtains, perhaps evidence that she had lodgers.

The twelve other sets of inventories, ten of them pairs, record houses in the possession of men. Two of them record the same house within a year with the

[17] L.A.O. Inv. 185A/194; 185A/135.

[18] L.A.O. Inv. 163/19; 177/155.

same furniture and similar valuations. The remainder record a number of houses separated by greater spans of time than those in the widow's sample. One pair is separated by a forty year gap, one of thirty three years, two of twenty six years and four with a gap of more than ten years. John Johnson a mercer of St. Benedicts died in 1671 and forty years later his successor of the same surname, also a mercer, died in the same house. The major items of furniture were the same and their valuation 37% less. The changes to the interior of the house were the replacement of leather chairs by cane chairs and the addition of silver and china.[19] In the two Tooley inventories of 1677 and 1688 the virginals still graced the dining room but again cane chairs had replaced the leather ones.[20] This pattern of general stability as far as the major items of furniture were concerned, with some change, but the emphasis on the addition of minor items such a linen or silver, is a fair generalisation from the evidence of all the inventories. Most of the evidence comes from wealthier households where change might be expected. This argues for an even greater stability in the major furniture of the lesser households. The one labourer pair of inventories which belonged to the gardener family of the Wises showed little change in furnishings over thirty three years and valuations of it which were one eighth less.[21] The two houses which have three inventory descriptions do not invalidate these generalisations. One of them belonged to the Watsons, the saddler/tanner dynasty and here there was no change between 1667 and 1677.[22] This house must have been recognisable inside throughout the decade with its fifteen beds, its linen and silver helping to furnish the dining room and its pewter on display in the hall.

Two more pairs of inventories record inns, the Angel in the Bail was described in 1698 and 1704 and another, the Reindeer, in 1666 and 1676.[23] The Reindeer was owned by the widow, Ann, for ten years after the death of her husband John Fisher in which time the valuation was increased from £378.50 to £743.95. In her time the room names were not changed and their furniture and function was retained. Indeed a visitor returning to stay in the Cross Parlour in 1676 for the first time since 1666 would have recognised the room from its major items of furniture but he would have been aware of a general improvement in this room and elsewhere. The furnishing throughout the inn was more lavish, eight looking glasses instead of two, seventeen chamber pots to twelve, four closestools to one, thirty one beds instead of twenty five. In the best room, the Kings Arms, six Turkey work chairs with cushions had replaced the wanded chairs and there were pictures on the wall and a mat on the floor that had not been there in 1666. The differences are not the result of casual appraising, both inventories show detail and care. If the Reindeer was improving the Angel seems to have been on the decline. The first of its two inventories recording the inn at the death of Douce (**45**) in 1698 is more detailed than the second in 1704.[24] Twenty rooms can be identified with the same name in each of the inventories and frequently these had the same number of beds and chairs in them. For all these rooms the second valuation is a half to a third less in value. It seems unlikely that this is an

19 L.A.O. Inv. 172/345; 203/100.
20 L.A.O. Inv. 188/69; 219A/31.
21 L.A.O. L.C.C. Admon. 1670/233; 1702/14.
22 L.A.O. Inv. 167/66; 219A/142.
23 L.A.O. Inv. 166/108; 177/141.
24 L.A.O. Inv. 198/2.

example of a deliberately undervalued inventory. Where valuations can be checked against similar quantities of pewter, ale or beer they appear to be fair estimates. Moreover the good quality accessories under Douce, such as Turkey work chairs and looking glasses, are not now appraised and such items would not be easily ignored. Changes in the Angel between 1698 and 1704 seem to have involved a decline in comfort in contrast to the accumulation of evidence that shows standards throughout the city were improving.

XIII

Appraisers and their valuations

The appraisers who valued the goods and chattels of the inventories made a surprisingly large group. They left 1664 signatures or marks on the 590 inventories and 831 individuals were involved. 63% of them helped with only one inventory, 14% were involved twice. Most of the remainder appear about five times with just a few individuals appearing more frequently. Alexander Luddington appeared most, twenty three times, Stephen Malton twenty one times and Richard Winne **(35)** twenty times. The last was a pewterer who appraised members of trades, professions and widows in seven of the Lincoln parishes. Luddington was a wheelwright and Malton was probably related to the chandler of the same surname. Both the readiness and the capacity to help were spread widely throughout the city.

It was expected that neighbours would help in the task of appraising and a consequence of this was that often the people involved were of the same social grouping or occupation as the deceased. Frequently a relation of the widow acted as a protector of her interests. In some of the nearby rural parishes churchwardens were expected to undertake the duty of appraisal in their year of office. In Lincoln the task of valuing shop stock would usually have been beyond the competence of a layman. In this same period in the Telford area there is evidence for the employment of men with similar business background to the deceased acting as appraiser when shop goods required expert knowledge.[1] In Lincoln there were examples of a similar commonsense solution to the problems posed by the more complicated inventories. Enoch Malton, a chandler, acted as an appraiser for several chandler inventories.[2] It is well to remember that much of the appraisal of ordinary households could have been done by a clerk with the so called appraisers acting more as witnesses to his accuracy than valuers. Indeed one 1705 inventory records witnesses as well as appraisers. These clerks must also have been numerous as the great variety in the wording of the preambles to the inventories show. Although these needed to do no more than give the name of the deceased and the date of the appraisal there are many variations in wording. The spelling in the inventories is usually good but punctuation is usually non-existent. Without exception the inventories appear to

[1] Trinder and Cox *op.cit.* p. 7.

[2] L.A.O. Inv. 161/24; 193/422; 201/234; L.C.C. Admon. 1680/82.

be effective working documents even though some of them involved several day's work on complicated accumulations of shop goods in a situation where dispute was always possible (**4**). In another way too the documents represent a recognised social obligation that seems to have been conscientiously fulfilled.

The appraisers seem to have come from a city population that was increasingly literate if the ability to sign one's name is taken as a measure of literacy. The percentage making a mark declines from 21% in the decade 1661–1670 to 20%, 17%, 15% and 13% for subsequent decades with the final years of the period 1711–1714 recording 8% of marks. This is a rough indicator as some, such as Edward Leatherland or Tom Townroe, used both signature and mark in their appraisals. It is a measure of male literacy, only six women acted as appraisers. Whatever reservations are held about the relationship between the ability to sign one's own name and literacy as it is now defined the trend is an impressively consistent one.

It was the responsibility of the appraisers to make a fair valuation of the goods and chattels of the deceased. There has been considerable discussion about their attitudes to this responsibility with some maintaining that assets of all kinds were consistently undervalued. The Lincoln evidence would not support this viewpoint because wherever it is possible to check the validity of valuations they seem to be generally consistent and closely related to the conventional prices of the time.

Some evidence to support this belief that appraisers were aware of current prices and valued what they saw at a fair price has already been considered. The stability of furniture appraisals in those pairs of inventories which describe the same house is one example.[3] Another is the consistency in the valuations for silver, brass and pewter.[4] Twenty five of the inventories value cereals and give its cubic capacity. These valuations can be related to the annual price returns of the Lincoln Leet Juries.[5] There are obvious difficulties in correlating the inventory valuations with the Jury prices. Complicating factors which are beyond recovery include evidence for the quality of cereal, the efficiency with which it had been stored and the time of year of the appraisal in relation to the state of market for a particular cereal. Overall the discrepancies between valuations and Jury assessments were insignificant. Eight of the valuations agree with the Jury prices, seven are somewhat below and ten are above. Rye was the cereal most at variance with Jury prices. Malt was valued in thirty three inventories and all but five of these valuations are based on what was obviously a generally recognised price of £1 per quarter. The appraisers seem to have been party to a widespread and generally recognised body of basic commercial knowledge, such as would have been normal in a market town. It gave them a framework which enabled them to value fairly and consistently.

There is confirmation of the reliability of appraisers' valuations in the administrators' accounts which survive for the period. These accounts were submitted by the administrators who had been appointed to organise the dispersal of the deceased's estate when no will had been left appointing an executor for this duty. The accounts itemise the cost of the various tasks

[3] See above p. lxxvi.
[4] See above p. lxxiii.
[5] Hill *op.cit.* pp. 225–6.

associated with the winding up of an estate. The actual cost of appraisal was usually charged at £0.15. The cost of the funeral, legal charges and the payment of debts were included. Less frequently the cost of arranging for the sale of the deceased's furniture, the hire of rooms for the storage of goods and the enormously expensive charges associated with the hire of horses were included.

There are twenty-five such administrator's accounts for Lincoln in the period, the latest for 1682. In only one of them does the administrator criticise and gain recognition in his final accounts for inaccurate valuation by the appraisers of a probate inventory.[6] The inventory had dealt with the goods of Edward Watterton, a rough mason, who died in 1674 with an estate valued at £81.08. A lead cistern, brewing vessels, pewter and a bedstead had been valued at £15.00. The administrator claimed they were worth no more than £9.28. His claim was upheld. An allowance for this, the payment of the administrator for his duties, for the funeral and the payment of Watterton's debts reduced his estate to a real value of £21.66. A reduction of this proportion was not uncommon. The appraisers acted of necessity as soon as possible after the death and could not acquire in the time at their disposal a proper account of the deceased's debts. Taking the Lincoln administration accounts as a group the total value of the appraised estates in them was reduced by 44% by the time the administrators' charges had been met and a final conclusion made to settling the debts of the deceased. It is an erosion of appraised wealth that needs to be remembered in all groupings of probate inventories based on levels of their sum totals.

[6] L.A.O. Ad. Ac. 42/64.

INVENTORIES

1. Joh Glen **L.C.C. Admon. 1661/74**

Barber 28.5.1662

	£	s	d
His purse and apparrell	13	0	0
In the Hall			
One paire of virginalls and the frame they stand upon	1	10	0
Two white earthen potts tiped with silver		2	0
Six littell bass bottomed Chaires one wanded Chaire one armed wooden Chaire one buffut Stoole and three littell stooles		10	0
Two littell Tables		13	4
One bacon flitch		10	0
One fire Iron with two end Iron and one paire of littell racks		6	8
One Gallow balke with two runing hookes		1	10
One hanging brasse Candlestick one littell brasse ladle two paire of Brasse Snuffers and one littell brasse flasske for gunpowder		2	0
Two drippin panns and two spitts		6	0
Foure fire shovells three paire of tongs one broiling Iron and other small Irons		6	8
One salt boxe			6
One bible with other littell bookes		3	4
One Iron Jack lines and weight		7	0
Six Cushons		6	0
One paire of tables		1	6
One Case of knives		3	0
Twenty foure pewter dishes great and Small one pewter Bason and one pie plate	3	10	6
One Iron pott		3	4
Three brasse panns great and Small		17	0
One brasse Scumer		1	0
One littell brasse Candlestick one Iron candlestick two tinn Candlesticks and one saucepann		1	8
One ould cupbord one lantherne two barells with woden dishes and trenshers and other small things		13	4
One frying panne		1	4
In the Still house			
One great Copper Still with a worme and a grate thereunto belonging	4	0	0
One great tubb one littell hen penn two washin tubbs two Kitts with other small things	1	0	0

	£	s	d
One great besen morter with a pestile and Clock		12	0
One temes one Searge one old Tubb one still and one worme	1	0	0

In the Chamber where Mr Robinson lodgeth

	£	s	d
One bedstead with a teaster one littel table one littell side table and one buffett Stoole	1	7	0

In the Lodging Chamber

	£	s	d
One high bedstead with a teaster and trundlebed	1	2	6
Two feather bedds one boulster and one pillow	2	10	0
One rugg one Coverlid and two paire of blanketts with one paire of old Curtaines and vallands	1	10	0
Six turkey wrought Cushons	1	4	0
Two littell Cushons and one Carpett		8	0
One draw table	1	0	0
One livery cupborde with three buffet stooles and one sid table	1	0	0
One high wooden Chaire for a Child and one low buffet stoole		4	0
Two painted basse Bottomed Chaires armed and two lesser Chaires		6	0
Two high covered Chaires two high covered stooles and one littell stoole		10	0
One basked voider one littell deske one old Seeing glasse and one trensher baskett		2	0
One small fire Iron and two end Irons		1	6

In the Clossett within that Chamber

	£	s	d
One diaper table Cloth two dozen of napkins one short diaper table Cloth five paire of sheets two Course towells foure littell table Clothes of pillowbears eight paire	3	10	8
One trunck one russe box one deske and one box thre dozen of trenshers one littel stoole and other small things		10	0
One littel Rapier		6	8

In the Childrens Chamber

	£	s	d
Two ould bedsteads		6	0
One feather bedd one boulster and Six pillows	2	0	0
Foure coverlids three paire of Blanketts one rugg two paire of curtains and vallands	2	4	8
One littel trunck three chists foure littell boxes two chaires and two littell stooles		18	6

One little long Settle and Smothing board for Clothes		1	6

In the Chamber where Mr Wright lodgeth

Six turkey wrogt stooles five covered chaires	1	18	0
One window curtain and one brush		3	0

In the Closett within that Chamber

Severall pieces of white earthen plates		4	0

In the Shoppe

One large chafer		6	8
Foure small brasse Chafers and one small pewter Chafer		7	0
One great brasse bason eleven small brass basons		7	0
Foure pewter besons		10	0
One brass Cock		2	0
One new case of tooles tippt with silver	3	6	8
Two old cases of tooles	2	0	0
One Charcole pann		3	0
One long Settele three Chaires one littel table one deske and thre Cushons		15	0
Linens used in the shopp nine frocketts twelve narrow clothes nine cappes eight head rubers twelve towells three branpokes	3	9	6
Powder and balles and other utensialls		6	8
One old citterne		2	6
One old Seeing glasse			8

In the other Shopp

In littell rundletts and strong water		6	8
One glasse case and glasses and other tryfles		6	8
One lease of a house in the parish of Saint Peeter at Arches in the Cittie of Lincoln held of the corporation of Lincoln	63	6	8
In plate one Silver boale and Six Silver Spoons	4	0	0
	133	15	9
	(133	17	2)

1 **Balles** – Balls of soap: wash balls.
Branpokes – implement for removing scurf from hair.
Broiling iron – an iron plate with hooks which allowed it to be hung close to fire.
Citterne – instrument of guitar kind strung with wire.
Cock – pipe with a tap in it.
Frockett – loose fitting smock.
Head ruber – a towel or brush.
Rundlett – small cask to hold liquor.

Smoothing board – the thick piece of iron that laundresses used in their smoothing boxes.
Teaster – the flat wooden roof of a four poster.
Virginalls – keyed musical instrument like a spinnet but set in box or case.
Worme – coiled tube connected to head of a still in which vapour is condensed.

2. Charles Clarke — Prob. Inv. 162/61

Blacksmith The Bail 14.1.1664

	£	s	d
His purse and Apparell	1	3	4
In ye parler next ye streete			
One table Six joynd Stooles one livery Cubbord one truckell bedd one wainscote Chest three Chayres with other (h)ushlements	1	6	8
In ye haule			
A long table and a little table one long forme twoe stooles seven bast chares one Safe	0	15	0
Pewter Case with puter and brasse and all other impliments	0	2	0
In ye Great Chamber next ye street			
Twoe little tables two little formes one livery Coubbard three bedsteads twoe with beding with other things	1	15	0
In ye little Chamber			
Twoe bedsteads with beding one livery Cubbard one chayre one little table with other things	2	6	8
In bills and bonds most of them desperate	39	17	0
In ye iner Chamber			
Twoe little bedsteads twoe trunks with other things	0	12	0
Lining Six payre of sheets Six pyllabears two table Clothes twoe dossen of napckings twoe towels	1	15	0
In ye beer house			
One lead with bruing vessell with other things	3	5	0
In ye yard			
One sowe and twoe pigges	1	6	8

In ye Shoppe

	£	s	d
One pare of bellowes one Sythe one vise fower hamers with other tooles	3	0	0
For five hundred of newe Iron	4	0	0
	63	2	4

3. Katerne Sewell **Prob. Inv. 164/90**

Widow (Dyer) 9.8.1664

	£	s	d
Her purse and apparell	5	0	0
In the Hall			
One high standinge Cupboard one litle table and 4 Chares and one Cupboard Cloth two Cushans and one Safe and one long table	1	10	0
In the Parlour			
One seeled bedstead with feather bed boulster 1 pillowe one paire of blanketts one Rugg and Curtaines and valence	0	4	0
One long table two other tables One forme 6 buffett stoolles and six Chaires two Carpetts 6 Cushiones one livery Cupboard with Cloth and other Utensills	0	4	0
In the best Chamber			
One stand bedd with feather bedd two boulsters 2 pillowes one blankett and one Coverlidd	2	10	0
Two Trundle bedds and bedding and two Chests and small boxes	2	0	0
In the Chamber over the parlour			
One stand bedd and one Trundle bedd one feather bedd 2 boulsters 5 pillowes 3 Coverlidds 2 pair of blanketts and two Mattrices 4 Chests and one presse	3	10	0
One suite of new Curtaines and Valence one Coverlitt and one new blankitt	3	10	0
In the servants Chamber			
Two stand bedds and beddinge to them	1	6	8
In the Corne Chamber or Store Chamber			
Malt and bread Corne	3	0	0

Wooll yarne hempe and Cheese	2	0	0
One Skreene	0	10	0
In the Kitchin and butterie			
Pewter and brasse	3	10	0
One Land Iron spitts Dripping pann Cobirons and one brasen Mortar	1	10	0
2 hoggsheads 2 barrells Tubbs Kitts bowles Cheese presse trenshars and other implements	1	10	0
In the Brewhouse			
One lead and brewinge vessells	3	0	0
The linnen			
Nyne peices linnen and hempen Cloth and other wearing linnen	6	13	4
Fowerteene loads of hay	9	6	8
Corne gotten and upon the Ground	5	0	0
Three Milch Kyne and 3 Calfes	12	0	0
2 quies on ye Comons	3	0	0
2 Mares 2 followers one foall	8	0	0
3 swine and one pig	2	0	0
One Waggon one Carte and horse geares and wood in the yard	3	0	0
Two payre of Tenters	4	0	0
In the presse house			
2 presses and 5 paires of sheares and other implements	4	0	0
One woodden belfrey and A furr Stack	1	10	0
Oniones and other rootts	0	13	0
One Skreene of Oake covered with stript stuffe	1	(..	..)
In the Warehouse			
Two Tunn of Wadd	35	0	0
3 hundred weight of fustick	1	18	6
2 hundred and halfe of redd wood	3	15	0
2 hundred of Allam	2	10	0
halfe hundred of Logwood	0	16	0
2 hundred of Copras	0	14	0
7 hundred of Madder	14	0	0
One parcell of Argell	0	3	4
Galbs	0	10	0
Indigoe	0	8	0
Brasill	2	10	0
Barkes and Woodwash	4	0	0
In the Diehouse yeard			
One Copper	18	0	0
One lead and one Seasterne	2	10	0

Three wadfatts and other Matialls	2	0	0
One stack of kidds in the yeard	3	10	0
Sixteene sheepe	4	0	0
In debts upon speciallty and booke Debts	20	0	0
Despate Debts and thinges forgotten	1	0	0
One lease att Canwicke	1	0	0
	219	14	10
	(203	2	8)

3. **Argell** – archil, lichens which yield a violet dye.
   Brasill – oriental or S. American tree providing a red dye.
   Fusticke – source of orange, brown and yellow dyes.
   Madder – plant providing yellow dye.
   Pressehouse – where cloth is given its final smooth finish with hot and cold pressure.
   Speciallity – debts which are legally binding.
   Tenter – fence like wooden structures on which cloth is stretched and dried.
   Wadd – woad.
   Wadfatt – woad vat.
   Woodwash – greenwood or dyer's bloom.

4. Benjamin Marshall L.C.C. Admon. 1667/131

Mercer 18.1.1665

	£	s	d
His purse and apparell	10	0	0
Five gold rings	3	10	0
Gold and money in the house	122	3	7
Silver plate, burnt Silver and broken silver one hundred fiftie Two-ounce weight	34	4	0
In the Greate Chamber			
Sixteen covered chayrs	3	4	0
Also one bedstead with a featherbed, curtans vallence rugg and bedding	10	0	0
A fire-grate, Edirons, Tongs, fire shovell, Two Tables and Carpetts a suit of stript Hangings A Looking glass A Skreen, A picture and Armes	4	16	8
In the Inner garrett Chamber			
One bedstead with Two feather beds, hangings rugg and coverings, A Table and carpett, Seven Chayrs and Stooles A fire-iron tongs and shovell	7	1	0

In the Outer garrett Chamber

Six chayres three stooles, A Violl, A Table and carpet with other implements	3	2	0

In the mens Chambers and paper chamber

One bedstead with an old feather bed a flocke bed, old hangings and coverings and old draw Table, old chists with other implements	4	2	0

In the Hall

Three Tables Three Carpetts thirteen Chayres, Eyght joynt stooles Nine green stuff qushions. A fire grate, tongs and shovell, with other implements, A Livery Cupboard and carpet Three fowling pieces, A clocke, a Spitt Jacke, A glass Case and glasses, An hanging cupboard A Case of knives, a standard, a lookeing glass	9	7	6
In New Linnen, A Large Holland Sheet, Two dozen and an halfe of Table Napkins Two Table Cloaths, Two damaske Side board cloaths Sixe Diaper Napkins and a Table Cloath A payre of fine holland sheets, an halfe sheet, seven course pilowbeares Three course sheets one payre of Linnen sheets Sixe Towells Sixe Linn Napkins and Two Damaske Napkins	9	15	0

In the Chamber over the pantree

One bedstead with hangings, rugg, feather bed and coverings	6	13	4

In the closett Chamber

A silver hilted rapier and girdle, white potts and glasses, Two Bibles with other small bookes, and six pounds of Hartshorne	2	1	0

In the Chamber over the pantree more

A stand bedstead with old hangings a Truckle bedstead with a Cupboard and a carpett, and potts, three old chayres fower stooles, A close stoole, and pan, a lookeing glass, a fire iron, a payre of Endirons of brass, a Truncke with other implements	3	8	4

In the Kitching chamber

A press a Truckle bedstead and Cannapre and three Chists	1	4	0
A Childes Carrall, divers Mantles, Suits of childes Linnen and coates	7	5	0

In Barnes Chamber

A bedstead with a feather bed, Coverings and hangings, Two Tables, Nine old qushions a Livery Cupboard with a Truncke and boxes	5	18	8

Linnen in the Kitching Chamber

Two dozen of Linn Napkins, Another dozen of Linn Napkins Sixe Diaper napkins five yeards of Diaper, Three Linn Table cloaths A payre of old sheets, A payre of Linn Sheets, Three other Table cloaths of Diaper, Two payre of Linn sheets Eyght Towells, fower Table cloaths, Sixe old napkins, fower fine pillowbeeres, Two payre of course sheets Two Table Cloaths, a Course sheete, Two pillowbeeres Sixe napkins and a Table cloath	7	16	0

In the Studdy in the Shop

Two nests of Drawers an old Table and a Chayre		6	8

In the pantree

A Great old Cupboard a joynt stoole, with divers glasses and white stone plate	1	0	6
In New and old pewther one hundred and fortie and three pounds weight	7	3	0
Three brass potts, Two Skellets, Two panns, a warming pann, a slice and a scumer, with some Tinn Implements	3	0	0
A Great brass Mortar and pestell, a Dreepin pan fower spitts, A payre of cob-irons, a payre of Endirons, a fire iron, tongs and shovel, a spitt-jacke with other small impements	3	10	0

In the Kitching more

A Table, Sixe old chayres, Two pastie peeles, Two shelves with other implements	0	10	0
Fower Brass Kandlestickes	0	3	4
A Great Copper, A little Copper, fower great brewing fatts, with other small Tubbs, soas, Kitts, stove potts, shelves, boules, Trenchers, a Lead Cisterne and old irn	13	3	4

In the Beare Celler

One Hogshead of small beare five Caskes, Sixe old Tubbs, Two Sacks, An old Table, a gantre, a Still, with other implements	3	2	0
A percell of coales		12	0

In the Stable

Three Saddles, old Tubbs, bridles, halfe a load of hey, An old Table, and old hangings in the garden house	1	15	0
Two Bacon flitches and a small pott of Butter	1	0	0
Sixtie New oake-boards with some joysts, posts and rayles, in Mr William Marshalls yeard	4	15	0

In the Shop, ware – Chambers and Cellers

Thirteene pound weight and an halfe of colored Silke £6 15s Two pound weight and one quarter of blacke silke, £1 5s. Two pound and an halfe of Hanke Silke, £17 6d. Eighteen ounce of slee Silke 18s. Twentie ounce of colored Naples Silke £1 0s	10	15	6
One whole piece of blacke ribbin £2 16s 0d. one other piece £2 5s. fortie sixe yeardes more £3 1s 4d. Twentie Sixe yeardes more £1 12s 6d Sixteen yeardes more in remnants 11s fiftie fower yeards of Smaller ribbin 18s. Two pieces of Small blacke ribbin 16s. Thirtie three yeards more in Small ribbin 11s. divers small remnants of small blacke ribbin 2s 6d. One boxe of old silver laces, and silke and Silver laces £1.	13	12	4
Fortie Seven yeards of colored ribbins in fower remnants £2 7s. Sixtie fower yeards more in colored ribbins £1 1s 4d. Ten yeards more in remnants 5s Eight pieces in Smaller colored ribbins £4. one other piece of colored ribbin 12s. fower pieces more of colored ribbin small £1 12s. Nine pieces of Smaller colored ribbin £3 3s. divers remnants of small ribbin 10s. one boxe of old ribbins in remnants £1. fower pieces of small ribbin £1. fower pieces of smaller ribbin 16s. five pieces of small colored ribbins 10s another boxe of Small remnants of colored ribbins 6s 8d. A percell of silke and silver ribbins 13s 4d	17	16	4
Three pieces of ferritt ribbin £2 4s. Three other pieces of ferrit ribbin 18s. fower pieces of smaller ferritt ribbin £1 12s five other pieces of smaller ferritt ribbin £1 10s. Two pieces of ferritt ribbins in remnants 6s. Twelve dozen of small ferritt ribbin £1. divers small remnants of ferritt ribbin 5s. Two pieces more of ferritt ribbin 12s	8	7	0

Three peices of Small Satten ribbin £1 4s Eyght dozen of Small Satten ribbin 13s 4d one pieces of Small blacke Satten ribbin 4s 6d in remnants of Small Satten ribbin 5s	2	6	10
Four gross of Silke Gallowne £4 12s Seven pieces of Silke Gallownes in remnants £1 11s 6d. A Gross and an halfe of thrid gallowns £1 1s. Remnants of thrid gallowns 6s 8d	7	11	2
One gross and one piece of Silke loop lace £1 2s 6d. in ordinary loope lace and Twist 13s. Three ounce of rich gimp 3s. ordinary gimps in remnants 1s. five dozen of Silke-laces tagg'd 7s 6d. remnants of lace fring and old ribbins 3s. Thirtie two silke laces 2s 6d one boxe of silke edgings £1. one boxe of ordinary edgings 2s 4d in Gimp laces 6s 8d. one gross and an halfe of cotton ribbins 10s. Twenty three piece of worsteed Caddas £1 14s 6d.	6	6	0
Nine papers of ordinary Bindings 12s. Sixe papers of the best bindings 10s. odd bindings 6s 8d. Eyght gross of thrid laces and an halfe £2. Twelv Gross of ordinary Thrid laces £1 10s. odd percells of thrid laces 2s 6d. Seventeen dozen of playing Cards 17s fowerteen dozen and an halfe of pinns with a percell of odd pinns £4 12s 8d	10	10	10
Sixe dozen and fower pound weight of Blacke and Browne Thrid £6 13s 4d. Seven dozen and fower pound of Number thrid fower pound weight of pieceing thrid, rich colored thrid, Two pound with one pound and an halfe of course colored thrid £1 9s 6d. Sixe dozen of Necke buttons 13s 4d	8	15	9
Thirtie five gross and eleven dozen of buttons of silke greate and small £2 10s. Two boxes of old fashioned buttons £1. Eyghteen Love, Curle and Taffitie Hoods £2 6s. Also more Twenty one Love, Curle, Taffity and ducap Hoods £2 4s	8	0	0
Twenty fower Ellns and an halfe of blacke and colored Tabbie in 4 remnants £4 18s. Twenty three Ellns and a quarter of Sarcenett £9 10s. Eyght ellns more in remnants £1 8s 8d. Some small remnants 3s 4d Thirteen Ellns of Taffitie in remnants £4 6s 8d	20	6	8

Fower Ellns of blacke ducap £2. Seven Elns of Allamood £1 15s. Twenty Ellns of black Sarcenett £8. Seventy five Ellns of black Cypress £4 7s 6d. Twenty three Ellns of Love £4 2s. Twenty one Ellns of blacke and colored Indian Silke £1 17s 6d. A percell of old blacke Satten capps and Masques 10s	23	2	0
Fortie seven yeards of silk moehayres £7 17s. Thirtie yeards in old blacke Callamancoes, Moehayres and wrought druggists £1 10s. Seventeen yeards of old fashioned blacke silks £1 10s. Small remnants of old fashioned blacke silks. Severall remnants of old halfe Silke druggests £2 13s 4d five yeards of blacke Cambetts £1.	14	12	10
Eyghteen yeards of blacke hayre Tamelletoes £2 14s. Thirtie three yeardes of colored hayre Tamelettoes £4 19s one piece of Callacine. one piece of bumbasine and one piece of worsted prunella £8. A percell of bumbasine and a percell of worsted prunella £3 10s. one percell of bumbasine £2. Seven remnants of blacke stuffs £2.	23	3	0
Three pieces of three-quarters stuffs £8 10s. Thirtie one yeards of worsteed Camletts £2 14s 3d. Ninetie five yeards of colored worsteed Camletts £8 6s 3d. Three pieces of Worsted prunellas £6 5s. Severall remnants of colored stuffs £1.	29	15	6
Fifteen yeards of Bowdied Tammie and Twenty five yeards of pincke colored Tammies £3. Severall remnants of Tammie 10s. Two remnants of stuff 10s. Ten yeards of bowdied Tammie 15s. fiftie two yeards of Ash colored Tammie £2 12s. Twenty five yeards of pincke colored Tammie £1 17s 6d. One hundred yeards of Tammie in fower pieces £5. Thirteen remnants of Tammie £1 10s.	15	4	6
Twentie Eyght yeards of black Shallowne Serge £2 6s 8d. Thirtie five yeards of blacke flaundress Searge £5 5s. Eyghteen yeards of flaundress Searge £2 10s 8d. Severall remnants of flaundress Searge £1 10s. Twenty Eyght yeards of padua Searge £3 10s. Severall remnants of padua Serge and Tammies £2.	16	19	8

	£	s	d
One hundred Ninety Nine yeards of Sempeternum £14 18s 6d. remnants of Sempeternum 3s. Eleven yeards of Bowdied Searge £2 15s. Ninetie Seven yeards of Taunton Searge £9 14s. Several remnants of Sagatha 5s. Several remnants of old fashioned Stuffs 10s.	28	5	6
Two pieces of parragon £4 10s. Seventy yeards of parragon in remnants £5 5s. Severall percells of phillip and Chena £1 10s fouerteen yeards of Green Say £1 8s. Thirtie seven yeards of green Say £2 15s 6d. Small remnants of Say 3s 4d.	15	11	10
One hundred fiftie five Ellns of Bagg Holland £34 5s 11d. One hundred Eyghtie Sixe Ellns small third Hollands £41 5s 6d. Two hundred sixtie five Ellns and a quarter of Isingham Hollands £30 4s 11d.	105	16	4
One hundred fiftie three ellns of Dowlas £10 2s 4d divers remnants of Dowlas £1 15s 4d. Thirtie Ellns of Lockrams £1 15s. Severall remnants of Cambricke £1 5s.	14	7	8
One hundred fortie five yeards and an halfe of Callicoe £6 4s 5d. remnants 3s 4d. Ten yeards of Scotch Diaper. Two percells of Callico and a percell of blacke coifes 10s one hundred thirtie nine yeards of blew linn £5 9s 7d. Seventie one yeards of colored Linn £1 10s 6d. Two pieces of Tufted Holland £1 10s. Twenty yeards of Tufted Holland £1 1s 10d. Two pieces of White Homes fustian 6s 8d. One piece and fower yeards of Colored fustian 17s. Nine pieces of Dymittie £7 13s.	25	6	3
Fortie yeards of Dymittie in three percells £1 11s 6d. Small remnants of Dimitie 5s 6d. One hundred Twenty five yeards and a quarter of Linnen cloath £7 0s 10d. one hundred seventie Eyght yeards of Canvas and wrappers £7 1s 9d. fortie yeards of Buckram in three pieces £1 16s 8d. fower remnants 3s 4d. Sixe yeards of french canvas 4s 6d. Seven Ellns of ossenbridge 3s 6d	18	7	7
Thirtie Eyght pound and an halfe of Severall Soarts of Outnall Thrid £13 8s 3d. Sixtie Nine pound of whited-browne Thrid £16 11s 9d.	30	0	0

Twelve gross of white Twist £1 4s. Heming Tape 8s 11d. Seventeen pieces of white London Tape 6s. Sixe dozen and ten pieces of colored Inckle £1. Two dozen of the best London white 17s. Two dozen and three pieces of Carnation colored Inckle 8s. Three dozen and an halfe of white Incle £1. five dozen of Manchester incle 4s. Sixe pieces of diaper Tape 3s 4d. Nine gross of whipcord laces 10s. Three New lookeing glasses 13s 4d.	6	14	7
Sixe tinn tobacco boxes 6d. fower copper boxes 2s. Twelve small brass boxes 6d. Three dozen of beggars Inckle. a percell of goose quills and white tagg'd laces 3s. Sixe Leather caps 6d. five dozen of padds and collers 6s 8d. a percell of past board packthred and brushes 4s 6d. A gross of handballs 1s. A blacke Spanish skin 2s. Eyghteen oyled skins 13s 4d. A percell of Combs 10s. A percell of bodys £1 6s 8d. A percell of pacthrid 5s. A piece of flannel 10s.	4	5	8
Sixe childrens Leading strings 1s. half a pound of sweet powder and balls 1s. Sixe hankeing baggs 3s. Three dozen of Inckhornes 4s. Two gross of Thimbles 1s 6d. A pound and a quarter of sealeing waxe 2s. Two dozen of Spectacles and sixe cases 2s 6d. fower papers and a small percell of hooks and eys 5s 6d. divers percells of gimp buttons decayed silver buttons, and old poynting and thrid buttons £1 1s 6d. Three cordivant skins 3s 4d. fower oyled cases 4s. Two pound of waxe Candles 1s 6d. Seaveing candles and girdles 1s 6d. Three pound and an halfe of soft waxe and old laces 2s 6d. A pair of Drawers and hatt cases 2s 6d. Three dozen of Bone £1 4s.	4	1	4
Seven pound of Spanish Tobacco £1 10s. fortie three pound weight in Cutt Virginia £1 15s 10d. Three hundred weight of the best Virginia Tobacco in the Leafe £15 3s 4d. Two hundred weight of the second soart of Virginia Tobacco in Leafe £5 5s	23	19	2
One hundred and an halfe lb. weight of the ordinary Soart of tobacco in leafe £3 4s 8d. One gross of glased pipes 1s 8d. Eyght gross of ordinary pipes 6s 8d. A percell of old caskes in the Cellers and Chambers 5s.	3	18	8

	£	s	d
One Barrell and three firkeins of the best soape £4 10s. Two Barrells and an halfe of ordinary Soape £5. one percell of Starch and fowerteen pound weight of knitting Needles 14s. Twelve gallons Two quarts and one pint of Strong waters called Anniseeds Water £2 10s. five gallons of Angelico water 16s 8d. wormwood water fower gallons 13s 4d. Stomach water Eyght gallons £1 6s 8d. of Aqua Vita Twenty Eyght gallons £2 14s. A pott of Anchovis 13s 4	18	8	10
Eyghty one pound weight of Honey £1 13s 9d. Two hundred and one quartram weight of fine pouder Sugar £8 3s 4d. halfe an hundred weight more of powder sugar £1 10s. Two hundred weight and fowerteen pound weight of a courser soart of powder sugar £6 1s. five hundred and an halfe hundred weight of the coursest powder sugar £10 9s. white Sugar Candy fower pound weight 5s. fower pound weight of browne course sugar 3s	28	5	1
Three dozen of pepper £1 16s. Two ounce weight of Saffron 6s 8d. one hundred and an halfe weight of raissins £3. one hundred weights of figgs £1. A percell of Currance raissins and soape in the Shop Boxes £1 6s 8d. one hundred weight of prunes 6s 8d. five pound weight of Cloves £3. Three pound weight of nutmegs 15s. one pound and an halfe of Mace £1 13s 4d. Eyght ounce of Cinnamon 4s. Twenty Eyght pound weight of ginger 7s 6d. fowerteen pound weight of Gunpowder 9s. Sixe pound weight of galls 4s. Two percells more 6s 8d.	14	15	6
Halfe an hundred weight of Rice 18s. fowerteen pound weight of Jourdan Almonds 9s. Two Baggs of Valentia Almonds 3s. five pound weight of french barley 1s 6d	1	11	6
Three pound weight of quicke-silver 10s. Three hundred weight of Alloms £3 13 8d. one hundred and an halfe weight of Copporas 10s. Halfe an hundred weight of brimston 12s. A quarter of an hundred weight of reedwood 6s 8d. A quarter of an hundred weight of powder blew 14s. Twenty pound weight of Indico £4 0s 6d. Two pound of stone blew 2s. Two percells of frankinsence 3s 4d. fower dozen Kandles 18s. Halfe an hundred weight			

	£	s	d
of treacle 9s. A quarter of an lb of Beeswax 13s 4d. A quarter of an lb of Liquorice 8s. A gallon of sweete oyle 3s 4d. Two hundred weight of Hopps £5.	18	3	6
Two Reeme of fine paper 12s. seven Reeme of ordinary writeing paper 17s 6d. Twentie fower Reeme of browne paper £2 8s. Three Reeme of large cap paper 13s 6d. Three Reeme of small cap paper 6s 8d. fower pound of Cumin seeds a percell of Carraway seeds and Annsseeds 3s.	5	0	9
Five dozen and Two payre of Cordivant mens gloves £6 0s 6d. one dozen and seven payre of mens white Kidds £1 0s 6d. Two payre of mens Bucks gloves 6s. Three dozen and fower payre of mens lambs and sheepe leather gloves £1 2s 8d. A boxe of old sheepe leather gloves 10s. A boxe of old Tannd gloves 6s 8d	9	5	4
One dozen of womens cordivant gloves £1. five dozen and seven payre of womens colored Kidd gloves £3 3s 6d. Three dozen and seven payre of womens White Kidds £2 1s 4d. fower dozen of white lamb-gloves £1. A percell of colored childrens Kidds 11s. one dozen and Eyght payre of maids Kidds colored and white 9s 8d. five payre of childrens gloves 1s. Seeventeen payre of childrens Muffs 2s. A boxe of ordinary gloves 5s	8	13	6
Fortie three payre of mens worsteed stockings £6 17s 10d fower payre of worsteed stirrup stockings 10s. Sixe payre of worsted Stockins for youths 12s. Three payre of mens white worsted 4s 6d. Eyght payre of bad woollen stockins mens 9s. Twelve payre of mens woollens 15s. five payre of worsteed womens stockings 15s. Two dozen and one payre of woollen Stockins for women £2 7s 8d. Thirtie five payre more of womens stockins woollen £2 3s 1d. Sixteene payre of girles stockins 13s 4d. Sixteene payre of childrens stockins 11s 8d. A percell of small childrens stockins 7s. A payre of womens Stockins Two payre of childrens and fower tops 3s 4d. Nine payre of socks 3s 4d.	16	12	9
Ten Childrens Coates 5s 4d fower childrens Coates 8s. Sixe childrens coates 2s 6d. Sixe childrens coates 13s 4d. one childs coate 2s five childrens coates 9s. Two			

childrens Coates £1. Nine childrens coates 3s 1d.	2	4	11
Twenty Eyght pound in greate brass weights 18s 8d. Sixteen pound in lesser brass weights 10s 8d. fowerteen payre of small brass scoales 14s. one payre of greate brass scoales 10s. one payre of less brass Scoales 4s. fower Setts of brass hanerdupois weights 12s. Two Sett of brass Troy weights. One Sett of Venice weights brass and a payre of gold weights 3s 4d.	3	12	8
A payre of Greate wood Scoales and an iron Beame £1 2s. one hundred and an halfe hundred of Lead weights £1 1s. Two Tobacco Knives and boards with an old Table in the Shop 13s 4d. A tobacco press £1 10s. Sixtie Nine Draw boxes in the Shop 11s 8d. Two nests of boxes in the Shop 18s. A window grate and a Map of England 5s. A greate press in the shop 6s 8d. Two greate presses in the ware Chamber 6s 8d. A Tobacco Hammer 1s 6d. Tobacco Sieves and panns 2s 6d.	6	18	4

Debts owing to the Testator in his Shop Book

By John Howton of Newarke payable in – months	19	0	0
Matthew Hebblethwaite of Lincoln	3	0	0
William Robinson of Lincolne	11	0	0
Mr. Henry Rands of North Carleton	3	6	0

Debts owing to the Testator in his Shop Booke

By William Foxe of the Cittie and Diocess of London Taylor	3	16	9
Mr Henage of the Cittie and Diocess of London	0	5	6
Mr Thomas Robinson of the Diocess of Litchfield and Coventre	1	10	0
Mr Eaton of the Diocess of Bangor	1	5	0
Mr Halford of the Cittie and Diocess of London	0	7	0
Sir John Bowles of the Cittie and Diocess of London			
Mr Thomas Dowse of the Cittie and Diocess of London	0	2	0
John Greenwood of the Cittie and Diocess of London	0	10	6
Debts owning by divers persons dwelling within the Cittie and Diocess of Lincolne amounting in the while to the sume of	210	16	0

of which Debts to the sume of one hundred and Twenty pounds ten shillings are desperate			
And the sume of Ninety pounds six shillings reputed good	265	12	6
The Funerall Expenses			
To the parson of St. Peters Church in Lincolne for the burying place	0	13	4
for also his Mortuary	0	10	0
To Thomas Gibson parish Clerke for his fees and the grave making	0	4	8
For Biskett	4	3	6
For Sacke and wine	3	0	8
For Sugar and Spices	0	10	0
Sixe payre of Cordivant gloves	0	18	0
For one Suite of Morning for the Executrix	2	7	9
For Bread	2	0	0
For a Coffin	0	12	0
Knowne Debts owning by the Testator To divers persons of the Cittie of London of the Town of Kingston Upon Hull and of the Cittie of Norwich and other places Upon bond and other wayes for goods and marchandises bought and received by the Testator in his life time and not discounted for by him.			
In all the Sume of Seven hundred fortie fower pound ten shillings	744	10	0
The Totall of all goods Chattells and Credebts	1203	15	5
The totall of the funerall Expenses and his owne debts	757	9	11
The charges of Viewing and Vallueing of the goods and makeing and double ingrossing the Inventory	2	6	8

4. **Anniseeds Water** – oil made from seed of anise.
Aqua Vita – spirits, probably gin.
Bagg Holland – coarse canvas
Bowdied – scarlet dyed.
Bumbasine – a material which was a mixture of silk and wool or silk and cotton.
Callacine – see above p. xlix
Cap paper – wrapping paper.
Chena – common worsted or woollen cloth.
Cumin seeds – from a Near Eastern plant valued for aromatic and carminative qualities.
Curl – a kind of woollen cloth with a curly surface.
Cypress – a transparent black lawn much used for mourning.

Ferritt ribbon – strong cotton tape.
Handball – ball for throwing in a variety of games.
Hancke silke – silk thread.
Hanerdupois – avoirdupois system of weights.
Hankeing bags – bags closed by a looped string.
Hartshorne – smelling salts.
Indico – indigo
Isingham Holland – canvas of unknown provenance.
Lockrams – linen fabric.
Looplace – an ornamented edging to lace.
Masque – mask.
Outnall – linen tape.
Parragon – ribbed woollen cloth much used for hangings.
Phillip – worsted or woollen cloth of common quality.
Powder blue – powdered smalt used in laundry.
Poynting – ornamental stitch; ribbon used as a lace.
Prunella – a durable stuff, originally of silk, later worsted, much used for gowns.
Quicke-silver – mercury.
Reeme – ream.
Saffron – dried crocus stigmata used as a dye and cordial.
Sarsenett – a fine silk material used for linings.
Say – a fine serge.
Scoales – scales.
Seaveing candles – rush candles.
Sempeternum – hardwearing woollen resembling serge.
Slee silke – silk ribbon.
Standard – a measuring rod.
Stomach water – a medicine.
Sweete oyle – olive oil.
Tamelletoe – see above p. xlix, probably camblet.
Tammie – an ordinary worsted.
Wormwood water – a bitter tasting cordial.

5. Thomas Lewis — Prob. Inv. 166/43

Labourer 9.1.1667

	£	s	d
His purse and Apparill	1	0	0
In the Hall			
One Cubard one table one forme 4 bast chares 4 buffitt stooles with other implements	1	0	0
In the parlar			
One bedstead one trundle bed 5 ould Cheest one small fether bed one Coverlid one paire of blankits with other implements	1	13	4

In the Kiching

One land iorn one gallow bauke with howkes tonges and other implements	0	3	6
2 brase pots 8 brase panes one Skelit one Skumer one brase Candle stick one brass ladle	2	1	6
For eight puter dublers fowre sawcers one flagon 2 puter candlesticks one bowle one sault	1	6	8
Two sithes one Spad one hatchit with bag and bottle and other smale implements	0	2	4
For three paire of hemping sheets fowre pillow beares six napkines	0	15	0

In the yard

Three Cowes	3	0	0

In the Chamber

Three loade of hay	1	0	0
	12	14	4
	(12	2	4)

6. John Featley **Di 38/2/10**

Doctor of Divinity. In his Dignity house of the Close of Lincoln 21.3.1667

	£	s	d
His purse and Apparrell	30	0	0
A Suite of hangings of Kidderminster with two Curtains of the same	1	6	8
Thirteen Rushia Leather Chaires	3	10	0
Three Tables with Carpetts	0	13	0
A Landiron with brasses a paire of Tongs a fire shovell a fire forke a fire grate Horse	0	8	0
A Screene with six foulds	0	13	4
A Larum Watch	1	0	0

In the Little Hall

A Table and forme	0	6	8

In the Dyneing Roome

A suite of Green hangings and three carpits of the same	6	5	0
A dozen and halfe of Turkey worke Chaires	8	0	0

A greate Lookeing glasse and three brasses	0	10	0
A Kidderminster Carpet	0	18	0
Three Spanish tables and two foote stooles	0	8	0
A Landiron with foure brasses a brasse fireshovell and tongs	1	2	0
A paire of endirons with foure brasses	0	12	0
The matting	0	15	0

In the Straingers Chamber

A Suite of Kidderminster hangings	1	10	0
A Downe bed Boulster and two pillowes	4	0	0
A Bedstead Cords Matt and Rodds	0	15	0
Serge Curtaines and Vallence head peice and Counterpaine Knobbs and tester	7	0	0
A large Rugg and paire of Blanketts	2	5	0
Foure Chaires and foure stooles suitable to the bed	3	10	0
A little Table and Carpet	0	8	0
A lookeing glasse with brasses	0	7	0
A Landiron	0	1	6
A Spanish Table	0	9	0
A Still and frame	0	10	0
Three Turkeyworke Cushions	0	6	0
Matting	0	8	0

In the Mens Chamber

A Bedstead Cord Matt	0	6	0
A featherbed and boulster and flock bolster	1	4	0
Two old Coverlids	0	5	0

In the Upper Straingers Chamber

A Bedstead Cord and Matt and Rodds	0	12	0
Striped Curtaines and vallence	0	13	0
A feather bed and boulster and two pillowes	2	0	0
A Rug and Blanket	0	13	4
A Spanish Table	0	9	0

In the Chamber over the Gate

A Bedstead Mat Cord and Rods	0	4	0
A featherbed two boulsters and two pillowes	2	10	0
A Coverlid and a blanket	0	5	0
A Trundle bedstead flocke bed and boulsters Blanket and Rugg	0	13	4
Striped Curtaines and vallence and window Curtaine	0	8	0
A Table	0	2	6

The Chamber over ye back kitchen

A Bedstead Cord Matt and Rods	0	5	0
A featherbed and boulster and pillow	1	15	0

A paire of Striped Curtaines Vallence and Rugg	0	10	0
A greate presse and a little presse	0	13	4
Two long Chests 8s and a little Chest 2s in all	0	10	0
Two greate Trunkes	0	8	0
Two little Trunkes	0	4	0
A Saddle and Bridle with bosses	1	0	0

In the Buttery

A little Table and Chest	0	4	0
Five Barrells and a Thrall with other implements	0	8	0

In the other Buttery

Three greate Barrells a thrall and a Salting tubb	0	10	0

In the Larder

A Safe dresser and other Implements	0	5	0

In the Garret

A Bedstead a Cord and matt	0	3	0
A featherbed and boulster	1	10	0
A Rug and Blanket	0	7	0
A Cradle and whisket	0	3	0

In the Chamber over ye Parlour

A suite of Kidderminster hangings	1	10	0
A Bedstead Cord Matt and Rods	0	10	0
A featherbed boulster and two pillowes	4	0	0
A paire of strip'd Curtaines and Vallence and Counterpaine	1	0	0
A Rugg and a blanket	1	8	0
Seaven Chaires and two stooles	1	4	0
A Table and Carpet	0	4	0
A greate Trunke	0	13	4
A Stove and nest of Drawers	0	12	0
A paire of Endirons fire shovells and tongs	0	9	0
Matting	0	10	0
Two wanded Chaires a Seller of Bottles and Close stoole Box	0	6	0

In the Inner Chamber

A Trundle bedstead and a Cupboard	0	4	0

In the Brewhouse

A Copper	3	10	0
A Brewing fat and other Implements	0	13	4

A paire of Rackes Landirons and Iron under the Copper and a Gally balke	1	0	0

In Stable

Foure horses	(..	..	..)
A Cow	1	6	8
A load of Hay	1	0	0
Corne	(..	..	..)
A hundred of bricke and tile	0	1	6
Five and thirty Deale	2	12	6

In plate

One hundred sixty five Ounces at five shillings per ounce	41	5	0
Two gold rings	1	0	0
A Watch	2	0	0

Pewter in the Kitchen

Seventeene stone at tenpence per pound	9	18	4
Of Lay pewter eighteene pound	0	9	0
Two Close Stoole pans a Candlestick and a bottle	0	11	0

Pan Mettle

Three stone and three pounds at 10d a pound	1	17	6
Pot brasse fifteen pounds	0	6	3
A warmeing pan and a brasse Ladle	0	6	0
A Skimmer and two small brasse Ladles	0	1	6
A paire of brasse Skales and weights	0	4	0
In lead weights five stone	0	5	10
A Jacke	0	10	0
Nine spitts	0	8	0
Cobirons and a Dripping pann	0	5	6
A Land Iron fire shovell and tongs with other Implements belonging to the Chimney	0	10	0
Three Iron potts and pothookes	0	8	0
Two frying panns	0	2	6
A Table two joynt stooles with other woodden Lumber	0	10	0
Six bells	0	12	0
A Lanthorne and foure smoothing Irons	0	4	0

In the Studdy

A Deske and Table	0	12	0
A Chest of Drawers	0	13	4
A greate Trunke and three small ones	0	12	0
Shelves and Matting	0	8	0

Lynnings			
Six paire of Holland sheetes att fifteene shillings a paire	4	10	0
A paire of fine sheetes	1	10	0
Two paire of flaxen sheetes	1	0	0
Seaven paire of Courser flaxen sheetes	2	6	8
Six paire of hempen	1	6	8
Three Cambricke pillow beares	0	5	0
Five paire of Holland pillowbeares	0	10	0
Six paire of flaxen pillowbeares	0	10	0
Two Dyaper Table Cloathes	0	12	0
Six flaxen Table Cloathes	1	16	0
Two Dozen Dyaper Napkins	0	16	0
Six Dozen of fine flaxen Napkins	2	14	0
Three dozen and an halfe of Course flaxen Napkins	0	14	0
Twenty Towells	1	0	0
Six Course Table Cloathes	0	9	0
Three sideboard Cloathes	0	5	4
A Scarlet Mantle with a Silver lace	1	10	0
A wrought Mantle and a tufted holland one	0	5	0
Two Damaske Napkins	0	3	0
A Hamocke	0	10	0
	207	16	1

7. Mr. John Towndrow **Prob. Inv. 168/76**

(Baker) 26.11.1668

	£	s	d
His porse and apparrell	5	0	0
In the Chamber			
Two stand beds with Cortaines and Valions one featherbed two feather boulsters and five pillowes one Ruge two Coverlitts two blankitts and one mattrice	6	1	6
In the same Chamber one long table one liveray Cobert and one Chist	1	10	0
In the same Chamber six bas-bothomd Chaires six quishions one paire of end-irons and one binch	0	7	6

In the meale-Chamber

Three strike of flower six strike of stuffing one mile to drese meale three ould tubs one strike and one peck measures with other Implements	2	5	0

In the garratt

Eight strike of wheate and at the mile twelve strike, more in the garratt five strike of Rye	3	0	0

In the Closett

One trundle bedstead some shelves with other Implements	0	6	8

In the Rye-meale Chamber

A leaven-strike of Rye-meale with a sive and other Implements	1	5	0

In the parlor

Two stand-beds two feather-beds two boulstor and three pillowes, two blankitts two Coverletts with Cortaines	4	3	4
In the same parlor one Closse-press one table three seelled stooles one Chist one box one seeing glase one forme with some other Iplements	1	4	6

In the shopp

Three dozen and a half of bread three basketts with shelves and other Implements	0	10	0

In the parlor next the buttery

One ould bedstead one flock-bed one boulster two pillows one blankitt and two ould Coverlitts one ould Chist with some other Implements	1	0	0

In the hall

Three little-tables one Cobert one long sadle two formes one Wanded-Chaire one ould Arme-Chaire three basbothomed Chaires three quishions one joyned stoole	1	9	2
In the same roome in pewter dishes 24 pounds one greate flaggon and five small ones one quart Kan one pinte and one half pint one Kandlestick and one beaker two Chamberpotts and one mustord-pot and one bason all of pewter	1	15	6

In the buttery

Six barrells and one kilderkin and one stand two wodden horses and one ould safe	0	18	0

In the bruehouse

One leade one washtub one geathering tub and one underbeck and one soa	3	10	0
In the same roome one trough to bake with, one brake one bakehouse table some peeles with other Implements	0	10	0

In the Kitching

One little Copper in the fornace foure brace pans and one brace pott one Iron beame with scoales and weights one dresserbord one stand with other Implements	2	0	4
Two paire of Linn sheetes and two paire of Linn pillowberes thre paire of hemp sheetes and one paire of harden three paire of hemp pillowbeares and line tablecloth one dozen of line napkins and one dozen of hempin ones	2	8	6

In the house

One Land Iron with end Irons one gallowbalke with hookes one paire of Racks one driping pann two spitts two fire shovells one frying pan one Chafeingdish eight Coople of roapes of ongons	1	8	0

In the yard

Six hundred of kidds 14 trayes one belferay and one leather	3	0	0
More in the yard 2 sowes with six small piggs	1	10	0
More in the yard two horses	4	3	4

In the Chamber

Neare a loade of hay	0	12	0
Ayle in the house	1	5	0
One rydeing-saddle and one pack-saddle and one paire of panyers	0	12	0
In the entry two shelves one meale trough	0	3	4
In Debts, but the most of them thout to be desperate	4	2	2
	58	1	4

7. **Brake** – kneading implement used by bakers.
Stuffing – grain of any sort.

8. William Norton Prob. Inv. 172/264

Maltster. St. Swithin 17.3.1670

	£	s	d
His Purse and apparell	20	0	0
In his Lodgings Parller			
One Great Stand bedstead	0	13	4
1 Rugg, 1 paire of blankets, 1 feather bed, 1 boulster and 2 Pillowes	4	6	0
2 Carpitts	0	10	0
One Trundle bedstead, 1 featherbed, 3 blankets 1 Coverlet	1	10	0
One Great table, 3 stooles, 1 forme	0	13	4
One Little table with a Cubert int 3 Chests 1 Great Presse for Cloaths	1	5	0
One wicker Chaire, 1 other Chaire, 5 Cushions, 1 Warming Pann with other Implements	1	0	0
In the Hall			
One old drawtable, 1 old Liverie Cubert, 1 forme, 2 Chaires with other Implements	1	0	0
In the Kitchin			
2 Cuberts, 2 litle tables, 1 Safe, one Long Settle, 2 Joynid Chaires, 5 other Chaires, and 3 Stooles	1	3	6
13 Pewter Dishes	2	5	0
2 flagons, 2 Pewter Canns, 2 Candlesticks 2 Pewter Cupps, 2 Bowles, 2 Poringers 1 Basin, 2 Chamber potts with other Smale peeces of Pewter	1	5	0
5 brass Panns, 1 brass Chafeindish, 1 brass Scimer, 1 ladle	1	6	8
2 brass Potts	0	15	0
2 Spitts, 1 paire of Iron Racks, 1 Iron Dripinpann. 1 land Iron, with other implements	1	10	0
In the Brewhouse			
3 old Steeping Tubbs, 1 brewinge Curb, 3 Soes, 1 Salting Tub, 1 Cymnill	2	10	0
In the buttery			
One Hogshead, 7 Smale barrells with other Implements	0	10	0

In the Nue Chamber

One bedstead Curtans and vallance 1 featherbed, 1 Blanket, 1 Coverlet, 1 Rugg, 2 boulsters, 1 pillow	3	10	0
1 Table with a Cubert in 't, Joynid Chaires 1 other Chaire 1 box	0	6	8

Lyinings

5 paire of Lyining Sheets	3	10	0
1 Duzen of Lyning Napkins, 2 diper napkins	0	15	0
2 Duzen of Hempen Napkins 10 pillowbears 3 paire of Harden Sheets, 7 paire of Hempen sheets	4	10	0
Eleven yards of bleatched Lyning, 40 yards of Lyning unbleatched	2	8	0

In the Stairhead chamber

2 stand beds and Beding, 3 Chests and other implements	2	0	0

In Severall Chambers

Dryed Mault, 148 quarters	162	16	0
Raw Mault upon the flore 30 quarters	30	0	0
Stept Barley in the fatts : 7 quarters	7	0	0
In the Barley Chamber 30 quarters of barley	30	0	0
3 Sacks of wheat	2	5	0
2 quarters of Rie	2	8	0
2 quarters of Oates	1	0	0
3 Sacks of Pease	1	4	0
24 Sacks	1	0	0
2 Strike Skeps, 1 Scrine, 36 yards of Hairecloth and one old Hairecloth and 4 Shovells	3	1	0
2 Loads of Coale	2	0	0

In the yard

One waine and wheeles 1 waine bodie, and 1 cart bodie, and Plough Geares	3	10	0
2 Horses, 2 paire of Oxen	23	0	0
2 Kyne and one Calfe	6	6	0
2 Swine	1	15	0
Woode	1	0	0
Hay	5	0	0
A cropp of Corne	10	0	0
In bonds bills and desprate Debts	100	0	0
	452	18	2
	(452	17	6)

8. Curb – framing round the top of a circular copper.
Cymnill – a kimnell or wooden tub.
Scimer – a shallow ladle.
Steeping tub – tub in which malt is soaked.

9. Francis Younglove Prob. Inv. 172/327

(Harness Seller) 25.4.1670

	£	s	d
His purse and apparrell	2	0	0
In the parlour			
Two high bed, with feather beds blancketts and Coverlids to them allso Curtaines and Vallance to each of them	4	0	0
Two Chests in the parlour two pairs of Lining sheets two pair of hempen-sheets one table cloth of Lining, with two dozen of Napkins	2	0	0
In the hall house or Kitching			
Halfe of the wooden goods	1	0	0
Halfe of the brass and pewter in the same Roome and one Jack with fire Shovell and tongs and hooks Also one Landiron two spits and one brass candlestick and one warming pan	2	6	8
In the chamber			
Two chests and one old safe	0	4	0
In the warehouse			
In Ropes thirty one stone at three shillings and four pence the stone	5	3	4
Also in the shop up street			
Hors collars and Beeils and one cant saddle and other wares	1	12	6
More in the warehouse			
Small cords and haire	1	0	0
One mill rop, and Three blind halters and one pair of till hancks and pack thread	0	14	0

In the shop

Two Carts, two winches twelve hookes and other impliments belonging to the trade and a pair of brass weights	0	12	0
Two bolts of sack cloth and fiveteen yards of haire cloth a paire of (t)ill hanks and a small peece of girt web	1	14	6

In the chamber

Twenty nine stone of hemp and thirteen stone of femble each at two shillings and four pence the stone	4	18	0
Also twenty and seaven dozen and a halfe of bast Teathers; at nine pence the dozen	1	0	6
Seaven score and ten pair of Beeiles for oxen	2	0	0
Also four dozen of flag collars	0	8	0
And four forkes	0	2	0
One horse and two sadles one hog and two tresles and one peece of wood at ye door	3	6	8
Ten milch Cows and one bull	28	0	0
In good debts and bad	15	3	6
	77	5	8

9. **Bast teathers** – rope beast tethers.
Beeils – cross bar of an animal yoke.
Blind halter – a bridle with blinkers.
Cant saddle – a side saddle.
Femble – hemp fibres prepared for use.
Flag – woven from rushes.
Forke – an animal yoke.
Girt webs – belt of leather or cloth which secures the saddle of pack to the horse.
Till hancks – hanks of coarse cloth.

10. Richard Hazelteine — Prob. Inv. 172/321

(Labourer) St. Michaels in the Mount (.. ..) 1670

	£	s	d
His purse and Aparell	0	10	0

In the house

One table: one frome: one Livera Cubert one long Sattle these things of valew	0	10	0
One wanded Chaire five bast Chaires	0	4	0
Two glas Cases one table basket	0	1	6

One Land Iron with other Irons to the harth	0	3	0
One broken puter flagon with other puter	0	5	0
One bras pot	0	5	0

In two other little Roomes

One old Cubbert one plaister trough one Sive with other small usefull things	0	6	8

In the two Chambers

One bedstead and beding	0	5	0
In the same Chambers 5 little chests and other small things	0	13	0
In the yard 3 stock of Bees and a little parcell opfell wood	0	16	0
One Cowe	1	0	0
One Sowe	0	10	0
	5	9	2

10. Plaister trough – plaster trough.

11. Eden Williams **Prob.Inv. 173/387**

(Bookseller) St. Martins 11.12.1671

	£	s	d
(app)arril	2	0	0

In the Parlor

(...) 1 boulster. 2 pillowes 3 blanketts one rugg (cur)taine and Vallence Curtaine rods and matt	3	10	0
(...)	0	15	0
(...) 1 low Chaire 2 stooles 2 Carpetts Irish (...)	2	12	0
(...) Cushions	0	9	0
(..m)app of London one hanginge shelfe and glasses	0	10	0
(..) Candlesticke	0	2	0
(..) irons one land Iron 1 pair frogs fireshovell and tongs	0	5	0
(Curt)aine and rodds	0	3	0

The Chamber over the parlor

(..) feather bed one feather boulster. 3 blankets (..) rugg Curtaines and Vallence and rods matt	5	0	0

(..) Cloth Chaire 2 Cloth Chaires Cloth stooles one wanded Chaire one (...)	1	4	0
(...) a paire of doggs with brasses bosses (..)	1	0	0
(...) severall glasses and earthen waires	0	5	0

The Chamber over the pantree

(...) one feather bed one feather boulster 2 (...) one old rugg Curtaine Vallence matt and cord	1	10	0
(...) one feather boulster (...) one flock boulster 2 Coverlides 1 old blanket matt and Cord	0	14	0
1 trunke 2 old Chaires one livery Cubberd and Cloth and other implyments	0	10	0

In the workeinge Chamber

(...) and the Lumber there	0	10	0

In the passage Chamber

(...) bedstead Curtaine and Vallence one Close (...) one Curtaine one Side table and Carpitt one old Chaire one Stand one box one glass case and glasses	0	13	0

In the Kittchinge

(...) tubb one dresser board one old forme one watring tubb one wash tubb 2 wooden horese one (..) boules 2 Kitts and other Lumber there	0	16	0

The Kitchinge Chamber

(..) tiles old boxes hampers and other Lumber	0	6	8

In the Stabble

A parcel of wood and other fuell there	0	14	0

In the Pantree

2 smale draw tables 1 great armed leather Chaire 7 other leather Chaires 2 leather stooles one bast Chaire	1	18	8

In the entree

One wainscott Chair one haire brush	0	2	6
One old cubbert one firr table and 2 Chaires	0	5	0
Severall dishes and other lumber	0	1	0

In the hall house

One Close bed one feather bed 2 feather boulsters one feather pillow 3 blanketts and one red rugg	3	10	0
One draw table and Carpett	0	13	4
One cubberd one Chest of drawers Cubberd cloth and cussions	1	10	0
One longe settle bed	0	4	0
5 bast Chaires	0	1	6
3 ioynt stooles	0	3	0
One deske and one looking glass	0	3	0
One screene one smale Child Chaire	0	5	0
One window Curtaine rod	0	(..	..)
One silver beaker 4 silver spoones one silver (...)	8	(..	..)
One lardge landiron and end Irons with bosses	(..	..	..)
2 Iron drippinge pans 3 Iron spitts	(..	..	..)
Brass and pewter	(..	..	..)
One Iron pott one Jack a paire of racks gallow balkes runninge hookes and other Irons	(..	..	..)
1 tinne Candlestick 2 haire brushes one grediron other Irons	(..	..	..)
12 pounds of flax and yearne	(..	..	..)
5 paire of linnen sheets at 6s	(..	..	..)
9 paire of Corse sheets at 4s	(..	..	..)
2 dozen of line napkins	(..	..	..)
1 dozen and 2 Corse napkins at 4d	(..	..	..)
11 pillow beares att 8d	(..	..	..)
8 table Clothes at 12d	(..	..	..)
18 towells at 4d	(..	..	..)
2 trunkes att	(..	..	..)

In the Celler

One hodghead one barrell one wooden (...) underbeck one baskets one funnell	(..	..	..)

In the little Shopp

4 Reames of Amsterdam Armes white paper	(..	..	..)
2 Reames 14 quire fools Capp paper at	(..	..	..)
1 Reame 18 quire of pott and piller paper at	(..	..	..)
1 Reame 17 quire of fine horne paper	(..	..	..)
1 Reame 12 quire of Venice paper at	(..	..	..)
11 quire of fine post paper lardge	(..	..	..)
2 quire and a halfe of imperiall paper at	(..	..	..)
12 quire of royall paper at	(..	..	..)
8 quire of Cullard paper	(..	..	..)
10 quire of branch paper att	(..	..	..)

10 quire of Silver paper at 9d	(..	..	..)
3 drawers of Maps at 2s	(..	..	..)
Smale bookes – ballads	(..	..	..)
1 skin 2 peece of Vellum	(..	..	..)
Halfe a rowle of London parchment	(..	..	..)
8 sheets of Lardge London parchment	(..	..	..)
2 drawers of smale parchment	(..	..	..)
1 drawer of Lincolne parchment	(..	..	..)
1 dozen and a halfe of Grantham parchment	(..	..	..)
1 dozen of smale London parchment	(..	..	..)
9 Lardge London parchments at 9d	(..	..	..)
2 dozen and a halfe of black boxes at 3s a dozen	(..	..	..)
2 dozen and a halfe of black lead pencills	(..	..	..)
3 pewter standishes	(..	..	..)
2 pound of hard wax	(..	..	..)
5 skins of greene Vellum	(..	..	..)

In the great shopp

99 bookes in folio smale and great new and old at 2s 6d	12	7	6
318 bookes in quarto smale and great new and old at 12d	15	18	0
1140 bookes in octavo at 6d	28	10	0
434 smale twelves 16° and 24° at 6d	10	17	0
3 old bibles in quarto att 7s	1	1	0
3 new bibles in quato att 7s	1	1	0
7 bibles in octavo att 4s	1	8	0
12 gilt bibles in 12° at 3s 6d	2	2	0
16 plaine bibles in 12° att 3s	2	8	0
2 plaine bibles in 24° att 4s	0	8	0
2 dozen of gramers att 7s	0	14	0
2 dozen and a halfe of psalters att 7s	0	17	6
12 single testaments att 12d	0	12	0
3 doble testaments att 3s 4d	0	10	0
10 paper bookes bound in octavo at 6d	0	5	0
10 paper bookes ruled in folio longe att 3s 6d	1	15	0
4 paper bookes unruled in folio longe att 12d	0	4	0
10 paper bookes in folio broad and 74° longe att	0	13	6
2 Common prayer books in 8° Cutts at 8s	0	16	0
1 Common prayer book in Cutts 12° one 24° Cutts	0	5	0
4 Common prayer in octavo plaine att 2s	0	8	0
(..) 12° plaines Comon prayer bookes at	0	2	0
(..) prayer booke 8° gilt at 2s 6d	0	2	6
(..) gilt at 2s	0	2	0
(...) at 18d	0	3	0

(...) at 12d	0	3	0
(...h)istorie bookes bookes and pamphlets	3	0	0
Shop on ye East side of ye streete			
(...) press 2 hand presses one plough one (....) old books shelves and other implyments	2	0	0
	145	3	4
(...Deb)ts owinge in ye debt booke	6	10	10
(...L)umber things unseene and forgott	2	0	0
	153	14	2

11. **Amsterdam Armes** - paper with the watermark of the city of Amsterdam.
Branch paper - ?
Cullard - coloured.
Cutts - unbound leaves.
Folio - printng paper folded once.
Foolscap paper - usually measuring 16.5 by 16.25 inches.
Greene vellum - unseasoned vellum.
Hand presse - printing press worked by hand.
Horne paper - paper with a horn watermark.
Imperiall - a quarto sheet of paper usually measuring 15 by 11 inches.
° - the abbreviation for 'mo' indicating the number of leaves that have been produced by folding a sheet of printing paper. Each leaf would have been printed on two sides to produce two pages of a booke. Thus 16° was the creation of sixteen leaves from four folds. 74° records the presence of seven quarto books so folded as to produce 'long' rectangular books.
Octavo - a book based on a sheet of printing paper folded three times to give sixteen pages.
Parchment - skin of sheep or goat prepared for writing.
Plough press - a long vice in which a book is clamped for the pages to be trimmed.
Post - quarto size paper or book.
Pott and piller - a size of writing paper usually 15.5 by 12.5 inches with a pot watermark.
Quarto - a book based on a sheet of printing paper folded twice to give eight pages.
Royall - paper sheets used for writing, printing and the making of cartridges.
Silver paper - a fine white tissue paper.
Smale twelves - small books of half or quarter octavo size.
Standishe - an oblong tray for writing implements.
Vellum - fine skin of calf prepared for writing, painting or binding.

12. George Shoosmith — Prob. Inv. 175/201

Glaissyar 8.4.1672

	£	s	d
His purs and aparell	2	10	0
In ye parlyar			
One high bedsteade Curtens and Valaces with a rugg and fetharbed two boulstares six pillows three blankites a payr of sheets mat and cord	4	10	0
One Trundel bed stead with a fethar bed one boulstar one rugg and Cuarlid with a pilloy and a payr of hempen Sheetes mat and cord	1	1	6
One Cubard Eighte Chayrs three Tabules and three trunkes one box and two stoules	2	0	0
One payr of greene Curtens and valance with three Tabell Clothes one Cubart Cloth four Corchans with a bibell and 3 or four othar boockes	1	2	6
One seeing glass a glass Case two baskites	0	10	0
One fyare Iarne with Endiarnes a payr of rackes and two spites with a galle bayck fiar shovell and tonges with sevarell othar Iarns and inplementes	1	1	4
The Closite with in ye parlar			
Three brasse pottes three Skellites foure pannes one warming panne four brass Ladelles with a littell brasse puding panne	1	13	4
Twelfe pewtar disses three basons three flagines foure Chambar pottes two Candalstickes two wine pottes with seavarell othar Implemantes	3	10	0
In plate two Cupes two spoones	3	0	0
In Linging sevne payre of Sheetes one duson and a half of napkings one Coubard cloth twelfe pillay bears two Tabell Clothes	3	13	0
In the garate			
One greate Chists with two windows of glasse and som Tilles with sevarell othar Implements	0	13	4
In the Shoope and back Shope			
For his Worcking Tooles in all	3	10	0
For Glasse in all	2	10	0
For Leade	2	10	0
All othar Implamentes in ye two shoopes	0	10	0

In ye kitchen and butery

Two brasse pannes one stille a fiarne forme galla baucke and hoockes and sevarell othar Implmantes	0	6	8

In John Benetis Chamber

A Livary Cubard	0	5	0

In ye yard and Stabell

One Lead in ye garden	1	13	4
One Cow	1	6	8
For wood and Stoones	0	10	0

In ye sabell

Two Lethars a Littell ould wood and Cooles	0	10	0
	38	17	0
	(38	16	4)

12. Fiarne – fire irons.
Galla baucke, gallebayck – gallowbalke.
Iarne – iron.
Pillay bears – pillow bears.
Tilles – covering of coarse cloth.
Valace – vallence.

13. John Dawsons — Prob. Inv. 175/234

(Farmer) St. Peters Parish in Eastgate 24.4.1672

	£	s	d
His purse and apparrell	5	0	0

In the Hall

One Cubbert 2 Tables and one furme Three Chaires and 2 Buffit stooles	1	3	4
One Kimnell one stand 3 Kitts a Churne and one Soe	0	11	0
Puter and Brass	1	10	0
One glass case with other imployments	0	3	4

In the Parler

Two Bedsteads with beding to them 2 little Tables Six Chaires 2 Chists 2 Buffit Stooles with other Lumber	4	13	4

In the Chambers

Two low Bedsteades and beding 3 Chists and a Trunk a Screele and other Lumber	1	13	4

In the Back Kitchin

Ten Axell trees with some bords and other plow timber	0	13	4

In the greate Barne

One Quarter of Wheate a Quarter of Barley a fan and a Ladder with other Imployments	2	6	8

In the foremost yard

A Bellferay with Corne on it	5	0	0
Waynes and waynes geares Cart and Cart geares Plow and Plowgeares Tumbrills with other trash	9	13	4
Two Sows foure Little piggs with the Poultery	1	10	0
Eighte Horses and Mares a Sucking foale and eighte Bullocks	40	5	0
Five Cows and Calfes 3 Steares	17	10	0
One Loade of Hay	0	13	4
Sheepe Eightscoare and fiffteene and aboute fifty lambs	30	6	8
Corne in the ground Tenn acre of Wheate and Rye thereaboute	15	0	0
Thirty Acre of Barley or there aboute	21	10	0
Pease and Oates 15 Acre or there aboute	7	10	0
Sheetes Pillebears and Napkins and other small Linnings	1	10	0
All other things not Seene or forgotten	0	6	8
	159	8	4
	(168	9	4)

13. **Axell trees** – beam on which wheels of a vehicle revolve.
Fan – winnowing implement.

14. William Kent **Prob. Inv. 175/29**

Gentleman (Maltster) St. Swithins (.. ..) 1672

	£	s	d
The purse and apparrell and some books and ready money	40	0	0

In the Hall

4 Tables, 5 chares, one napkin press with brass Land Iron and bosses and other utensills	3	5	4

In the Parlor

2 Spanish tables 2 guilded Leather Carpetts, 16 Rushy chairs and cupboard and a Sute of brasses	4	17	4

In the Kitchen

16 Pewter dishes, 3 dozen and halfe of Plates with other such like things as spoons and pottingers	7	15	7
10 Candlesticks 3 Copper Canns a Chafer 3 pie plates with other necessarys	3	10	0
One clock one Jack one Birding peice and spitts etc	10	0	0

In the Buttry and Cellar

3 brass pots 7 brass pans 2 brass plates, 4 hogsheads 2 horses one pair of scales and brass weights	7	8	0

In the Chamber over the Parlor and little roome by itt

4 bedsheads 4 feather bedds one flock bed with bed furniture 2 chests 3 trunkes etc.	13	0	0

In the Chamber over ye Hall

One french Bedstead with other furniture aboutt it with hangings, 8 chairs and stooles, 2 truncks one Chest with 12 pair of Linnen sheets 8 table cloths, 1 dozen of diaper napkins, 1 dozen of towells and other utensills	20	0	0
In plate one tanker, and cupp 14 spoons and a wine cupp	12	0	0
One brass Land Iron and a still and other Lumber in the little roome within it	3	3	6

In another little Chamber

One Bedd and bedding etc	10	0	0

In the Brewhouse

One Lead Mashtubb with other vessels and utensills	6	0	6

In the malt house and Chambers

2 Cisterns	16	0	0
2 Skreels and severall measures	10	0	0
In malt uppon the Kilne and in the Chambers and sold since the Testators decease	262	10	0

In the yard

In Coals and wood and other fewell	1	10	0
3 quarter and 1 sack of oats sold since the Testators death	1	8	0

Uppon the Comons

One Gelding and one Cow	7	0	0
In desperate debts	20	0	0

In his grounds att Newbell

Hoggs and shearings	32	0	0
One hundred twenty four ews and 3 rams	76	4	0
Thirty eight Hoggs att Scamton	19	0	0
2 oxen 2 Cows and 1 calfe with beast tumbrells sheep tumbrells and other fencing	30	0	0

In the Marsh att Skegnes

250 sheepe	171	0	0
The sheepe fold and fencing there	2	0	0
Money for beasts received at London since the Testators death	164	0	0
4 acres of Harrowed land fitt for seeds	1	0	0
	951	4	6
	(954	11	9)

14. **Hogg** – young sheep not yet shorn.
Shearings – sheep after first shearing.
Skreel – a screen for dressing grain.

15. Mary Nickinson **Prob. Inv. 174/21**

Widow. St. Swithins 29.5.1673

	£	s	d
Her purse and apparell	5	0	0

Goods in the Parlor

One draw table a livery Cuberd a Cubbert table two joynt chaires four joynt stooles a press for to press cloaths in six nedle

work stooles fifteen Cushions a paire of endirons and landirons a wheele and other implements	3	7	4
In the entry			
Four barrells and other implements	0	7	6
In the Hall			
One long table two formes seaven buffitt stooles and the irons in the chimeney four old chaires a little table and other implements	1	5	6
In the Kitchen			
Three spitts a gallo balke a horse and other implements of iron	0	7	0
More wooden implements	0	3	0
In the brew house			
One Copper a tub and two Soes	2	0	0
A paire of Quernes a Lether a firr deale table an axx	0	9	0
Six pans six pots a possnitt and other brass	3	10	0
Pewter and two bras candle sticks	3	11	8
One silver bowle and six silver spoones	4	0	0
In the little Chamber over the Kitchen			
A Screen one trundle bed with beding and other lumber	1	9	8
In the Chamber over the Hall			
Two pillows a yellow bed bedstead with two fether beds four blanketts a counterpaine with Curtaines	4	6	8
An other bed with two fether beds two boulsters two coverlids one blankett with bedstead and hanging	3	10	0
Four chests and other truncks	0	16	0
Three little firr deale boxes one wanded chaire and other implements	0	4	6
Two guns	0	5	0
In the gallerys			
One beam and Scales a leven tub a paire of cobirons	0	10	0
Corne bowles and other implements	1	0	0

In the Chamber over the Parlour

A red bed with two fether beds two boulsters four pillows two blanketts one Coverlid one green rugg with bedstead and red curtaines	7	14	0
A yellow bed with two fether beds three boulsters two pillows two blanketts four coverlids with curtaines and bedstead	5	12	0
Twelve Coverlids and blanketts	1	16	0
Five pillows a wollen Coverlid a varder and three other Coverlids	3	1	0
A paire of curtaines with vallance and Counterpaine	1	10	0
Two pair of green stript blanketts	1	12	0
Two paire of blanketts	0	15	0
Two green Carpetts a course Coverlid	0	19	0
Two paire of blanketts two pillows	0	19	0
One blankett and new cloth and bras in the Cuboard and a paire of Strip Curtaines	1	4	0
A Cubert a table and thre chests	1	5	0
Four Trunckes a cabonett and bookes	1	14	0
A broad trunk of Linin a Sea chest a box a trunck of course Linin	20	0	0
A bedstead and two pillows	0	10	0
Two mayres and one foale	3	5	0
One Lease Holden of the Dean and Chapter of Lincoln	14	0	0
A stock of bees and two pooles	0	10	0
Debts without specialty	35	0	0
	106	8	10
	(136	18	10)

16. Sissie Peacock **L.C.C. Admon. 1673/85**

St. Benedicts 31.12.1673

	£	s	d
Purs and aparrill	1	0	0
the hall Hous			
1 cubbert 2 table	0	18	0
1 furme 6 chares	0	10	6
Pewter 26 at 10d per lb	1	1	8
1 warminpan and 1 Chaffindish	0	7	6
4 Cusshons at	0	2	0
1 landiorne and andiorne at with sorm other hookes at	0	6	4
1 pewter Case and other impplements	0	2	0

in the parler

1 table 4 buffit stooles at and 1 Cubbert	0	16	0
3 Chares and tw Cusshon	0	4	0
in the Chamber			
3 beds and bedstead with other things beloning theareunto	4	0	0
4 pare of sheet and other linning	1	10	0
2 Chist and other meteralls	0	10	0
in the Brewhouse			
1 lead and other vessels belong to brewing	3	10	10
Milke shop			
1 pare quearne at	1	0	0
Sorm rops and Coller and soum tooles	1	0	0
in the stable			
Fewile and foether	1	0	0
in the yard			
11 swine at	2	13	4
1 hors at	4	0	0
1 mare and fole at	1	0	0
1 ould bote	1	10	0
7 bese young and ould	10	0	0
Thinges seene and not seene	0	10	0
	37	12	2
Their wose lefte owing by ye desesed	12	0	0
	25	12	2

16. Bese – beasts, cattle.

17. Thomas White — Prob. Inv. 174/228

(Wool Merchant) St. Mark 3.2.1674

	£	s	d
In the Hall			
One table one forme and seaven joynt stooles	0	17	0
Six chaires one long settle two short forms	0	10	4
One glass case and six white mettle plates	0	2	6
One land iron fireshovell and tongs and a paire of endirons and other irons	0	15	0
One cupboard and a litle table	0	7	6

In the parlour

One long table, six chaires 4 cushions	0	19	6
One paire of tables, one little table and carpet and ten pictures, one glass case and thre plates	0	6	0
One skreen and cloth	0	4	0

In the great chamber

One bedstead 2 ruggs six blanketts, curtaines and vallence	3	8	0
Two feather beds and bolsters and pillows	4	13	4
One liverie cupboard three leather stooles and arme chaire	0	10	0
One little chest pictures and voider basket and other Hushlements	0	3	0

In the little chamber

One bedstead, feather bed, bolster and pillowes	4	6	8
One cupboard and cloth 3 chaires and 4 stooles and one lookeing glass	1	0	0
Six chaires 2 stooles curtaines and vallence	4	0	0
One table and chest and other Huslements	0	10	6
One Iron and brasses	0	7	6
One chest of linnings	4	10	0

In the Kitching chamber

One bedstead bedding and furniture	1	10	4
One chest and a desk and a chaire	0	5	0
Two silver cups and one spoon	2	13	0

In the Kitching

Pewter and brass	5	8	6
One warming and candle stiks	0	6	8
One driping and one iron pott, spitts cobirons and other irons there	0	13	4

In the brewhouse

A Lead, brewing vessells and leaden cistern	6	3	4

In the cellers

4 hogshead and other small barrells	1	0	0

In the Stable and yard

Two horses and 4 swine	8	13	0

In the wooll chamber

Four packs of wooll and pack clothes	24	0	0
Scales and weights and firdales	1	0	0
In good debts	134	15	3

	£	s	d
Purse and Apparell	30	0	0
Things seen and not appraised	0	10	6
	244	9	9

18. Elizabeth Bate **L.C.C. Admon. 1673/7**

St. Michael on Mount 28.2.1674

	£	s	d
Her purse and apparell	1	13	4
In her Lodging Chamber			
One Seild Bedd one fether bed one Boulster two Pillowes one Rugg one payre of Blanketts with Curtaines and vallence	4	0	0
One Trunke with some small Lynnen (vizt) one paire of Hempin Sheets one paire of Linnen Sheetes a dozen of Napkins and a paire of Pillowbeares	1	11	0
Three Little Boxes and a Warming pan	0	5	0
Six Lether Chaires two seild Chaires one Livery Cupbord and Carpett two Matted Chaires and five Cushions with other implements	2	0	0
Three Pewter dishes one Pie Plate one Bason one pewter Poringer and salt and some small pewter	0	6	8
One paire of Racks 2 spitts a dripinpan fire Shovell and tongs	0	6	0
One Screene one Closestoole with a pann and other implements	0	10	0
Things unseene and forgotten	0	2	6
	10	14	6

19. John Atkinson **L.C.C. Admon. 1675/5**

Tanner (..).6.1675

	£	s	d
Purse and Apparrell	1	0	0
In the first Tub at the southwest end of the tanyard 25 Hids			
In the next toub of the south row 15 Hids			

In the thre Round toubes more of the sam Row 19 Hids			
In the midell Rowe thre toubes and In them 31 Hids			
Fower toubes on the north sid and in them 37 Hids			
In the owes 5 Hids			
In the Limes 25 Hids			
In the Stabel 6 dry Hids			
In all the broken and Hole 16 dicker and one Hid vallued at fifty six powend seaven shillings	56	7	0
In the owes 4 doussen of Calf skins			
In the Lymes and toubes A Leaven dousson in all the hole and 200 of calf skins valeued at	5	0	6
Bark in the bark Howes valeued at	5	0	0
Thurty yards of Lining Cloth valeued at	1	0	0
One maire valued at	1	10	0
One Cow valeued at	1	0	0
Desperat detes never to be got	10	0	0
	80	17	6

19. **Bark** – used for tanning.
Dicker – a bundle of ten hides or skins.
Hids – hides.
Limes, Lymes – part of a tanner's workshop where skins were steeped in lime and water to whiten them.
Owes – the solution of bark used to tan hides.

20. Jefre Wood L.C.C. Admon. 1675/111

(Labourer) St. Martins (.. ..) 1675

	£	s	d
We praysed his purce and Aparrill	0	15	0
For his worckings tooles	0	5	0
One bedsteade and beding and A pare of Curtins and A Rug and A Blanckit and two pare of shetes	1	6	8
One table and A furm	0	4	0
One Trunck and a bocx	0	2	6
One square table and a bocx and A Chist	0	4	6
One Cubbert	0	3	0
Thre Chares	0	1	6
One quart one Chamberpot 2 Candellstick 2 Cupes	0	3	6
Tow Cusshans	0	0	6

One pot one skelit one pan one warmin pan	0	5	0
One landiren A pare of tonges and A fire scumer and A Gallaback and All other small thinges	0	4	0
One pare of bellowes and a friing pan	0	1	0
One kit and A tub	0	1	0
One seing Glas one bras Candelstick And A tin dripin pan and A tin Candelstick	0	2	0
	4	1	2
	(4	2	2)

20. Furm – form.

21. William Atkinson — Prob. Inv. 177/144

Tayler 11.1.1676

	£	s	d
His purse and apparrell	4	0	0
In the low Roome			
One long Table foure buffit stooles	0	15	0
One Press Cubbert and a long Saddle	0	12	0
One Screene Six plaine Chaires and a little Table	0	12	0
Ten Pewter dishes	1	10	0
Three flagons and two pint cans	0	13	0
Three Candlesticks	0	8	6
One Bason One Chamberpot with other small pewter	0	6	0
Three Brass Pots	1	4	0
Foure Brass Pans	0	14	0
One Warming Pan 1 brass candlestick and a Scummer	0	6	0
One Land Iron with end Irons One fire shovel one paire of Tongs One paire of Cob Irons with other implements	0	14	0
One seeing glass 1 hour glass 2 Bybles	0	7	0
In the Best Chamber			
One Standing bed with fetherbed and bolster Two pillows and Curtaine and other bedding	5	0	0
One Trundle bed with fether bed bolster and two pillowes and other bedding	2	0	0
One Livery Cobert and One Square Table	1	0	0
One Chest and One Wanded Chaire	0	13	4
Six green Chaires and foure Cushens	0	13	4

One Silver Cup and a Silver Spoon	2	6	8
One Land Iron with brasses 1 fire shovel and a paire of Tongs 1 paire of bellowes	0	17	0
One Creddle One seeing Glass and a brush	0	8	0
Foure Earthen plates and a dish and 2 Candlesticks and two dosen of Trenshers	0	4	0

In the Middle chamber

One bedsted with hangings and other bedding	0	14	0
Three paire of linnen sheets 4 paire of pillowbers and 6 Napkins	1	10	0
Six paire of Hemping Sheets	0	18	0
Two Cheests 2 Truncks	0	12	0
One Cubbert Table and six little boxes 1 pillion seat	0	9	0
One Cushen 1 little Carpet with other implements	0	4	0
2 Leven Tub and 2 Kits	0	3	0

In the Shop

One Shopboard One window frame One Chest 2 paire of Sheares and 1 Iron	0	8	0

In the yard

One Stock of bees	0	5	0
	30	12	10

22. John Langforth **Prob. Inv. 179/222**

Whitesmith St. Martins 7.10.1676

	£	s	d
His purse and apparell	5	0	0

In the Hall

Pewter. 12 Dishes. 1 Bason. 11 flagons. 9 Poringers 5 Candlestickes. a pint and a gill Cann. 2 Salts. 2 Sawcers. 12 Spoons	2	10	0
Brasses. 6 panns. and a posnett. a warmeing pann a Ladle	1	0	0
Irons. A Landiron and 2 Endirons. 3 Spitts a Gallowbalke, 1 hooke a paire of pothookes, fireshovle and tongs. 1 Jack, 3 wire and 2 tinn Candlesticks, 1 Iron	1	10	0
Wood. A Cupborde, a Table, a Dresser, 8 Chaires with basse bottomes	0	13	4

In the Kitchin and Brewhouse

A Coper and grate, a gathering tubb. 3 litle Tubbs 2 Soa's, 2 wand Copers, a skope, ye Quernes 3 Kitts. a Wyre Kidle, a paire of bellowes, dishes and Earthen panns, 2 shelves and a litle table	7	1	2

In the Buttery

Fower Hoggsheads. 2 Barrells. 2 Kilderkins 3 woden Horses. a litle stand, trenchers	1	5	0
Ale 2 Hoggsheads	3	0	0

In the Shopp

A paire of Bellowes, one Stithy. 3 paire of Vices 2 hand hamers, 3 fore hamers, 4 small hamers 12 fyles. 5 New Jackes. 2 hand vices, 6 screwplates. 4 paire of Tongues. a boare bench-wheele, a fowling peece a birding peece and a Muskett, a paire of pistolls and Holsters, 4 paire of Casting frames, other old tooles, and Irons. 3 Gun lockes. a Bench and old locks two Chafing dishes	13	10	4

In the great Chamber

A Ceiled bedstead Matt and board a fetherbed two bolsters, 2 pillobers a paire of Blankets, one Covering one Rugg a paire of Curtains, Rods and Vallence	4	(..	..)
A Truckle bedstead, a flock bed, and bolster a paire of blankets, and a Coverlett	(..	..	..)

In the midle Chamber

One halfe headed bedstead Matt and Coard one Mattresse, one flockbed, two fether bolsters, 1 pillow, 1 blankett, and one Coverlett	0	14	4
A table and Carpett, 2 formes, a Chest, a trunk a Napkin presse, 1 Safe and 2 baskett	1	4	0

In the Lane Chamber

Two bedsteads, Matts and Coards, 1 fetherbed five bolsters, five pillowes fethers two blanketts, 2 Coverletts, 1 Rugg 2 paire of old Curtaines, and Vallens, with Curtaine Rods	4	10	0
A litle table a Cradle 2 Chaires 1 foot pace	0	8	4

In the Lane

A parcell of wood	1	0	0

In the yarde

One Grinding Stone and frame 4 Stoopes and 6 Tressles, 6 boards, and 3 blocks, a Swine Stye	0	15	0
One house of office	1	10	0

In the stable

One horse bridle and sadle, and a Cowe	4	10	0
Hay and Cowfodder and two fleakes	2	2	0

fewell

A loade of pitt coale, and other fewell with two hundred of Kidds	1	0	0
Five Swine and small piggs	2	13	0
For things unseene old wood, Iron and all other Hustlements and things forgot	0	13	0
In the Shop booke debts good and badd	2	10	0
	72	0	3

22. **Boare bench wheele** – a drill?
Casting frame – structure to hold moulds for casting iron or a mould to receive molten iron for casting.
Ceiled bed – a canopied bed.
Fleake – a wattled hurdle.
Fore hamer – a sledge hammer.
Screwplate – a device for cutting the threads of screws.
Skope – scope.
Stithy – a stiddy or anvil.
Wand copers – staves.
Wyrekidle – a seive.

23. John Wignall — Prob. Inv. 219A/183

(Brickmaker) St. Buttolph 19.12.1677

	£	s	d
Purse and apparrell	13	6	8
At the kilne 14000 of tile at	9	2	0
8000 of Brick there at 10s a thousand	4	0	0
Fewell and other stuffe there at all	1	10	0
Brick and Tile at home in the yard	4	6	0
In debts by bonds and Bills	220	0	0

In the Chamber over the Kitchen

One bed with Bedding and Livery Cupbord with other implements	4	0	0
2 Chests with Linnen	2	0	0

Malt in the Corne Chamber	5	0	0
Wheat and Rye in the same Chamber	2	10	0
A Screell and other implements there	0	13	4

In a little lodging at the staires head

A Chaffe bed and other small things	0	5	0

In the Buttery

4 hoggs heads and other implements	0	1	8

In the parlour

A Table and Six stooles and a forme	1	0	0
5 basse chaires and a wanded Chaire	0	6	0
2 small deskes and other implements	0	3	4

In another Buttery

1 presse Bedsted and Bedding	1	0	0
1 old Table and Chest	0	2	0
3 hoggsheads and a Barrell and other things	1	3	4
A Bible	0	6	8
Brewing vessells in the Brewhouse	1	10	0
Other woodden ware there	0	6	0

In the Kitchin

Eight brasse potts and posnetts	2	13	0
4 brasse panns	1	6	0
2 warming panns and a drippin pann	0	15	0
2 Copper canns	0	4	0
3 Spitts 2 payre (.....) and 2 Land irons	1	(..	..)
16 pewter dishes 6 porringers 3 flaggons	3	(..	..)
3 candlesticks a pewter cup and a Bason	0	(..	..)
(......................................)			
3 horses and a Mare	7	10	0
Hay in the yard	3	0	0
2 swine	2	0	0
Wood in the yard	2	10	0
Giests in the yard	1	10	0
60 firdales	2	0	0
A pair of wheeles	0	10	0
2 Carts and geares	1	10	0
Paveing stones	1	10	0
A lease of a small peece of ground held of the Deane and Chapter	2	0	0
Coales and other fuell	3	6	8
Plate given by will unto the Child	5	0	0
	317	3	0

23. Giests – joists.

24. Mr. Edward Fawkes **L.C.C. Admon. 1679/79**

Alderman and Upholster 29.3.1679

	£	s	d
Purse and aparrell	7	0	0
In the House			
One Table 2 stooles 1 Elbow Chare	0	7	6
6 score pound of pewter at 8d a pound	4	0	0
3 Brasse potts 66 pound at 4½d a pound	1	4	9
In pan brasse and brasse Candle stickes	1	18	0
7 bast Chares	0	2	4
1 Land Iron 2 end Irons 2 drippin pans 4 spitts fire shovell and tongs with other small things			
In the Parler			
11 set worke Chares at 6s 6d	3	11	6
1 ovill table 1 Lether Carpett	1	0	0
1 Credle Iron with brasses	0	9	6
In the Street Chamber			
One Bed stead 1 fether bed 1 bolster 2 pillows 2 ruges 3 blankets curtains and vallants	3	13	4
2 Tables 5 buffet stools 7 Lether Chares	2	14	0
2 Trunkes 1 old wanded Chare and a stand	0	13	4
6 paire of Lin sheets	3	0	0
4 paire of pillow beares	0	8	0
2½ dussen of Lin napkins	1	0	0
36½oz. of silver plate 4s 10d an oz.	8	16	5
2 Table Cloths	0	8	0
12 Case Knives	0	6	0
In the Little Chamber			
1 bed stead matt and cord 3 bolsters 1 downe bed	1	4	0
1 bad ruge 2 old blankets	0	3	6
2 old credles 1 Childs Chare 2 bast Chares	0	5	0
2 old Trunkes and other Implyments	0	2	6
In the Litle Clossett			
One Table one Carpett glasse botles and sume earthen ware	0	10	0
In the Garett			
One Truckle bed 2 stooles 2 Chists	0	18	0
One bolster one blanket 1 Credle	0	13	4

4 wrought Cushons 1 paire vallants 1 cubert cloth	0	10	0

In the seller

8 hogsheads strong bear 1 wood Horse 1 salting tubb	8	4	6
1 maire at grasse	3	0	0

In the shop

7 10 qts ruges 22s	7	14	0
5 9 qts ruges 18s	4	10	0
4 8 qts ruges 15s	3	0	0
4 Credle ruges	0	15	0
6 yards of print ½ bredth	0	6	0
10 small draft beds 9s	4	10	0
2 Jacke draft beds 7s 6d	0	15	0
6 Coverlids Lacie 7s	2	2	0
4 Large Diaber 7s	1	8	0
1 small diaber 5s	0	5	0
3 blankets 1 9 qts 1 8 qts 1 corse midle	0	16	0
2 bed and bolsterers 6 qts	2	0	0
2 6 qts qts and ½ beds	1	10	0
2 6 qts beds	1	6	0
1 Stand bed EW	0	12	6
2 Corse beds TW	0	16	0
1 bolster 5s 6d	0	5	6
15 yards tikeing 12d	0	15	0
16 yards tikeing 11d per yard	0	14	8
16 bakes and 16 seats	2	16	0
9 set worke Cushons 9s dussen	0	6	9
6 volure Cushons	0	9	0
8 yards of mockadee	0	10	8
50 yards of Drugest	2	10	0
1 Russey Hide 2 Bassells	0	11	6
36 tufted fringe ……..	6	6	0
88 yards 7 qts stufe	6	12	0
51 yards 6 qts stufe	3	0	0
4½ yards 8 qts stufe	0	9	0
5 score and 13 yards of print	10	0	0
1 Close stoole	0	4	0
40 oz. tufted fringe at 4s a pound	0	10	0
21 pair of stoole and small stringe 3s 6d	3	14	0
8 Hand fringes	0	16	0
Some remnants fringe		2	0
1 Quilt 1 packe cloth	0	10	0
6 Chare frames	0	9	0
Shelves shop table and other implyments	0	5	6

In booke debts due to the deceased	10	0	0
	141	12	3

24. Bassell – tanned sheepskin.
Bakes – backs.
Draft bed – a bed in the process of construction.
Jacke bed – a shorter bed than normal.
Mockadee – a woollen cloth which imitates velvet.
Print – cloth which has a wavey pattern created by applying hot plates against the cloth resting on a carved wooden block.
Qts – quarters, presumably quarters of a yard, but not in some contexts obviously applicable to beds.

25. Henery Mitchell — Di 39/1/134

(Haberdasher) 14.4.1679

	£	s	d
His Purss and Apparill	6	0	0
Gloves			
1 dozen boys Cullered Lambe at	0	3	0
3 pair boys Cullered Lambe at	0	1	0
9 pair boys Cullered Kidde at 7d	0	5	3
6 pair boys wash Leather	0	2	0
Gerles			
5 pair gerls Cullered and white Lambe at	0	1	8
22 pair gerls white Kidd at	0	12	10
17 pair gerls Cullered Kidd at 9s 11d	0	9	11
Mens			
8 pair mens tanned gloves at 5d	0	3	4
10 pair mens Cullered Sheepe at	0	7	6
12 pair Illmister at	0	8	0
13 pair more Cullered and white	0	8	0
3 pair mens buck leather	0	9	0
16 pair mens Cullered Sheepe at	0	10	8
26 pair mens Insemd Cordivant at	2	3	4
24 pair Drab Cordivant at	3	0	0
52 pair mens Cullered Kidd at	4	3	4
27 pair mens white Kidd at	1	18	3
5 pair mens Cullered Kidd	0	8	4
Weomens			
24 pair weomens Illmister and Cullered	0	16	0
26 pair weomens white Kidd	1	16	10

48 pair weomens Cullered Kidd at	3	12	0
3 mens and weomens black Shamey at	0	9	0

Lining and Diaper

6¾ yards Diaper at 3s yard at	1	0	3
12 yards Osinbridge at	0	9	0
7 yards Osinbridge moore at	0	5	3
10 ells hamburg Cloth at	0	13	4
12 ells Dowlays at	0	16	0
7½ ells Dowlays more at	0	8	9
14 ells Dowlays at	1	8	0
6½ ells Holland at	0	10	10
16½ ells Holland at	2	6	4½
9 ells Holland at	1	2	6
7½ ells Holland at	1	3	4
4 ells Holland at	0	11	4
2¾ ells Holland at	0	6	9
2½ ells Holland at	0	5	10
3¾ ells Holland at	1	17	6
1 Remnant Holland at	0	4	0
8 yards Callico at	0	8	0
15 yards musling at	3	0	0
6 yards Cloth	0	2	6
2½ yards Callico	0	2	6
Severall Remnants Camrick	0	3	0
6 pair Cotton gloves	0	12	0
2 pair Childrens Muffes	0	1	0
1 pair mens Cotton Hose at	0	3	10
2 pair mens Cotton Stirrups	0	5	4
2 pair mens threde Stirrups	0	5	0
5 yards Lace at	1	4	2
2 yards Lace at	0	13	0
7½ yards Lace at	0	11	3
2 yards Lace at	0	5	4
5 yards Lace at	0	7	6
8½ yards Lace at	0	17	0
2¾ yards Lace at	0	6	4
5 yards Lace at	0	10	0
6 yards Lace at	0	5	0
16 yards Lace at	1	4	0
5 yards Lace at	0	4	2
6½ yards Lace at	0	8	3
5 yards Lace at	0	0	11
9 yards Lace at	0	0	9
5 yards Lace at	0	5	0
54 yards Lace at	1	11	0
9 yards Lace at	0	12	0
25 yards Lace	0	7	4
6 yards Lace at	0	8	6

2 yards Lace at	0	5	0
16 yards Lace at	1	4	0
5 yards Lace at	0	6	8
5½ yards Lace at	0	1	8
10 yards Lace at	0	4	0
5 yards Lace at	0	17	6
10½ yards Lace at	1	5	0
Bone Lace at	1	5	0
Moore bone Lace at	1	0	0
In bone Lace moore	3	13	0
2 yards Lace at	1	11	0
1½ yards Lace at	1	10	0
1 pointe at	1	0	0
1½ yard Lace at	0	18	0
6 yards Lace at	1	15	0
3 yards Lace at	0	9	0
5½ yards lace	0	15	0
2 yards Lace at	0	5	0
¾ yard Lace at	0	5	0
2¾ yards Lace at	0	8	0
10 yards Tiffiney at	2	5	0
9 muffes at	3	6	0
1 plush Cape at	0	18	0
2 gownes at	3	15	0
4 Silke Cusnitts at	0	2	6
1 nest of truncks at	0	2	0
21 peeces tape at	0	14	0
12 peeces round twist at	0	4	0
2 peeces Diaper fillitin at	0	2	4
In tapes	0	6	0
12 peeces purle at	0	17	0
½ peece London fillitin at	0	1	0
18 horne Comes at	0	10	0
10 horne Comes at	0	3	4
18 box Comes at	0	6	0
4 Ivory Comes at	0	6	8
14 Dandrife Ivory Comes at	0	14	0
12 Ivory Comes at	0	8	6
13 Iovry Comes at	0	7	0
6 torta Shell Comes at	0	6	0
7 plaine Cornatts at	0	17	6
4 Lacest Cornatts at	0	2	0
3 pair Lacest Cuffes at	0	7	6
2 pair Lacest Cuffes at	0	16	0
5 pair Lacest Cuffes at	0	9	6
6 pair plaine Cuffes at	0	6	0
2 pair Lawne Cuffes at	0	5	0
2 pair plaine Cuffes at	0	2	0
2 Laces for Cornatts at	0	10	0

4 Lacest Cornatts at	1	2	0
5 Lacest Cornatts at	1	5	0
4 boys Cornatts at	0	6	0
3 plaine Cornats at	0	3	0
7 bands at	0	3	6
7 Coller bands at	0	3	6
4 Twillted Stomachers at	0	10	0
3 head rowles at	0	15	0
4 piners at	2	0	0
1 lacest band at	0	10	0
4 Coiffes at	1	0	0
1 sute lacest Childe bed linings	2	0	0
4 sutes Childe bed linings at	3	4	0
6 fanes at	1	10	0
3 fanes at	0	6	0
8 fanes at	0	16	0
15 Scotch and Roman Necklaces at	0	10	0
8 Counterfit Amber at	0	4	8
3 glass necklaces at	0	2	6
2 Oringe necklaces at	0	5	0
Weomens Sleeves at	2	0	6
7 lacest Coiffes at	1	15	0
3 flowerd Cornitts at	0	6	0
3 Lacest Cornitts at	0	15	0
34 yards birdey at	1	5	6
5½ yards pertian Taffitey at	0	19	0
2 Capes at	0	0	6
2 Shirtes at	0	16	0
2 Shirtes moore at	0	16	0
2 Shirtes moore at	0	9	0
1 Shirte at	1	0	0
2 pair Sleeves at	1	0	0
2 pair Sleeves at	0	8	0
2 pair Sleeves more at	0	13	0
2 pair Sleeves more at	0	16	0
Pair Sleeves more at	0	4	0
2 bossomes at	0	12	0
2 bossomes at	0	6	0
6 pockit hanckerchiffs at	0	8	0
2 hanckerchiffs moore at	0	7	0
7 Caps at	0	4	8
3 bossoms at	0	6	0
2 hancerchiffs moore at	0	3	0
17 pair Socks at	0	5	8
9 gawess Hoods at	0	18	0
20 Hoods at	1	10	0
2 Run Hoods at	0	5	0
2 Erminion Hoods at	0	9	0
2 moore Hoods at	0	7	0

2 moore Hoods at	0	7	0
3 hoods at	0	13	0
2 hoods at	0	11	0
12 paire eare Knots at	0	9	0
2 Caps at	0	2	0
12 vizorns at	0	12	0
3 small brushes at	0	1	6
Nettin needls and pins at	0	1	6
2 pair gold garters at	0	10	0
5 pair garters at	0	6	4
6 pair buckells at	0	6	0
Thimbles Tweezers brushes tooth picks	0	5	0
Gimpe at	0	10	0
14 necklaces at	0	2	4
2 pair little Coiffes at	0	3	0
15 pair pendance at	0	7	6
124 papers of patches at	0	12	0
1 Dressin box 2 powder boxes and 2 patch boxes	0	12	0
3 lute Stringe hoods at	0	18	0
14 Ducape hoods at	1	15	0
3 hoods at	0	10	0
Lacest hoods at	4	8	0
1 Longe lacest Scarfe at	1	5	0
12 round Scarfes at	1	10	0
6 white Sersnit Scarfes at	0	9	0
6 birdey Scarfes at	0	4	0
1 Ermin Scarfe at	1	7	0
12 lacest Scarfes at	2	14	0
3 lacest Scarfes moore at	0	13	6
4 lacest Scarfes moore at	0	8	0
9 Scarfes moore at	0	6	0
8 peakes at	0	2	8
A bando and vaile at	0	9	0
Cutt paper at	0	17	6
1 Reame paper moore at	0	7	0
17 quire and 4 quire in all 21 quire gilt paper	0	13	4
8 quire Small gilt paper	0	2	8
3 Ivory busks	0	3	0
5 busks moore	0	1	3
4 purses	0	4	0
Lookin glasses	1	13	4
4½ dozen nomber thrids	0	18	0
9lb nuns thrids	7	13	4
Pins in generall	1	9	8
3 dozen and a pair Cards	0	10	0
Soft wax 3d	0	0	3
Harde wax	0	1	5

13 Sattin and Cullerd Capps	1	6	0
Ribbin Knotts	0	2	6
1¾ yards prissiner	0	5	3
2 peeces Tiffiney	3	5	0
15 yards of Tiffiney moore	0	15	0
5 yards Tiffiney moore	0	5	0
2½ yards bone	0	5	0
5¾ yards allamode	1	4	0
4 pair bottons	0	2	8
2 pair 1 botton	0	11	0
1 Sett buckells	0	9	0
5 pair pendance	0	10	0
2 pair pendance	1	4	0
1 pair pendance moore	0	18	0
4 dozen and 7 Silke laces	0	18	0
5 dozen Silke loop lace	0	10	0
3 dozen Silke loop lace moore	0	5	6
5 pair bunches ribbin	0	12	6
18 peeces open tapes at	0	9	0
3 peeces open tape at	0	18	0
21 yards open tape at	0	7	0
Necke laces	0	2	6
18 hed rowles	0	9	0
Spanish painte	0	5	0
8 Come Cases	0	1	0
3½ peeces Cillver Ribbin	1	15	0
3 peeces Cillver Ribbin	2	17	0
2 peeces Cillver Ribbin	3	0	0
1 peece Cillver Ribbin	3	0	0
1 peece Ribbin moore	1	10	0
1½ peece Cillver Ribbin	1	7	0
1½ peece Cillver Ribbin	0	9	0
5 gross 2d Sattins	3	0	0
4 gross 2d Sattins	2	8	0
1 peece Sattin	0	4	6
4 peeces Sattin ribbin	1	8	0
1½ peece Sattin ribbin	0	18	0
5 Come brushes	0	1	8
3 groses of Shoe lace	1	10	0
20 gross of halfe peny Sattins	4	10	0
In taffity and flowerd ribbins	71	13	8
Seaverall Holland toys	3	0	0

In ye Hall Chamber

1 bedstead and bedin with furniture at	5	0	0
1 dozen red Chaires	2	8	0
The red hangins	2	0	0
2 Stands and glass Case	0	3	0

Fier Iron Shovill and tongs	0	10	0
In plate	11	0	0

In ye Clossitt

In white ware and other things	1	10	0

In ye Kittchin Chamber

1 heigh bedsted and furniture at	3	0	0
1 Trundle bedsted and bedin	2	0	0

In Lining

4 pair linen Sheets	1	10	0
5 pair Ceoarse Sheets at	1	5	0
3 linen Sheets moore	0	15	0
3 dozen linen napkins	0	15	0
1 dozen and 9 Diaper napkins	0	17	6
3 Diaper Table Cloths at	0	15	0
6 pair holland Pillowbears	0	18	0
Some other linins	1	0	0
1 Crimson Scarfe at	1	10	0
Trunks boxes with other Lumber	1	0	0

In the Kitchin

1 fier Iron tongs and fier Shovills with End Irons	1	5	0
1 warming pann	0	2	6
1 Jacke	0	10	0
1 Spitt	0	1	0
Chaffin Dish with other Irons	0	2	6
2 Tables	1	0	0
2 Leather Chaires	0	18	0
2 bass Chaires	0	1	4
2 Carpetts and hangings	0	10	0
1 glass Case	0	1	0
1 Case knives	0	4	6

In ye Seller

1 bed pann	0	4	0
11 puter Dishes	1	7	0
2 Chamber potts	0	1	0
12 platts	0	12	0
1 musterd pott	0	0	6
2 Kettls 3 Skellitts at	1	0	0
2 Iron potts	0	3	0
1 Table 1 Tearse 2 beare barills Juggs and bottls with lumber and Implements	0	10	0

In ye Stable

1 Pillion Seate and Side Sadle with ye furniture	0	15	0
1 horse to Dry Cloths on	0	2	0
Halfe a Challder Coales	0	8	0
Boxes and washing tobs and other lumber	0	10	0
1 gelding Sold at	16	0	0
1 Little gray horse	3	0	0
2 bridles and Sadls with the furniture	0	10	0
1 Saddle with houlsters and pisstols and furniture	3	5	0
3 Swords	2	10	0
In good debts	20	0	0
	379	6	7½
	(379	19	7½)

25. Bando and vaile – loose turnover collar made from two narrow strips of linen.
Birdey – spotted, a spelling of 'birds' eye'.
Bone lace – patterned linen thread.
Bossomes – fabric between sides of dress covering the chest.
Busk – piece of wood, whalebone or steel passed down front of corset to stiffen it.
Cillver ribbin – silver ribbon.
Cornatt, cornitt – part of a headdress consisting of lappets of lace hanging down sides of the face.
Cusnitt – pin cushion.
Dandrife – dandruff.
Eareknot – a bow of ribbons worn as an ornament.
Erminion – ermine or an imitation of it.
Hambro – Hamburg.
Head rowle – a cushion or pad used to construct the elaborate and fashionable female hair styles of the time.
Illmister – Somersetshire cloth.
Insemd – ?
Necklace – ornamental lace worn at the neck.
Nettin needles – wooden needles used to make net like textiles such as stockings.
Patches – a small shape of black silk or court plaster worn on the face as a fasionable adornment.
Peakes – the projecting front of a headdress.
Pendance – hanging part of an earring.
Piner – a coif with two long flaps.
Prissiner – unidentified textile.
Purle – thread of twisted gold or silver wire used for embroidering.
Run hodds – draw string hoods?
Sersnit – sarsenett.
Spanish painte – cosmetics.
Stomachers – ornamental covering of chest worn under lacing of bodice.
Tiffiney – a thin silk.
Twilted – quilted.
Vizorn – mask; strengthened peak of a headdress.

26. Robert Pearson **Prob. Inv. 180/236**

Waterman – St. Swithins 28.8.1679

	£	s	d
His purse and apparrell	3	0	0
In the house			
One Bedstead with the featherbed and boulster 1 pillow one greene rugg with all other furniture belonging to the same	3	0	0
One Cupboard 4 joynt Chaires 2 Tables 2 Chests one Oake press 2 boxes one joynt stoole 5 bass bottam'd Chaires	1	15	0
Ten pewter dishes 2 flaggons 3 canns with other Small peices	1	6	8
Three brass potts 2 Panns one brass Candlestick one warming pann one Chaffing dish with other Smalle things	1	0	0
One Land Iron 2 end irons one paire of Cob irons 2 Spitts with other things belonging to ye Chymney	0	5	0
In the Chamber			
One Stand bed with feather bed and other furniture belonging One Trundle bed 3 oake Chests one pair of Linn sheets 6 pair of hempen sheets 6 paire of Pillow bears 4 pair of napkins 12 yards of Linn Cloth 12 pounds of flax	5	0	0
Fouer strick of wheate with other Lumber	0	10	0
In the Corne Chamber			
Two quarter of white pease with other things	1	10	0
In the out houses			
Ten thousand of Turfs	1	0	0
Coales in yard and out house	10	0	0
Two boates with Sailes rops and other materialls	8	0	0
A Lease	10	0	0
	46	6	8

27. Abigaile Watson **Prob. Inv. 180/242**

Widow. (Saddler) St. Peter Arches 1.9.1679

	£	s	d
Purse and Apparell £12	12	0	0
4 gold rings at 20s	1	0	0
In the Shop			
In Garth Webb 136s	6	16	0
In Glew 21s 9d	1	1	9
In hyde Leather 20s	1	0	0
In Gray Thred 11s	0	11	0
In Spurrs 25s 2d	1	5	2
In ye Little Cupbord for Leather and Plush	1	0	11
In Whipcord 26s	1	6	0
In Staples and Rings 4s 6d	0	4	6
In Calfe Skins and 1 Dog Skin	3	10	11
In Swine Leather 42s 6d	2	2	6
In Does Leather 3 peices of Cordevant and pylion Skins	0	15	0
In Horsse Clothes; and Stufe for Horsse clothes, 2 Skins A small parcell of Cotton; 1 pare of Holsters	1	7	2
In Collar Buckles; and other Irons for Harniss with Barrs; Nailes and chaines for Harniss	2	19	8
In Bridle maker Ware	6	15	8
In Setts with a Roole; a pylion Cloth and Silver and Gilt Buckles	1	14	10
In Brasse Buckles for Bridles with Starrs; bosses Bullion Nailes and belt buckles; Garter and Shoe Buckles; with Portmantle Socks	2	6	1
In more Buckles; Bosses and Revitts Dogg Couples; with Iron Nailes and Thongs	1	17	1
In Bridle Bitts of all sorts	1	15	0
In Sturrops of all sorts 42s 4d	2	2	4
In Snaffles of all sorts with 2 Mussrooles	2	7	6
In Garths with a sursingle and A Cloak Bagg	0	19	9
In Portmantles; Sadlecloths and a furniture	1	18	5
In Garth Buckles with Curry Combs and Maine Combs	0	14	3
For Thirty six Sadles £14	14	0	0
In old Sadles with Gray and Green Stuffe	1	2	0
In Whips 111s and 6d	5	11	6
In Belts and Girdles	4	5	2
In Gold and Silver thred; with Silver Chains and Galloome	2	14	2

	£	s	d
In Pylion Seats; Malpylions padds Sashoons and Camois Baggs	0	13	8
In Worsted fringe and Binding with Tapes Courses Canvis and Soivitts	0	8	1
In Spanish Silke with fringe	2	11	3
In plates and Chaines with a bridle bitt and bosses	1	8	0
In Sadle Trees in ye shop and Stables with Side Sadles	4	19	10
For working Tooles; with straining boards and a vice with other Implements	1	5	0
In Panill cloth 10s 10d in Springs 15s	1	5	10
In Lyning Cloth with 3 peices Diaper	31	8	5

In the House

	£	s	d
25 pewter dishes small and great 63lb at 8d	2	2	0
4 pewter Candle sticks; 5 flaggons; 2 Cans 10 poringers; 2 Basons; 2 pye plates 5 other small plates, 9 Sawcers 3 Salts 1 Mustard Pott at 45lb at 9d per lb.	1	13	9
2 small edgd Chamber potts 2s 10d	0	2	10
9 Occimins Spoons at 18d	0	1	6
8 Brasse pans without Hingles 40lb. at 8d	1	6	8
3 Brasse Potts 34lb. at 5½d per lb	0	15	7
6 Brasse Candlesticks at 6s	0	6	0
1 Warming Pann at 3s 6d	0	3	6
Tynn Waris; 1 Coarer 1 puding pann 1 Apple Roaster; 1 pastry pann 1 Sawcis pann 1 pan cake slicis 1 Cheese plate; 1 Candlestick 1 Dridger all of them	0	2	10
1 Jack with Cord; and other Implements belonging	0	9	6
1 fire Iron; with end Irons 1 Gantrey; 2 running hooks; 1 Grate fire Shovell; 3 irons; 2 pair Tongues 1 pestill; 4 Spitts 1 Cutting Knife 1 fire Horse 3 forks 1 Broyler, 4 Smoothing Irons 1 Candle Stick 1 pigg plate; 11 Skewers; 1 Chafeing Dish 1 pair Snuffers with a Smoothing Iron grate 1 Iron Driping pann with an Iron to set before it	1	4	9
One pare of Bellows 12d	0	1	0
One Lanthorne 8d; 1 Bookcase 6d	0	1	2
10 Cushions made and unmade up at 8d	0	6	8
8 Bass and Wanded Bottom chaires at 6d	0	4	0
1 Livery Cupboard and 1 Table Cupboard	0	10	0
1 press for Clothes at 5s	0	5	0
1 Pewter Case with frame and Drawers	0	12	0
1 Small Table with a Carpitt	0	2	6

1 Long Settle 3s 4d 1 Looking Glass 4s	0	7	4
1 fold up Bedstead 18s	0	18	0
4½ dozen Trenchers 2s 3 Water Kitts and Bend Kitt 2s 6d 6 Noggins 6d	0	5	0
1 stand to Wash on 8d; 2 Stooles 18d	0	2	2
2 Close Beaters 8d 1 Brasse Ladle 10d	0	1	6
2 Small Silver Cupps; with 2 Silver Spoons; weighing 9½oz at 4s 11d	2	6	8
1 Case of Knifes 16d	0	1	4
1 dozen of Glasse Bottles 2s	0	2	0
2 feather Beds; 2 Bolsters; 2 pillows; 2 Arm Pillows weighing 10 stones 5s 6d	2	15	0
1 Rugg; 3 Blanketts, 1 pair Sheets 10s	0	10	0
12 Bushell of Coales 12s	0	12	0
2 Washing Tubbs 4s	0	4	0
1 Serge 2 Temsses; 1 Siev 12d	0	1	0
2 Wheeles and 1 Reeles 3s	0	3	0
1 Hand baskett and 2 Voiders 12d	0	1	0
2 Tearses at 2s a peice	0	4	0
In Drincking Glasses 1s with other Lumber	0	1	6

In the Parlour

5½ dozen Course Napkins 3s 6d	0	19	3
2½ dozen Diaper others years old 3s	0	7	6
1 dozen plaine 6s	0	6	0
½ dozen Diaper at 8s a dozen	0	4	0
5 pare and 1 Lynning Sheet at 7s 6d at pare	2	1	3
1 dozen Pillow Beeres 10s	0	10	0
1 Callycoe Sheet 6s	0	6	0
2 Diaper Table Clothes at 10s	0	10	0
3 Diaper Napkins 3s	0	3	0
16 ordinary pillow Beers at 5s	0	5	0
10 ordinary Table Clothes at 18d	0	15	0
20 Course Towells at 3d	0	5	0
7 pair Hemping Sheets at 4s 6d	1	11	6
2 pair Courser at 3s	0	6	0
1 feather bed with Bolster 2 pillows weighing 7 stone 7lb at 7s 6d a stone	2	16	3
1 other feather bed with Bolster and Pillows weighing 8 stone 3lb at 4s	1	12	10
1 Bedstead 5s	0	5	0
1 Rugg with a Coverlett 13s 4d	0	13	4
7 Blanketts at 18d a peice	0	10	6

In the Stables

In Pitt Coal 20s	1	0	0
In Tanned basens Dryed 26s	1	6	0
In Hains of severall Sorts 25s	1	5	0
3 Stools	0	1	6

In Stifening and other Lumber	0	10	0
In Debts supposed good	80	10	11
In Desperate Debts of which a Bond is in part for 40s	23	2	7
A Lease of 4 Houses	40	0	0
	288	0	10
	(325	0	10)

27. **Arm pillow** – cushion.
Barr – ornamental band on a saddle.
Basens – piebald hides.
Bend kitt – tub bound with iron.
Bullion nail – decorative stud or nail.
Camois bag – saddle bag.
Close beater – clothes beater.
Curry comb – comb for rubbing down horses.
Dridger – a box with a perforated lid to sprinkle powders.
Hains – fences.
Hingle – means whereby bowl could be suspended or attached to trivet.
Malpylion – a mail pillion or side saddle.
Manecomb – comb for rubbing down horses.
Mussroole – the nose band of a bridle.
Noggin – small drinking vessel.
Portmantle – case or bag for carrying necessaries on horseback.
Ring – harness attachment.
Roole – bridle band.
Saddle tree – framework that forms the foundation of a saddle.
Sashoon – a stuffed leather pad worn inside the leg of a boot.
Sett – the filling of hair beneath the ground seat of a saddle which gives the top seat a proper shape.
Snaffles – a simple form of bridle bit.
Soivitt – metal buckle on saddle tree from which stirrup leathers and girths hang.
Staples – metal harness attachments.
Stifening – canvas or whalebone used as a backing or strengthening.
Straining board – a stretcher for shaping leather which forms seat of a saddle.
Sursingle – a horse girth, usually of a kind that go over pack as well as horse.

28. Henry Wanleste — Prob. Inv. 180/248

The Close 6.9.1679

	£	s	d
In the Bedd Chamber			
One Landiron with brasse bosses fire Shovell and tonges one Seeing glasse and one Picture	0	12	0

In the Hall Chamber

One Iron grate with endirons and brass bosses, one litle table two Leather Chaires three stooles some small pictures the hangings of the roome with the window Curtains being greene baise	0	14	6

In the Litle Closett in the Hall Chamber

One dozen trenchers with some shelves	0	2	6

In the Hall

Three basse chaires one table and a brass candlestike	0	2	0

In the great Parlor

Two Chaires A fire iron with two brasses and two old enirons some old pictures	0	11	0

In the Litle Parlor

One deske a Close Stool and pann	0	7	6

In the boarden garrett

Bedsteads and in the Litle garret next to one bedstead and in ye next garrett to that one Chist	0	6	0

In the Chamber over the new roome

One truckle bedd with 2 Coverlidds a pillow and a blankett a Land iron and end irons thereto belonging and a small hanging shelfe	0	6	8

In the Kitching Chamber

Foure wooden Chaires	0	2	0

In the Kitching

Sixteen pewter dishes one flaggon nine pewter chamber potts one dozen and a halfe of plates 4 pewter Candlesticks 4 brasse Candletsicks and 3 iran Candlesticks and one brasse hanging Candlesticke 4 brasse potts one Copper pann 3 brasse Skellets and one Little pann a warming pann a brass morter and pestell the Jack and Spitts a Kettle a sauce pan a Cullinder a Skimer a bason	3	8	2
Reckon and hookes the Iron Rainge and endirons with other small iron utensills in the Kitching Chimney and fire Shovell and tonges	0	18	4
2 small Gunns	0	10	0

	£	s	d
2 Litle tables 4 basse Chaires 2 dressers a Stoole 4 pewter porringers with other small utensills	0	5	0
In the Stable and Chamber over it			
Racks and Maungers and a Load of hay or thereabouts	1	0	0
Fewell with Stocks and blocks in the yard	1	0	0
In the Cellar			
Halfe a hogshead of ale and 5 emptie hogsheads ith the horses they stand upon	2	0	0
In the Passage			
One old Cupboard	0	3	4
One old gray horse	2	0	0
The Racks and Mannger in the Stable over the way	0	6	8
Seaven Swine Valued at	5	4	0
Pullen in the yard	0	2	6
His Purse and apparrell	3	0	0
	23	2	2

29. William Browne — Prob. Inv. 180/252

Goldsmith 21.1.1680

	£	s	d
His purse and apparell	100	0	0
In the Hall			
Two and twenty pewter dishes small and great at	2	4	0
Foure and twenty flagons small and great at	1	10	0
Thirty six pewter porringers at	0	18	0
Two dozen of pewter plates and one dozen of chamber potts at	1	0	0
Three brasse potts and foure brasse pans and 2 brasse skelletts at	2	0	0
Three pewter pye plates at	0	2	6
Foure pewter candlesticks and two brass candlesticks	0	8	0
One Cupboard with cloth and cushion at	0	5	0
Two litle tables and one dozen of chaires and one furme	0	11	6

One grate landiron with endirons 2 iron horses one fier shovell and tongs 2 warmeing panns 6 spitts 2 cobirons one Jack with severall other implements in the said hall at	2	10	0

In the roome next street

Two litle tables fourteene wood chaires at	1	14	0
Foure stooles and one landiron with endirons	0	7	0

In the parlor

One dozen of Rushy leather chaires at	3	0	0
One table one chest and one trunke and one boxe	0	15	0
One landiron with endirons and some other small goods at	0	16	0
Two bedsteads, two featherbedds, two bolsters two pillowes sixe blanketts 2 coverlidds with curtaines and vallens all at	5	0	0
One Trundle bed with matt and cord at	0	5	0
Three paire of sheets 2 other matts and cords att	0	15	0
One great bible at	0	8	0
Three window curtaines with iron rodds	0	6	8

In the litle Chamber next the Street

One bedstead one fetherbed one bolster 2 blanketts one rugg with curtaines and vallens att	3	0	0
Nine leather chaires at one wanded chaire at	1	10	0
One landiron with brasse bosses and one paire of tongs and a litle table	0	17	6

In the Garrett over the said litle Chamber

Two halfe headed bedsteads 2 featherbedds 2 bolsters one coverlid and 2 ruggs with Matt and cords at	2	10	0
One litle table and 3 bass chaires at	0	1	6

In the great Chamber next the Street

Two bedsteads, 2 fetherbedds, 4 bolsters 2 paire of blanketts 2 ruggs with matts and cords and curtaines and vallens all att	8	0	0
One table and one litle livery cupboard and 5 chaires	0	10	0
One landiron with endirons and fireshovell and tongs	0	5	0

In the Chamber over the hall

Two bedsteads, 2 fetherbedds 2 bolsters 4 pillowes 2 blanketts 2 ruggs with matts and cords and curtaines and vallens	4	10	0
Two tables 2 carpets and 5 cushions att	1	5	0
Three chaires and one chest	0	5	0

In the Garrett over the parlor

Two halfe headed bedds, 2 fetherbedds, 3 paire of blanketts 2 bolsters 3 pillowes, one coverlid and 2 ruggs all att	2	10	0
One Trunke one chest and 4 chaires at	0	15	0

In a litle Chamber

One Trundle bed one fetherbed one blankett one coverlid and severall other things all att	1	0	0

In the Chamber over the Parlor

One bedstead with curtaines and vallens all att	3	0	0

In the Buttery

One horse 5 hoggesheads and ale in the same hoggesheads	5	0	0

In the Brew house

One Copper and Grate at	10	0	0
One Mash tubb 2 gethering tubbs one under becke one soe and severall other things	1	10	0

In the kitching

4 hoggesheads 2 chaires with severall other things and a little landiron and some vinegar and small beare	2	0	0

In the Court

All the pittcoals and seacoales att	2	0	0

In the Stable

One guelding att	5	10	0
All the hay	3	10	0

In the yard

Three peeces of wood	0	10	0

In the great Stable

Servall peeces of wood and stoopes and railes and other things at	0	6	8

In the Buttrey next the parlor

Twenty dozen of linnen sheets at	6	6	8
Two dozen of pillowbears and eight dozen of napkins	5	0	0
Foure table Cloths att	2	0	0

In another Chamber

Thirty five quarters of barley att 15s per quarter	26	5	0
Fifteene quarters of Mault at	14	0	0
Sixe strikes of beanes and 6 strikes of oats at	0	18	0
One Screene one strike one shovell and 6 Sacks att	1	0	0

In the Shopp

All the plate both Silver and gold and all the gold and all the gold rings and all the broken silver and silver lace and other things of value, all appraised att	300	0	0
All the workeing tooles in the said shopp belonging and appertaining to a Goldsmith valued at	20	0	0
Severall goods chatells forgotten, and not in view	3	0	0
In good debts	60	0	0
In debts which are desperate	20	0	0
	643	11	0

30. Henry Corbet **Di 37/3/112**

Doctor of Physick. St. Margaret in Close 9.11.1680

	£	s	d
His purse and Apparrell	40	0	0

In the best parlour

Foureteene Chaires and one Couch a stove and fire Irons belonging to it, a Chimney peice and a door peice with two Tables a Glascase and two Window Curtaines	10	6	8

In the little parlour

	£	s	d
One round Table foure Chaires one Long stoole, one fire grate one old presse with ye hangings and other huslements within the said parlour	2	10	0

In the Hall

One Table six leather Chaires one forme and a screene	1	13	4

In the Kitchin

The pewter and brasse and fire Irons and other householdments there	25	10	0

In the Brewhouse

One Copper and grate with the Brewing Vessells and other things there	12	3	4

In the Dairy and smallbeare Buttery adjoynenig to it

One Table some shelves with small beare vessell and other things there	1	6	8

In the Seller and the roome over the same

For Caskes, Glasse bottles and other huslements there	5	0	0

In the Dyneing Roome

One Table with a Leather Carpet twelve Chaires and foure Cushions Guilt Leather hangings a Chimney peice and some pictures belonging to the staire Case and one fire grate	26	10	0

In the matted Chamber

The Bed and bedding and furniture thereunto belonging with the hangings of the Roome, Chaires and other things there	26	0	0

In the Store Chamber

In plate	52	0	0
In White Mettle flint glasses and other things there	3	0	0
In Linings	13	3	4

In the best Chamber

	£	s	d
The bed and bedding and furniture to the same belonging with ye hangings Chest of drawers Dressing boxes Chaires and other things belonging to the same Roome	62	0	0
In a little Roome within the same Chamber a bedstead bed and bedding and other furniture belonging to the same	5	0	0
In the boyes Roome			
One bed and furniture thereto belonging	1	10	0
In the yellow Chamber			
One bedstead with two feather beds Curtaines, and the hangings of the Roome with Chaires five pictures and other things there	12	10	0
One bed to bee removed from one roome to another	3	0	0
In the Red Chamber			
One Bed and bedding two tables six Chaires the hangings about the Roome and other utensills there	9	10	0
His Library	30	0	0
In the Garretts			
Severall small things there	1	10	0
In the Cole house			
Coales and other fireing with some old plaister there	2	10	0
Three Geldings a Mare and a foale	30	0	0
A Coach and Harnesse	13	0	0
For a Cowe	2	0	0
For an old Cesterne in the yard	2	5	0
The lease of the House wherein the deceased lived and the house adjoyning to it	300	0	0
In ready money	100	0	0
In Debts oweing to the said deceased	100	0	0
	893	18	4

31. George Biron **Prob. Inv. 182/33**

(Farmer) St. Martins 23.5.1681

	£	s	d
His purse and apparrell	10	0	0
In the Chamber over the entrie			
One bedstead Curtaine and Vallence a boulster and 2 pillowes a paire of blanketts and a rugg natt and Cord	2	10	0
A bed tickinge with some feathers	0	13	4
One smale feather bedd	0	15	0
One wainscott Chest one livery Cubbert one table 2 buffet stooles and a deske	1	0	0
2 leather Chaires and one glass Case	0	5	0
A Cubberd of white earthen plate and a Seeinge glasse	0	7	6
One land Iron and flower de luce brase Candlestick	0	13	4
One table Cloth and Cubbert Cloth	0	3	0
One sword and scabberd	0	1	6
All his linnen beeing 2 paire harden sheets 2 pairs of linne sheets	0	16	8
3 pillow beares	0	3	0
6 huccaback napkins	0	3	0
14 other napkins	0	4	8
1 diper table Cloth one line table Cloth 2 other table cloth	0	6	0
3 Corse pillow beares and other old linnen	0	2	0
A percell of bookes beeinge 15 bookes	1	0	0
In the north Chamber			
One bedstead Curtaine and Vallence one feather bed 2 blanketts one rugg one boulster natt and Cord	1	15	0
One livery Cubbert 2 Chests one Chaire table	0	17	6
8 bumble Chaires	0	4	0
In the Chamber over the hall			
One feather bed one flock bed 2 ruggs 2 blanketts one flock boulster	1	0	8
One paire of iron racks alanthorne a leaven tubb and other implyments	0	5	0
In the Shopp and Seller			
One Kilderkine one horse wood and Coales beastcoupe washinge tubbs shovell spade and other implyments	0	14	0

In the Kitchinge

One livery Cubbert one smale table one wanded Chaire 5 bumble Chaires one paire of bellowes	0	14	0
One Jack land Iron end Irons one Spitt fire Shovell and tongs Iron forke drippinge pan and other implyments	0	15	0
46lb of pewter at 8d	1	10	0
One warmeinge one smoothinge Iron 2 heaters	0	3	6
One brase pott one brase pott ketill 2 brase panns one brase skellit one brase Can one brase Candlesticke	1	2	2
4 flicks of bacon and one Cheane of bacon a peece bacon and aneats tongue	3	13	4
4 Cheeses	0	4	0
Severall earthen vessells a Kitt and wooden waires and other implyments	0	3	4
2 stone of tallow	0	5	8

In the stable

14 Deale bords at 10d	0	11	8
2 maires 2 horses and a swine	10	0	0

In the Close

6 beasts	21	0	0
2 other beasts	3	0	0
43 ews and 43 lambs in houghton feilds	20	0	0
2 sheepe 1 ewe and 1 lamb	2	15	0
9 dozen and 3 skins of 12s 6d a dozen	5	15	6
Debts owinge by his booke	5	0	0
Mr. Dempster Uppon bill	7	0	0
Other things Seene and Unseene	0	10	0
	108	3	4

31. Cheane – chine of bacon.
Flower de luce – fleur de lys.

32. John Leach **Prob. Inv. 182a/230**

Gentleman (Grocer & Brewer) 7.1.1682

	£	s	d
His purs and Apparrill	10	0	0
In ye hows			
6 Rushey Lether Chares A Couch Chare A Table Cobards Jack Andirons Hookes with other things	3	10	0
In the Shopp			
Suger 300 waight sweetmeats Aloms and other things	20	0	0
In a Little Roome by the stares			
10 puter dishes puter plates six bras pans 2 bras potts A payer candlesticks, A Safe with other things	2	10	0
In the Chamber over the hows			
A bedstead, fether bed boulster and pillows Rug blankitts Curtaines 2 Chests, with Lining sheets Towels napkings 4 Chares and other Things	5	0	0
In the Chamber over the Shopp			
Hangings of the Roome 13 reeded wrought Chares and stooles A bedstead, fether bed, boulster, pillows, and other Beding Curtains with Severall other Things	5	10	0
In the Garratts			
A bedstead fether bed boulster, beding with severall other Utinsells	2	0	0
Att John Johnsons hows			
A french Bedstead mat, cord, Cortaine rods A long Table Two Joyned forms Another Table A glas Case A peuter Case dresser 2 hodgsheads A Copper and Grate 3 Larg brewin Tubs underbeck, Soe and other Things	11	0	0

At Widow Armstons hows

	£	s	d
A bedstead fether bed, boulster, pillows, Curtains, vallians, beding, Tables, Cobard, puter Brass, potts and pans, hodgsheads, Barrills, Rackon hooks with many other utinsells	6	0	0

At the Brewhose in Much Lane

	£	s	d
A Copper 3 Larg Tubs underbeck A Iorne grate A Soe and other things	7	0	0
For 90 quarters Malt	80	0	0
Rents in Tennants hands	17	0	0
In Bonds and good debts	60	0	0
In desperate debts	70	0	0
	299	10	0

33. William Peart **Di 39/2/53**

Gentleman (Coffee House Proprietor)
St. Mary Magdalene 21.3.1682

	£	s	d
His purse and Apparrell	10	0	0

In the Hall

	£	s	d
Foure tables, two formes nineteene basse bottom'd Chaires and one Buffet stoole	(..	..	..)
One paire of tables	0	6	8
One Screene one Carpet with Curtaines and Rods	0	15	0
One Grate, one paire of Andirons with fire shovells and Tongs, one Jacke one brasse hanging Candle sticke and one paire of Bellowes	1	16	6
Pewter and brasse with Spitts and Cob Irons	8	4	6

In the Scullery

	£	s	d
Copper and Tyn Coffee pots and Coffee dishes with other Lumber	1	6	8
Tyn ware	0	5	4

In the Cellers

	£	s	d
Ale and Beare with hogsheads and Barrells	8	12	0
For Meade and Cyder and glasse and Stone Bottles	6	12	0

For flaggons and Quarts and Pintes, pots and Glasses and other things there	3	6	8

In the Brewhouse

The Brewing vessells with Bucket and Band, a paire of Cobirons and other things there	3	13	4
For a table and other things in the Stont	0	6	8

In the Celler Chamber

Two Bedsteads with feather bedds Bolsters Curtaines and Vallence and other furniture belonging to them	6	18	4
A Coffee Mill, a Roaster, a pot of Honey one table three formes a livery Cupboard, one box of Tobacco and other Lumber	6	13	4

In the Chequer Chamber

One high Bedstead one Truckle bedstead with two feather beds Curtaines and valence and other furniture belonging to them	6	13	4
One Table one forme five Chaires one Deske two Voyders and a seeing Glasse	1	5	6
One Chest of Lynnens	12	3	4

In the Garret

Two feather beds and bedsteads and other furniture belonging to them	3	13	4
One table one forme four Trunkes two Boxes, one Close Stoole and pann Trenchers and other Lumber	1	10	8

In the Best Chamber

One featherbed and bedstead with a paire of Broad Cloathe Curtaines and vallence and a pair of Stained Callicoe Curtaines and vallence, both vallences with Silke fringes, a Counterpaine to them both with other furniture	10	10	0
Two tables and Carpets fifteen Chaires and Stooles, two Window Curtaines and Rods, one paire And Irons with brasses fire shovel tonges a grate and other Lumber	4	0	0

In the little Chamber next ye best Chamber

One Bed and Bedstead with the furniture thereunto belonging One Table and Carpet with five Chairs and other things in a Closet in the same Roome	4	10	0

Six Silver Spoones and a little Silver Cupp	3	3	4
His Bookes	3	10	0
In the Stable			
For Hay and Straw and Beanes and Oates	3	0	0
In Bills and Bonds and ready Money	40	0	0
For things unseene and forgotten	1	13	4
	157	15	2

33. **Stont** - place, platform, booth.

34. Richard Ellis — Di 38/1/86

(Whipmaker) 24.5.1682

	£	s	d
His purse and Apparell	1	4	0
Old Whips	0	0	0
3 hunting Whips and short Whipp supposed to be left for mending	(..	..	..)
Seeing Glass	0	6	0
2 brushes	0	0	6
1 feather bed, Pillow, bolster and old land Iron, brass morter	1	10	0
12lb. of whale bone	0	12	0
1 belt 12d	0	1	0
9oz. Silk	0	9	0
Old watering pot	0	2	2
Water bowle	0	0	3
Wheel for twisting and venis weights	0	8	0
A twisting Wheele 18d	0	1	6
2 Carpets 18d	0	1	6
1 Shirt with other linen	0	9	0
9 Clock strings	0	9	0
Collourd Crewlls 33lb at 2s 6d	4	2	6
Picture in frame	0	1	6
Brass wyre	0	1	0
Brass Candlestick	0	0	6
Whip frame two weights	0	8	0
Cat Guts 3 boxes with honner resp etc	0	12	0
Wings and Quils	0	0	1
1½lb more whale bone	0	1	6
Gold Ring	0	2	6
Counters Shelves Glass case Coat of arms box of drawers with other appurdenances Winders quills for Silke etc	0	18	0
Single money	0	0	1½

Box comb	(..	..	..)
Scales and Weights	0	2	0
Chair and Cushion	0	1	2
Cross Stool	0	0	6
Yard Wand	0	0	2
Pair of Scales	0	1	0
Mortar Pestell brass	0	1	0
Buffe belt	0	1	0
Silk	0	1	0
Large broad Ribbon	0	0	6
Silver spoon	0	1	4
[One whip almost finished – Challinged and not charged to Account]	[0	5	0]
Library	0	6	0
Window grate	0	2	0
Parcell of old boxes with other Lumber	0	2	0
7 Ounces of Odd Silk	0	2	6
Samples – old	0	1	6
Silk Bellt	0	1	0
2 Pewter Dishes waight 5½lb	0	3	2½
1 old Cubord	0	1	6
1 small silver Cupp	0	2	0
	13	17	4
	(13	13	0)
Mistake was in setting down the pewter dishes but now rectifyed and add 1s 7½d	–13	18	11½

34. Crewll – thin worsted yarn used for fringes and laces.
Honner resp – a rasp for sharpening tools.
Twisting wheel – a device for plaiting thongs.
Wing – in this context probably the bird's wing from which quills were taken.

35. Mr. Richard Winne L.C.C. Admon. 1683/127

Alderman (Pewterer) St. Martins 12.3.1683

	£	s	d
His purse and apparrell	6	0	0
In the parlor next ye street			
One feather bed 2 blanketts one boulster 2 pillows 2 coverlidds one bedstead Curtens and Vallens cord nat and twilt	3	0	0
One Draw table 3 Joynt stooles	0	18	0
6 red leather Chaires	0	18	0

One livery Cubbert one Cuberd Cloth 2 wrought Cushons	0	8	0
One Joynt Chest one black glass Case	0	5	0
Window Curtaines and rods one pickture Close stool and pan	0	7	0
2 bibles and other smale bookes and implyments	0	10	6

In the hall or house

One draw table one forme 4 stooles Joint	0	13	4
One smale white table 6 bast Chaires one wanded Chaire one little wooden Chaire	0	8	0
One Jack Cords pullies and weights	0	15	0
6 spitts 2 paire tongs 2 hookes one grate fire shovell one horse one smoothinge Iron one pestell one Iron forke one brass to draw on shoos 1 paire racks	0	16	0
One land Iron one gallow balke 2 end Irons 1 runing hooke one paire tongs 1 slice 1 paire bellows 1 window Curtaine rod, Curtaines and a table Carpett	1	2	6
One brass sconce 2 brass candlesticks	0	8	0
One brass and one tin puddinge pans	0	1	6
One warmeinge pan	0	1	0
2 tin Covers 13 glass bottles 1 grater 1 water bottle	0	3	0
47lb of pewter att 8d	1	11	4
One tin sugar box one tin Candle Case with implyments	0	1	6

In the Inner parlor

One feather bed one boulster one pillow 1 paire of sheets 2 Coverlids 2 blanketts one bed stead one Curtain Matt and Cord	1	10	0
One press Cubberd one press to hang Clothes in, one Joint Chest one old Chest	0	16	0
3 thrum Cushions 2 smale feather pillowes one glass Case	0	6	0
One black and yellow low stoole and implyments	0	1	0

In the Kitchine

2 pans one Iron pott one brass stewinge pan one fryinge pan one skellitt one scummer 1 sauce pan	0	12	0
1 paire of Iron racks 1 land Iron and great Iron nayles	0	6	0
3 pewter Chamber potts 1 tin dripping pan	0	2	0

3½ dozen trenchers one water Kitt 1 brass pott Kettill	0	6	6
1 water tub 1 low stoole and other implyments	0	1	6

In the Stable

One horse and hay	1	10	0
One wheele barrow and grinding stone	0	3	0

In the best Chamber

One feather bed one feather boulster 2 pillowes 2 blanketts one red rugg a pair of red Curtaines and vallence bedstead and Curtaine rods Cord and natt	4	10	0
2 Armd Chaires 5 wrought Chaires 10 stooles	1	17	6
One lookeinge glass one table one fram of gilt leather	0	8	6

In the next chamber to ye best Chamber

One bedstead Curtaines and vallence 2 boulsters one paire of sheets 3 blanketts 1 Coverlidd 1 natt	1	15	4
4 Spanish tables	1	6	8
One trundle bed natt and Cord	0	4	0
3 Joint Chaires and a little stoole	0	7	0
2 mantles 1 Cradle rugg 1 wainscot chest	0	12	4
3 paire sheets linen 3 paire hempen sheets 16 huckaback napkins 19 linen napkins 1 damaske cubbard Cloth 2 towells 3 table Clothes	1	14	10

In the workeinge Chamber

One wheele and frame workeinge tooles and a pair bellowes	0	12	0

In the Shopp

49lb of sad waire at 9d pewter	1	16	9
68lb of hollow waire at 10d	2	16	8
21lb of lay at 8d	0	14	0
130lb of Kettills at 10d	5	8	4
36lb of Iron drippinge panns and fryings pans at 4d	0	12	0
46lb of new brass potts at 6d	1	3	0
1 milne brass weigh 11lb at 7d	0	6	5
41lb of Iron potts at 1½d a pound	0	5	1
One Copper bottom weigh 14½lb at 10d	0	12	1½
14lb of brass morters and a Copper Can at 15d	0	17	6
A Chafinge dish weigh 1½lb at 15d	0	1	10½
3 warminge pans 11s one fryinge pan 2s 6d	0	13	6

2 sauce panns	0	2	0
4 tin Cullanders 3 tinn dish covers 3 tin cans a tin box	0	6	11
2 tinn drippinge pans 1 tin pasty pan 1 warming pan bottom	0	3	8
8½lb of old lay at	0	3	6
1 still topp weigh 7½lb at 5d 1 still bottom weigh 13lb	0	4	2½
One lardge beame and scoales	0	10	0
3 warminge pan frames 2s 11 stone lead at 15d	0	16	4½
13lb of brass weights at 10d	0	10	10
One Iron pistoll one sugar box and other implyments	0	2	6

In the yard and Mr Freestones back dore

One leadon Ceasterne	0	13	4
6 peeces of wood	2	14	0
	59	4	5

35. **Ceasterne** – cistern.
Hollow ware – utensils which are bowl or tube shaped.
Milne – mill.
Sad waire – solid utensils.
Thrum – a fringe.

36. Thomas Eure — Prob. Inv. 185A/194

Gentleman (Farmer) 19.6.1684

	£	s	d
His purs and apparrell	30	0	0
In ye Hall			
One Long table one forme	2	0	0
In ye Kitchin			
Twenty eight pewter dishes	3	6	8
One duzen of trencher plates	0	8	0
Two pye plates	0	2	0
One Still	0	6	8
One Chamber pott and other old pewter	0	2	0
Three brass potts and a posnett one sauce pan	0	11	0
Six brass kettles one scumer	1	10	0
Foure brass candlesticks	0	3	4
One brass morter and pestel	0	2	0

One warming pan	0	3	4
One Jack with lines and weight two spitts two cob Irons one frying pan	2	0	0
One Land Iron with fire shovell and tongs gallow bawke and rackon hookes a payre of bellows	0	13	4
Two dripping pans	0	6	8
One little table	0	2	0
Foure Chaires one wanded Chaire	0	7	0
One duzeen and halfe of trenchers	0	1	4

In ye Brewhouse

One Copper and grate three tubs and other Implements for brewing	3	10	0
One washing tub one kitt one chicken pen with other lumber	0	5	0

In the little parlour

Two tables with leather Carpets	1	6	8
Fifteene leather chaires	3	1	0
One Landiron with fire shovell and tongs	0	12	0

In ye New parlour

One stone table with frame	0	12	0

In ye parlour over ye cellar

Two feather beds one pillow one bolster one rugg one blanket one payre of sheets one bedsted	2	0	0
Two tables three wainscote chaires one bass chaire one forme	1	6	8

In ye Cellar

Eight barrells foure horses	0	13	4
One leaven tub three temses	0	6	8
Three dozen of glass bottles	0	5	0

In ye pantry

One table one glascase one little Cupboard 2 Joynd stooles	0	6	8

In ye best Chamber

One downe bed and bedsted two pillows three blankets a payre of Sheets	9	0	0
Curtains and vallenc and counterpaine	2	10	0
Six Chaires	2	0	0
One table and carpett	0	6	8
The hangings	1	2	0
One lookeing glass	1	10	0

Window curtains	0	8	0
Fire shovell and tongs	0	2	0

In ye pantry Chamber

One feather bed and bedstead one bolster one pillow two blankets one payre of sheetes one Coverlid one rugg	3	10	0
Curtains vallenc window Curtains cupboard Cloath	0	6	8
One table one livery cupboard three chaires	0	8	0

In ye little Chamber

One feather bed and bedsted one bolster one pillow two blanketts one coverlid a payre of sheets curtaines and vallenc	1	10	0
One table one chaire one Lookeing glass	0	4	0

In ye Kitchen Chamber

One feather bed and bedsted two pillows one bolster two blankets one rugg a payre of sheets	2	10	0
Curtains and (va)llenc	1	0	0
Hangings	0	7	0
One table	0	4	0
Five Chaires	0	5	0
In plate one silver tankard one dozen of spoones two salts one little cup one porringer	14	0	0
One skreene one stoole	0	6	0

In ye garret over ye Kitchin

One bed and bedsted one blankett one coverlid a payre of sheets a table an old Chest	1	0	0

In ye Middle garret

One Chest with foure dozen of huckaback Napkins ten payre of sheets two payre of holland sheets one dozen of cours Napkins foure table Cloaths four payre of pillow bears	5	0	0

In ye Corne Chambers in the low house

15 quarter of rye more or Less	15	15	0
4 quarter of Malt more or Less	4	0	0
6 quarter of Oates more or Less	3	12	0
5 quarter of wheate more or Less	7	0	0
4 quarter of beans and fitches	2	13	4

In the Chamber over ye stable

One load of hay more or less	1	0	0
Wood in and about ye yard	1	6	8
In Coles the value	1	0	0
In brick tiles and reed the valu	0	18	0
The bucket and band and 2 troughs	0	10	0
2 lead cisterns	5	0	0

At Colbey

Six oxen	24	0	0
Five horses and a Mare	18	0	0
15 load of hay more or less	7	0	0
3 Swine	1	0	0
Cart and Cart geere wayne and wayn geere plow and plow geere with other Implements thereto belonging	5	0	0
Pease and beans on ye hovell	2	0	0
Corne on ye ground in barly	12	0	0
Rye	1	16	0
Peas	1	0	0
Oats	1	10	0
Firr deale boards 50 att John Laws house and more at hom	2	10	0
Three horses with Mr Saunderson and a Colt at Colebey	30	0	0

In Leases

Fabrick Lease his dwelling house	54	0	0
Chaunters Lease Hotchkinson house	20	0	0
Parrish Lease Pyms house	20	0	0
In bills and bonds and good Security	600	0	0
For things which may be omitted	0	6	8
	947	11	4

37. William Evison **Prob. Inv. 186/237**

Gentleman (Timber merchant) 16.5.1685

	£	s	d
His Purse and Apparrell and some other small things	123	7	6½

In the Chamber over the Hall

Two Bedsteads and two feather bedds with Curtaines Vallants and beding thereunto bellonging	6	10	0
One chist of Drawers and a little table	0	10	0

A frame and a Box	0	16	0
Five Chares one Stoole	0	14	0
One Seeing Glass	0	2	0
One Rapier	0	5	0
A trunk and a Chist and some other small things	0	8	0

In the Closset belonging to the Hall Chamber

Two Hatts and a Hatt Press	0	13	0
One Seeing Glass	0	8	0
Two Boxes a Trunk and Severall other things	0	8	0
Some small peeces of Silver a little Box	0	10	0

In the Parlor Chamber

A Cabbenit and frame and stands	10	0	0
A Bedstead a feather bed with Curtaines and Vallents one Rugg two Blankets one Boulster two Pillowes	0	0	(..)
One Seeing Glass	0	5	(..)
One Trunk	0	0	(..)
Five chares one Couch one Stoole	1	0	(..)
One Paper window	0	2	(..)
A Wastcoate and Coate left in Paune	0	6	(..)
One fire Iron a fire shovell and Tonges	0	15	(..)

In the Chamber over the Kitchin

Nayles and Nayle Boxes	1	10	(..)
One Bedstead and bed with beding	0	12	(..)
One other bedstead and bed with Beding	0	10	(..)
Two Screenes with some boards and other Things	0	5	(..)
Twelve Glass Bottles	0	2	(..)
A Ballance	0	3	(..)

In the Parlor

One chist of Drawers	0	16	(..)
One Sideboard Table a paire of stands a Looking Glass frame	2	0	0
One clock and a Case	1	10	0
Three Dutch Table leaves	1	0	0
Twelve Leather Chares	1	16	0
A fire Iron and Brasses	0	10	0
A little Dressing Box	0	5	0
One other Side board Table and Stands	0	4	0
Three Duzen of Trenchers	0	8	0
One Mortar of Marble Seaven Plats one Bason one Jugge a Possitpot a Pasty peele a wooden Oatmeale Trough with other small things	0	5	0
Three Pistills	0	15	0

In the Hall

One Gunn	0	12	0
One oak table and frame	0	8	10
One Forme and Stoole	0	3	0
Two little Tables	0	3	6
Five Wanded Chares	0	2	4
One great Wanded Chare	0	1	0
A fire Iron and what belongs to it two creepers three fire shovells and Tonges	2	0	0
Three Spitts and other Irons An Iron Chafingdish two cleavers	0	6	8
Four Stone of Puter in twelve dishes and two pye Plates	2	0	0
Fourteene Puter Plates	0	10	0
Two Puter flaggons	0	10	0
Three Puter Chamber pots a paire of Puter Candlesticks three Brass Candlesticks	0	10	0
Six Puter Porrigers and Potts 1 Salt	0	2	0
Three Puter dishes 12 pounds and a ½	0	9	0
Two Puter Tankers	0	3	0
Two Tinn Bakeing Panns two tinn Dripping Panns a tinn fish Plate two Cullenders with some other peeces of tinn	0	3	0
The Earthern Ware in the hall	0	4	0
Six Cushons	0	6	0

In the Hall Buttrey

One Brass Pann one Brass Pott with a brass cover two Brass Skellits a Copper Coffey Pott a Brass Warming Pann a Copper Can a Brass Ladle	1	2	6
Four Beare Barrils	0	12	0
A Wooden Boule and a Tray two wooden Saffes a Shreding Block	0	6	0
A Hatchet and a Belt	0	1	0
Three Knives three Meat forkes	0	3	6
One Kildrekin a Barrell a hand Basket	0	3	0
One Puter Bason	0	1	0
A fanchin	0	6	6
One Bible two Comonpraire Bookes and other Small Bookes and other small things in the Hall	0	10	0

In the Kitchin

One Copper and Brewing Vessell	1	15	0
One Jack	0	6	0
One Brass pott three Brass Panns one Iron pott a Brass Skellit	1	0	0
One Spitt and Irons belonging to ye Kitchin Chimney and other things there	0	6	8
Two Iron Dripping Panns	0	3	4

A Chickin Penn	0	3	0
Four Occimy Spoones with wearing Trenchers with all other Huslements whatsoever	0	6	8
In the shade next the House Wainscot and other Matterials to ye vallew of	5	10	0

In the Cooper Shop

Firkin Staves with other things	5	0	0
Gists against ye Shop with other small peeces	2	0	0
One pile of Oake Boards consisting of 60 in Number	2	10	0
More Gists	1	5	0
One parcell of Lumber Wood	0	10	0
At the Shop Side a parcell of Boards and timber	1	0	0
Norway Oake boards with Lathes and other Necessaryes	4	10	0

In the little Shop

Small peeces with other Necessaryes	1	10	0

In the Chamber

Two New Tables with other Matterialls	3	0	0
A parcell of sawne Timber next the Pailes	4	0	0

In the upper shop

And what Materialls is in it	3	0	0
A Waggon	5	10	0
One Carte	1	10	0
20 Short square Loggs in the yard	2	0	0
One peece of Elme	1	10	0
Lumber Wood at the yard end	0	10	0
All the Gists and other Sawne Timber at the yard End	4	0	0
At Tyles Becks thirty and five Ends of Oake Wood	7	0	0
At Bardney thirty and Nine Ends of Oak and one of Ash timber	7	10	0
In Whashingbrough Long Stongs and upon the Greens twenty and two ends of Ash Wood	6	0	0
At Washingbrough ferry eighty and five Ends of Ash wood with some other peeces in Heighenton close and else where	6	0	0
Eight peeces of oak two peeces of yew in Sinsill Ditch	2	0	0
Two Mares one filly	7	0	0
One Cow	1	6	8
Wood bought at Ingleby with wood unmeasured	50	15	0
With all other Materialls whatsoever	1	0	0

	£	s	d
Ten quarter of Oates	5	0	0
For some cloathes of Mrs. Evisons	1	0	0
For sheets Napkins and other Linings	2	10	0
All good and bad Debts	80	0	0
With Tooles and all others things not before valued	2	0	0
	(c.£404	0	0
	no total given)		

37. **Fanchin** – a bill hook.
Gists – joists.
Saffe – safe.
Shreding block – pruning block.

38. Robert Burtons Prob. Inv. 188/70
Gardener (Weaver) St. Martins 9.7.1688

	£	s	d
His purss and Apparrell	10	0	0
In the parlor			
One Beddstead with Curtaines and vallance with feather Bedd Boulster and pillows Blanketts and Rugg	5	0	0
A Trundle Bedd and a paire of Blanketts five Chares Two Chests, one side board Table, Two Stooles	1	0	0
Six paire of Linn Sheets six paire of Linn pillow beares Two dozen of Huckaback Napkins Two Huckaback Table Cloths and Two Linn Table Cloths	5	11	0
Tenn paire of Hempin Sheets and dozen Napkins, foure paire of Hempin pillow bears Two paire of Harden sheets	2	15	0
Silver Cupp and Spoone	2	0	0
A Chest of Drawers and a wanded Chaire	1	0	(..)
In the House			
An Andiron with fire shovle and Tongues and end irons with other irons belonging to ye house with reckon hookes	1	6	8

Fifteen pewter dishes a dozen of pewter plates, foure sawsers foure flaggons, foure pewter porringgers Two pewter Tankards Two Candlesticks, Two Mustard pots, Two pewter Measurs one pinte and Gill with other odd pewter things	4	0	8
Foure Brass panns Two smaller Brass pans and one saws pann Two brass potts a Warming pann	1	10	0
One Cuppboard with earthen plates and possett pott	0	8	4
Dresser Board and Two pewter Casses Two Tables six bast Chares Three paire of Scales and Weights with other lumber	1	0	0
In the Shopp			
Two Loomes with Gears and other matearialls belonging to a Weaver	2	0	0
In the Chamber			
Two old beddsteads with Bedding and a pillion seat with other Lumber	2	0	0
In the Yard att home			
For Cherries and Berrys and other Garden harbs and Rootes	4	0	0
In the Great orchard			
For Ceries and Berries and Corrans and Young Trees and Roots and other Garden harbs	10	0	0
In the Nurrsey Yard			
For pease and Beanes and other Roots and harbs	0	10	0
In the Cherry holt			
For Cherries and Beanes and other things	3	0	0
In the Hopp Yard			
For Berries and Carriatts and other things	1	0	0
One cow	2	0	0
Two Mares	(..	..	..)
One pigg	(..	..	..)
In the out house			
Two wheele Barrows and foure parre of paniers	0	10	0
One Corporation Lease of Two houses on Green hill in ye parrish of St Martins in ye City of Lincolne	20	0	0
Things not seen or forgott	0	2	6
	87	6	2

39. Thomas Hill **Prob. Inv. 187/13**

(Confectioner) St. Markes 16.7.1688

	£	s	d
Purse And aparill	3	0	0
Towe Horses and a fole	6	0	0
One Hogeshead of Treakell	5	0	0
2 Pack sadles and 3 pare of panyers	0	10	0
2 Emte Hogesheads and 3 pare of Tresels	0	4	0
5 Hundrd of Kides and a Belferah with sum Lumber	1	15	0
For 2 Loade of Meales	0	18	0
For 10 Qarter of wheate	11	0	0
For a Millone to dres meales with 4 Tubes and 2 Strikes	2	0	0
All the meterales Belonging to ye Back house	1	0	0
A Bage of Ginger and Ginger Bread and oather Lumber	1	0	0
In ye Hous			
For Brase and Puter	4	1	0
For 2 Cuberds	0	8	0
A dreser Board and Puter Case	0	3	0
A Landiorne and oather Iornes Belonging to ye Range	0	10	0
A warnin pane	0	5	0
3 boxes with Sweetmeats in them	0	13	4
1 Table and Hafe a dusson of Cares with sume Lumbr	0	6	8
In ye Towe Chambers			
2 Stand Beds and a Trundell Bead and furnituer to them all	8	10	0
For a Liverrah Cuberd and a Table in ye Littell Chambr with Ten Chares	0	10	0
One Wandin Chare and a Voyder	0	4	0
One Locking glase and Glas Case with a Boxe	0	5	0
A littell Land iorne	0	3	0
1 Longe Table with a furme and Stoules Beloning	0	6	(..)
3 Chistes and 3 Boxes	0	7	(..)
8 pare of sheets Coarse and fine	2	0	(..)
8 pare of pillow beares Coarse and fine	1	0	(..)
3 Table Cloathes with 1 dusson and a hafe of Napekines	0	13	(..)
The Earthone ware with 1 dusson of Bottles	0	8	(..)
A Skole Beame with The Weytes Belongin	0	7	(..)
	53	7	(..)

39. **Belferah** - belfrey.
Kides - kids.
Millone - mill.
Skole - scale.

40. Roger Wood — Prob. Inv. 188/163

Glover St. Botolph 29.8.1688

	£	s	d
Purse and aparill	2	13	4
In the house			
One pres 1 pare of drawers and glascase 2 small tabels 5 chares one stoule one small glascase and a few bookes	0	13	4
6 puter dishis one flagin one pinte can one poringer 2 cupes 2 sasers one bowle 3 earthondishes 4 stone plates 2 stone candel stikes one salte	0	15	0
In the parler			
One bedstead with fetherbed 3 blankites one boulster 2 pillows one coverlide one pare of Curtines	3	10	0
One Chist one Trunke one seinglase	0	3	4
One pare of lininge shetes 4 pare and a halfe of hempin shetes 6 pilla covers 7 napkines one Tabelcloth 6 towiles	1	7	0
One small bras pot 2 small panes	0	7	6
One Landiran with other Iranes one pare of belas one smouthin iron	0	5	0
In the Chamber			
One small bed with beding to it 3 ouldd chistes one tabel Leafe	0	10	0
In the Shope			
Lether and gloves	6	0	0
One horse sadel and bridel	2	10	0
One cowe	1	10	0
One Cimlin one searge one temes and sume other Implomentes	0	8	0
	20	12	6

40. **Cimlin** - tub.

41. Edmund Fleare **Prob. Inv. 188/99**

Bodyes Maker 6.10.1688

	£	s	d
His Purse and Apparrell	79	12	4
In his lodging Chamber			
One standing Bed with beding Curtaines and other furniture	2	0	0
One Silver bowle and a Silver botkin	2	10	0
Two Chests	0	6	0
Six red basings	0	6	0
Five ends of ticking at 14s 6d per peice	3	12	6
One end of ticking	0	10	0
Seven ends of ticking at 11s per peice	3	17	0
Five ends of ticking at 14s per peice	3	10	0
Two ends of ticking at	1	3	0
One dosen of bodyes	1	0	0
16 paire of bodyes	1	10	0
Three dosen of bodyes	5	0	0
In the Shop			
A parcell of Sticht bodyes	1	4	0
51 paire of unsticht bodyes	1	6	0
Thirteene paire of gray thrid green hole bodyes	1	12	6
Twelve paire more of the same	1	10	0
Five paire more of the same	0	12	6
Six paire of childrens bodyes	0	3	0
Eight paire of womens bodyes	1	0	0
Ten paire more of the same	1	5	0
Eight paire more of the same	1	0	0
Foure paire at	0	8	0
Five paire more at	0	12	6
Six paire more at	0	15	0
Nine paire of girles bodyes at	0	12	0
Seven paire of womens at	0	14	0
Tenn paire more	1	5	0
Six paire more at	0	12	0
4 paire at	0	7	6
10 Stomichers	0	5	0
2 paire of bodyes	0	2	0
Thirteen paire of bodyes	1	12	6
Seven paire at	0	10	6
Six dosen and a half of Eether bodyes	3	0	0
Six ends of white ticking at	3	12	0
Thrid at	1	10	0
Silk	0	8	0

A dosen of skins	0	4	0
Seventeen dosen of whale bone at 16s per dosen	13	12	0
Debts good and bad	1	0	0
Other small things seen and valued	1	0	0
	146	11	10
	(141	11	10)

41. **Basings** – foundation, base.
Bodyes – female underbodice usually stiffened with stays of bone.
Botkin – bodkin.
Eether – Easter (?)

42. William Houghton Prob. Inv. 191/16

The Castle of Lincoln 13.1.1695

	£	s	d
His purse And Apparrell	10	0	0
Inn the Best chamber			
One fether bed with the furniture there unto belonging and the hangings in the Same Roome	6	0	0
One Clocke	2	10	0
One table, Six Chaires one Landirne one Lookeing glass and Sevrall od things	2	10	0
Inn the Closett			
Severall Bookes and plaite and Severall other od things	2	0	0
Inn the Dining Roome			
Three Beds and all the furnighture to 'em	10	0	0
One form and Large press	0	13	0
Inn the Little Pantrey			
Severall pewter dishis and plaites and other od things	6	10	0
Inn the two Bed Chamber			
Two beds and ye furnituer to 'em and foure Chaires	6	0	0
Inn the fare Chamber			
Three beds and furnituer to 'em a Landirn and table	5	0	0

In the Great Chamber			
One table foure Chairs and Severall od things	1	6	8
Inn the three bed Chamber			
Three beds and furnituer to 'em	4	0	0
Inn the Little Room			
One fether bed and furnituer to 'em	1	10	0
Inn the trellis Roome			
One fether bed and furnituer to it and Levintub	1	10	0
In the Kitihon			
Two tables one form one Landirn a dresor two Chairs a Kitt and severall od things	4	0	0
Inn the first Roome			
Two tables one Bedstead and a Chist of drawers a press and Eight Chairs one Landirne and Severall other od things	6	10	0
Inn the Ale Seller			
5 hogseads of Ale and 8 hoggseads 2 pipes three Horses 23 flagons and severall od things	15	15	0
Inn the small bear Seller			
Three Hoggseads and a Chist and Irnes and two tubs and soes and severall other od things	7	10	0
Inn the George			
One table and Six Chairs and Severall other od things	0	10	0
Inn the Little Gaite			
Two bedsteads and a table and Chaire	0	2	6
Inn the County House			
Hay Kids billits and Severall other things	2	0	0
Inn the Grand Jury Chamber			
Wheatt Chees and other things	2	0	0
Inn the Little Chamber			
Two Chists and beans	0	6	8
Inn the Little House in Castle Yard	10	0	0
The hay upon the hufell and hufell and swinsty	6	0	0
Inn the Stable			
One Chist a Rack and Manger	0	8	0

Inn the Coale House

The Coales a Racke and Manger	4	0	0

Inn the old Brew House

One Little Coper one Landirne two dresers a pair of Querns	3	2	6

In the Yard

Two Geldings three Mairs and two fooles	30	0	0
14 Swine	9	6	8
Two Seasterns foure Swine troufs	4	6	8
The Coales in the Coale hole	2	6	8
The Lime in the Saleporte	5	0	0
The Wood in the Yard	15	0	0
The Brikes at the Dore	7	0	0
The Coper at the Gaits	12	0	0
The Wood and Lether at the Gaits	2	10	0
The wood in the towers	5	5	0
The Copper Mashtub Gathering tub and Severall other things	16	0	0

The Garrett Next the Gaits

Two beds the furnituer to em 47 paires of Sheets and severall other Linings	21	10	0

In the other Garrett

Three bedsteads a pair of Querns and Severall other things	4	0	0

Inn the old Garrett

Severall od things	0	10	0
The two two towers	15	0	0
Severall od things at the office	0	10	0
The three Maidenheads	11	0	0
The New Stables	60	0	0
A House at Hikeam	5	0	0

Inn the New Stables

A Stiddy and bellows Rax and mangers	2	13	0

Inn the Chamber

Tools and Severall od things	5	10	0
Severall things in the Garrett	1	0	0
Inn Good Debts	77	1	8
Inn Debts desperatt	55	0	0
Things unseen	1	6	8
Brawne and Bacon	5	0	0
	485	3	2

42. **Brawne** – meat.
Hufell – hovel.
Maidenheads – spoons with ornamented handles.
Pipe – a cask containing 126 gallons or two hogsheads.
Stiddy – anvil.
Trellis – lattice or grating.

43. Michael Drake — Prob. Inv. 192/368

Clerk. St. Swithins 31.3.1696

	£	s	d
His Purse and Apparell	10	0	0
His Library	10	0	0
A Silver Cup, four Spoons and a Taster	2	10	0
In ye Matted Chamber			
Ye bed, Fetherbed, hangings and other things belonging thereto	4	0	0
Three Trunks, a wanded Chair a Table and a Stand	0	13	4
Ten pair of Sheets, a dozen and a half of Napkins and Six Table Cloaths	2	0	0
Ten pillow bears	0	5	0
In ye Lodging Roome			
Two Feather-beds, a Flock bed and all things thereunto belonging	3	0	0
Two boxes with some other things	0	2	0
In ye Passage			
A Press, two small chests and a Trunk	0	6	8
In ye Parlour			
Two Tables, five Chairs and four Stools with some other things	1	0	0
In ye Buttery			
Three small barrels, some bottles a Kit and some other things	0	10	0
In ye Kitchin			
Seven pewter dishes, six plates a Flaggon, two basins, three porringers, a pint pot two or three small peices of pewter	1	6	8
Four brass pots, a Kettle pot, five small bad brass pans and a small brass skellet	0	15	0

A warming pan, a frying pan, a brass morter a ladle, two brass Candle-sticks and a Scummer	0	10	0
A Couch chair, six chairs, six cushions, a stool frame, eight woodden bowles, two small Tables and a Cupboard	0	13	4
Two Spits, a Grid-Iron, a clever, two pair of Tongs, a fire Shovell, a pestell, and Fire Irons with some other small things	0	14	0
	38	6	0

44. John Dring — Prob. Inv. 192/362

Joyner. Saint peeters in ye arches 4.12.1696

	£	s	d
The purs and aparell £30 plate £2	32	0	0
Bed Chamber			
The feather bed pillars and bolsters blanckits and roog	5	0	0
The bedsted and cornish cortins and vallents cortin rodds cord and map	3	0	0
The chist of drawers the cheeses the Looking glassees and pictures	3	14	0
Cradle and roogs	0	15	0
The Clossit			
Bedsted and all belonging to varnish fish skin brushees	3	12	0
The Seeled Chamber			
The wallnuttree chist of drawers and Looking glassees	10	12	0
The fenered tables and stands side bord tables and combox	3	10	0
The bedsted ye great with bossees and other things	1	9	0
The Mens Chamber			
The feather bed roog and blanckits all things belongin to it	4	0	0
The cuttin screwes with ye box to it the chist with the tooles all	2	1	0
The Litle chamber			
The table feet that is in it	0	11	2

The garrat

The coffins and bedsteds cheere frames turning frames a still and pot to it	5	0	0
The 2 sawes stoole feet black wood and molds staing stoole wheele rack Bird cage baskit and bock bocks all comes to	2	4	4

The parlar

The ovell wenscote tables and the side bord tables and Litle table all	8	3	0
The chist of drawers ye bedsted one greate with ye froggs and galla boake	5	8	6

The hall

The tables in ye hall wenscote and elme one with the other comes to	4	15	0
The wallnut chist of drawers stooles pewter case a cooller washing tubs and other things	9	7	0

The Kichin

The pewter 2 douzen of plates 11 pewter dishees 2 tankards 1 flaggin 2 candlesticks	3	17	0
The tables and cheeres 3 guns one pair of wooden srewes glew a ston and half all	3	11	0
The brass pots and Kettles candsticks and copper can warming pan fryin pan sawspan	1	18	0
The spits tosting Irons smoothing irons glew pots nest of drawers	0	13	6
The driping pan glas botles a paire of folding dores with the hingees	1	1	0
Three douzen of Locks one douzen paire of duftale hingees 3 douzen of dripls	1	9	5
Three douzen of scuthings 7 douzen of squaes coffin Locks	0	10	5

The back Kichin

The washing tubs temes scip and other neasesary things for ye Kichin	0	16	6
The oake bords old Iron turning fram other odd ends of stufe all	2	11	0
The foale and the hay	1	19	0

The Sellar

The end of wood and five barells	1	17	0

The Yard

The bed post bed rales bed sides and all other peicees with a buring wheele and bords	2	15	0
The stufe in the summer house	1	10	0

The Wood house

The oake quarters elme bords wallnuttree plancks and other peicees	5	0	0

The Hay Chamber

The dale bords and five score and ten of quarter dales comes to	11	11	2
The oake plank and bord the paire tree plank and bord	1	10	6

The Shop in ye Street

The coffins the wenscote bords the bass bords and peicees of bords	2	9	4
The stools and cheere feet and rales 2 gun stocks with other peicees	0	17	0
The molds and patterns squares and leavell frames of tables screwes and boxe	0	16	0
The chist and all tooles in it and in the shop hatchits hansawes hammer holdfasts Long plains for plaines smoothing plaines cornish plaines belection plaines ogees hollow and rownds plaines plowes growing plaines spring plaine files rasps and burring tooles screwes and screw plates wimble and passer stock and small kits mortis chissell and all sort of chissells and formers and gougees the turning fram a vice the benchees all things in it	9	16	7

The old house Where they came from

The oake plank the Wallnuttree plank the partree plank the grindle ston and other waist wood in all	4	7	1

The Timber

The oake timber by Saint Sweethings Church the sawpitt The foure trees comes to in all	6	13	4

Elme wood

The elme wood att Stamp end 20 peicees comes to in all	3	0	0
	174	12	4
	(175	12	4)

44. Bock – a saw buck.
Buring wheele and tools – grinding implements.
Cheere – chair.
Combox – comb-box.
Cornish – cornice, the ornamented projection on which curtains are hung.
Cuttin screwes – bits

Dripls – projecting members of a cornice.
Duftale hingee – hinge with outer edges wider than hanging edges.
Fenered – veneered.
Fish skin brushes – for giving a varnish grain on wood.
Gougee – gouges.
Hansaw – handsaw.
Holdfast – clamp.
Map – mat.
Passer stock – holder for a gimblet.
Patterns – templates.
Planes
Belection – used to make projecting decorative mouldings especially those of bedsteads.
Cornish – used particularly for ornamenting cornices.
Growing – function uncertain.
Hollow – for concave or hollow woodwork.
Ogee – produces a continuous double curve, one convex, one concave.
Plowes – a plough plain which made a grove in the shape of a rectangular prism.
Spring – function uncertain.
Rownds – used for making beading.
Roog – rug.
Scip – a scoop or ladle.
Screw plate – a hardened steel plate used to cut the threads of small screws.
Scuthing – key hole plate.
Squae – square.
Staing stoole wheele – ?
Turning fram – a lathe.
Wimble – gimblet.

45. Robert Douce — Prob. Inv. 193/394

Gentleman (Innholder) Angell in the Baile 15.6.1698

	£	s	d
His purse Apparrell and good debts	20	0	0
The Lease of years in being of the Angell	20	0	0
In the chamber called the Hart			
Seaven Chairs a Table Cupboard and stand two feather bedds boulsters and pillows two bedsteads Curtaines and Vallens with Ruggs blanketts Quilt hangings of the roome and other things	13	12	0
In the Angell			
Seaven Chairs one Table one bedd with the bedding thereunto belonging and hangings of the Room	10	10	0

In the Crowne

	£	s	d
Ten Chairs two Stooles Livery Cupboard two bedds with bedding Curtaines Vallens hangings of roome and other things	(..	..	..)

In the Darnix

Six Caine Chairs two stools Table and Cupboard two bedsteads with beds and bedding belonging to them Ruggs blanketts hangings of the roome and other Utensills	10	4	9½

In the black Swan

Two bedsteads two feather beds boulsters pillows curtains rods vallens ruggs and Curtaines two chairs a stool and Cupboard	10	6	5

In the Bell

Three featherbeds boulsters and pillows ruggs blankets Counterpaines bedsteads and two Chaires a Stool Cupboard and other Utensills in the room	8	19	7½

In the great Sun

One bedstead featherbed boulster pillows curtains and vallens rug blanketts Counterpaine hangings of the roome eleaven chaires a slate Table and other things	13	17	9

In the little Sun

Three featherbeds boulsters pillows ruggs blankets three Bedsteads a table two formes two chairs with other utensils in the roome	11	5	3

In the Green Chamber

One featherbed boulster curtaines valens bedstead Closet shelves and other things	4	10	0

In the great Cross

Twenty two Turky work Chairs four Tables and a Looking Glass	(..	..	..)

In the Little Cross

One featherbed boulster pillows hangings of the bed Counterpaine blankets hangings of the roome two Caine chairs a table and looking glass with other things	14	0	0

In the Nursery

Two feather beds Curtaines Vallens Rugg Coverlid blanketts two bedsteads three chaires a table and other goods	3	9	0

In the Study

One feather bed boulster Pillows Bedstead vallens curtaines six cane Chaires a Table 2 stands and other goods	9	5	5

In the Starr

Nyne Chaires one Table one press bed Ironworke curtaines fringe feather bed boulster pillows and other things	7	18	8½

In the office

Six cane chaires one Table one feather bed boulster pillows curtaines vallens bedstead counterpaine and blanketts and other things	12	9	10

In the new buildings

Five chaires one Table bedstead flock bed boulster pillows blanketts and other things	4	0	0

In the Red Lyon

Two feather beds two boulsters pillows bedsteads curtaines vallens rugs blanketts three chaires one Table with other things	4	10	6

In the Great Green

Nynne chaires one bench one table hangings of the roome with the two bedsteads two featherbeds Bolsters pillows ruggs blanketts Curtaines vallens and other things	12	10	10½

In the Little Green

Two chaires a Table two bedsteads two featherbeds boulsters pillows blankets Rugg Quilt and other things	6	3	0½

In the Mitre

A Looking Glass Cupboard Drawers and Plate	10	0	0

In the Hall Chamber and Hall Chamber Closet

Hangings Shelve and a Table	3	0	0

In the hall and Closet over the Porch

One bedstead Shelves three tables and a chair	0	10	0

In the Little Hall

A particon one Table and one forme	0	8	0

In the Drying Roome

Seaven Spanish Tables two Dressers hen pen Troughs window Shutts three Close Stooles and other Utensills	5	0	0

In the Drying Chamber Closet

A presse and Shelves	0	6	0

In the further Parlour and Nearer Parlour

Sixteen Chaires and three Tables and other Things	5	0	0

In Bowseys Closet and the Barr

One press Basketts Punbowl two cupboards Slate booke Chest of Drawers shelves and other things	3	0	0

In the Kitchin

A Table a Dresser with Cupboards a Horse for Linnen with Cords and pullies shelves Chopping block and scuttles with a Jack	5	11	0
Seaven hundred and fifteen pounds of all sorts of pewter	35	0	0
Two warmeing panns and a stew pan	1	2	0
Two Copper Canns two Sconces and 3 bras stool pans	1	0	0
All the Candlesticks a plate Chafindish and brass morter	2	10	0
The Barr bell and rope	0	5	0
Nyne pair of Doggs four Grates a purr peice of Iron ten pair of Tongs fireshovells spitts gridirons and other things	9	10	0
The Kitchin Grate and Grate before the fire with a parcel of Iron things with a Mill	2	0	0

In the Little Kitchin

A Table forme and benches and two brass Pans	3	4	0

In the Larder

Three Dressers a Safe and Shelves	1	0	0

In the Bowsers

A Table Bench and particon all the Knifes and forkes	0	16	0
Eighteen Yards of Hangings in ye 3 new rooms Six sash window Shutts	5	0	0

In the Brewhouse

A Copper, a little Copper for washing with Grates A Gathering Tubb and Guile the Tunnel scope, Tub, Kitt, Copper covers slings, Spouts and dressers and other things	24	10	0

In the Ale Celler

Six Tun one quarter of Cask the bellows, Corks, one Leather pipe Three Cocks a Tarrier two Tunn Tunnels a hamer two Gimbles Canes and other small things	11	10	0
An east dish and tap Tubs Screw Filters and Barr board a pulley the horses in the wine Celler and ale Celler with a Table shelves and Cupboard	2	0	0

In the small Beer Celler

Four hogsheads a horse and Tap tub window shutts Glasses mugs Canns Salts graters and brushes with all the Locks in the house and fourteen hogsheads of Beer and ale	35	0	0

In the Wine Celler

Canary Claret Tent and White wine port and sider	30	0	0
Empty Cask	0	16	0

In the Stables and Yard

All the racks mangers and standings in the Stables with the measures forke and shovell one round Cistern one square Cistern with a Cistern for swillings a spout a well Brandreth and stone trough and a Buckett rope	6	10	0

In the bowling Green

Eight paire of boules two Sacks and a rouler with all the fences belonging to the Green	5	10	0
All the Linnen belonging to the house	35	0	0
The Cock pitt penns and other things	12	0	0
Malt oats beans Swine and one Maire	14	10	0
All other Utensills unseen or forgotten	0	12	0
	493	2	6½

45. **Bowser** – the inn servant responsible for taking money.
Canary – a sweet white malmsey from the Canary Islands.
Claret – wine from Bordeaux region.
Darnix – cloth hangings.
East dish – yeast dish.
Gimble – connecting links of machinery.
Punbowl – punchbowl.
Purr Piece – poker.
Slate book – used for recording debts.
Spout – overflow pipe.
Tarrier – instrument for extracting a bung from a barrel.
Tent – red Spanish wine.
Tunnell – a funnel.
Window shutt – shutter used to secure or darken a window.

46. Elizabeth Littleover — Prob. Inv. 194/102

Spinster. St Mary Magdalens 10.11.1699

	£	s	d
Her Purse and Apparrell and ready Money and Wages due	7	4	0
A set of Curtaines and a paire of Blanketts and one Rug	1	0	0
Eighteen yards of Hempen Cloth at Eight pence a yard	0	12	0
Three sheep at Benniworth	0	15	0
	9	11	0

47. Thomas Feris — Prob. Inv. 194/289

Glover (Tanner and Brewer) 15.4.1700

	£	s	d
Purs and aparill	30	0	0
In the Hall			
3 ovill tables 30s. 14 chares 10s. 12 pickters 9s. one fire iron and endirons and hookes and other irons belonging to it 16s 8d 2 spits and a pare of belowes 2s 6d	3	8	2
In the best Chameber			
One bedsteade and fetherbed and boulster and pillowes and hangings and other furniture belonging to it	10	0	0

4 pare of Lin shetes 40s 7 paire of hempin sheetes and 3 pare of pillow beares and 1 boulester draure 30s 4 pare more pillow beares 8s 4 table cloths 20s 3 duzen and 9 napkins 30s 4 window curtins and rods 6s 8d	6	14	8
One silver tankerd and 2 silver cups and 6 silver sponres	11	10	0
One seeing glas 15s one chist of draures 15s 9 chares 16s one fire grate and shovell and tongs 5s	2	11	0
In the seccond Chameber			
One bed steade fether bed and boulester and furniture	4	0	0
One small bedsteade and 1 coverled and 3 chists 1 trunk one voyder and some other small things	0	15	0
6 chares in the same roume	0	6	0
One plush side sadle and pillion seate	2	10	0
In the third chameber			
One bedsteade and furniture and other small things	1	6	8
In the citching			
16 pewter dishis containeing in weighte 65lb at 8d a lb	2	3	4
24 plates at 9s per dozen is	0	18	0
2 flagons 5s., 5 candlesticks 6s., 1 frying pan 4s, one dreser 12s, one table and 3 stoules and 3 chares 5s	1	12	0
2 bras potts 8s., 4 Ketles 25s., 4 scellits 4s., 1 coper pan 12d., 1 iron driping pan 18d other small things 10s	2	9	6
In the brewhouse			
One leade and brewing vesills and soe and other tubs and 7 barills	2	10	0
25 quarter of malte at	26	0	0
Guds in the shop			
5 duzen of wimins gloves 30s., 7 duzen and a halfe of mens gloves £2 9s, 20 pare of dogskin gloves 18s, 3 duzen of boyes gloves 8s, 9 paire of brichis 27s., 43 drest dog skins 35s., 47 drest Calfskins £3 10 6d, 10 buck skins £4 0s 0d, 10 doe skins 35s, 10 fanne skins 5s, 6 horse hides 24s	12	9	6
Five score white sheepe lether at £2 5s 0d	2	5	0

50 tannd sheepe lether at 1 5 0	1	5	0
50 calfe skins lether at 1 5 0	1	5	0
52 calfe skins lether at 2 10 0	2	10	0
Skins in the pitt and the brand	5	1	0
A horse and a Cow at	7	0	0
A malt screene at	0	10	0
Meterealles belonging to the trade	0	5	0
Dets gud by bond in all	38	18	6
More upon bond	12	0	0
More in lent monyes	10	0	0
More in lent moneyes	5	10	0
Dew more for rent	3	5	0
The house they now live in being a lease vallew	50	0	0
The banks lying of each side of the south bar gates	60	0	0
A house upon the bridg being the citys Lease	35	0	0
Other dets more in the booke	5	0	0
More in lent monyes	15	0	0
More as a bill doth apeare	5	10	0
	393	10	4
	(387	10	4)

47. **Brand** – torch or linstock.
Brichis – breeches.

48. Elizabeth Manby — Prob. Inv. 195/20

7.5.1701

	£	s	d
The Purse and Apparrell	700	0	0
The farthermost Chamber			
One Bedstead one fetherbed one Bolster three Blanketts one Rugg and one Quilt and one Counterpain Curtains and Vallence	6	0	0
In the same two Table Nine Chaires Eight wrought Cushons	1	15	0
In the same Room one Landskip in a frame one fire grate one fireshovell and Tongs with the Tapestry Hangings and one looking Glasse two Window Curtains and a Rod and one Table Cloth	4	5	0
In the passage Chamber			
One Bedstead one Pillow One Rod three Curtains	0	12	0

In the Maids Chamber

One Bedstead and fetherBed two Boulster one pillow two Blankitts two Coverlids Matt and Cord	2	5	0
In the same Roome Seven pillows Eight Blanketts one Chest one little Table one Box one dressing Glass	2	14	0

In the Middle chamber

One Bedstead and fetherbed one Bolster two pillows three Blanketts with Curtains and Bed Cord and Matt and Twilt	5	0	0
In the same Roome five Chaires one Table one Dressing Box with Tapestry Hangings	2	10	0

In the Dineing Room

One lookeing Glass one Table one Squab tenn Chaires ten damask Cushons one damask Carpett and a Damask Couch Bed	9	0	0
In the same One fender two paire of Cobirons with brasses three pictures in frames four Window Curtains with some Chiny ware	4	0	0
In the same Roome Three peices of Tapestry Hangings	8	0	0

In the best Chamber

One Bedstead and fetherbed one Boulster four Blankitts and one Counterpain Curtains and Vallance	8	0	0
In the same Roome one Cabinet and Tee Table	5	0	0
In the same Roome five Chaires covered with Velvet one Nest of Drawers one Trunk two Tables and one Box	2	10	0
In the same Roome one lookeing Glass with some Chiny and Shells	2	0	0
In the same Roome one Stove fire shovell and Tongs and Dogirons	1	10	0
In the same Roome three peices of Tapestry Hangings and one Truky work Carpett four Window Curtains one Table Cloth one Picture	6	0	0

More in the Best Chamber

Severall pieces of Silver plate	50	0	0
In the Stair Case fifteen pictures	3	0	0

In the Hall

Fourteen Turky work Chaires one Ovell Table	2	0	0
One Grate two Cobirons with Brass Bosis and one Sconce	1	0	0

In the Kitchin

One Iron Grate three Spitts one Jack one Grid-iron fire shovele and Tongs with hooks and Gallow Balks and severall other Irons	4	10	0
One Copper and Grate	3	10	0
One Mash Tub with all other brewing vessells	1	0	0
Four large Brass pans two small ones one Copper Boyler four brass potts one brass flower pott one fish plate and severale other Brasses	8	10	0
Two pewter Dishes three dozen of plates	4	0	0
One pewter Searston	0	6	8
One Table Six Chaires with other Utensills not seen	2	0	0

In the Seller

Six Barrills about four Chalder of Coales and other fewele	6	0	0
Table Linnings Sheets and pillowbeares and other Linings	4	0	0
	861	7	8

48. Chiny ware – china.
Landskip – a landscape painting.
Squab – mattress like cushion.

49. Richard Green **Prob. Inv. 195/245**

(Brewer) St. Swithins 14.6.1701

	£	s	d
Purse and Aparell ten pounds	10	0	0

In ye Hall

One Ovel table and 18 Leather chares	3	10	0

In ye Kitchin

For Puter and Brass	6	13	0
The Jack ye Landiron and other fireirons	3	10	0
Two Little tables 6 chares and all other furniture there	0	12	0

In ye back Kitchen

3 pott Kettels 1 drippin pan and other things	1	10	0

The Chamber over ye hall

1 Bed and furniture thereunto belonging	8	10	0
7 Cain chares	2	10	0
1 Chest of Drawers A Side board table and Stands	1	0	0
1 Looking Glass	1	5	0
1 Grate Iron Brass fireshovel tongs and horse	0	13	0
Window Curtains and hangings about ye room	2	5	6

The Chamber next

1 Bed and furniture	5	10	0
A Trunk of Linnin	4	10	0
4 Chares and other things there	0	16	0

The Chamber over ye Kitchen

1 Bed and furniture	4	10	0
Some Chares and A Little table and Look. Glass	0	17	0

In ye Closet

Plate, 1 Tanker 1 Cup 6 Spoons	11	10	0
Glasses and other things there	0	15	0
1 Chest of Linnin more	10	18	0

The Chamber over ye Sellar

1 Bed and furniture	6	0	0
1 Chest of drawers 1 table and 4 chares	1	11	6

The back chamber

1 Couch chare and other odd things	0	10	0

In ye Sellar

Ale and Cask	8	15	0
Empty cask	4	0	0

In ye brew house

A Copper and Grate	16	0	0
Tubs and others	8	0	0
Coak	3	0	0
A Clock	1	10	0
A Steel Mill	1	5	0
For hops and other things in a back Room	5	0	0
Malt 160 Quarter	160	0	0
1 horse and Mare	9	0	0
Two fabrick Leases	200	0	0
In mony in Bills in Bond and book debt Good and bad	150	0	0
For all other things seen and unseen	1	10	0
	670	16	0

49. Steel mill – a grinder.

50. George Wright **L.C.C. Admon. 1702/1**

Chandler Bale 3/4.8.1702

	£	s	d
For Purse and Apparrell	5	0	0
In ye Hall			
For a fier Grate and Irons belonging to it	1	2	0
For 6 turky work Chairs 2 tables 2 Stands pictures potts and other Small things	0	16	0
The Parlor			
2 tables 9 Caine Chairs 1 turky Chair pictures and potts of ye Chimney peice	2	8	8
The Pantory			
3 puter dishis Candlesticks and Snuffers	0	12	0
The Kitchin			
For fier Irons and Irons belonging erthen dishis	0	13	0
For a Copper Grate 1 Dozen plates 2 kettles 2 brase panns 2 Sauce panns salting tub frying pan temse and Serdges	2	7	0
For 1 Dozen of trenchers Chopping blocke etc	0	3	0
The Chamber next Street			
For a bedd bolster 2 pillows bedstead hangings and blankitts	4	0	0
For hangings in ye Roome 6 Chairs Stooles and Stands and Glasses and things over ye Chimney 2 little glass and a side bord cloth	0	19	0
The Green Room			
The Green feather bedd 2 bolsters 2 pillows 2 blankitts twilt bedstead hangings	3	0	0
(.....) bed bolster pillows 3 blankitts Coverlitt hangings bedstead	3	0	0
Chest of drawers Cubbord 3 Chairs and white potts	0	16	0
The Garett next Street			
1 feather bedd bolster hangings a table and odd things other Garet	1	4	0

The Clossitt

3 pair of sheetts 3 table cloths 1½ dozen of Napkins and other corse things	2	10	0
For 4 Silver spoones		4	0
For 2 Mairs and a Cow	6	10	0
For Coals hay and other odd things	3	0	0

The Raft house

200 whole deals 1 parcel half deals Scafle deals and others	11	12	8
5 score and 16 poles 1 barrele of tarr and Reed	5	18	0
For Rotton Store Rudd and Rozin Spanish white and allome	0	18	0

The next ware house

For 55 bunch of Latts (at 9d) Irne. 1 barrel of tarr	4	18	9
For 4 dozen of Sythes 3 barrill Crowne Sope at £4 6s and 1 firkin of ordinary at 16s	17	10	0
For half hogshead of Leaf tobacco	12	10	0
For 18 dozen of quart bottles at 2s 2d 6 dozen flagg broomes at 4s	3	3	0
For Rudd Charcoale and birch beezams	0	16	0
For a Counter and Sheles Spanish white and Empty Caskes	1	12	0

In ye Beezams house

For 48 bunch of birk beezams at 16d	2	14	0
For 3 Crates of Muggs and potts Cork links and a parcell of bottles	1	17	0

The Whiteware Chamber

For white ware and other potts and 12 lb of turky yarne	8	9	7
For 21 dozen of Candles at 4s 6d	4	14	6
For potts and Glassis in another Chamber	1	0	0

The Passage

For 10 dozen of small Muggs	0	10	0
For pots and Glassis	2	4	0

The Corse pott Chamber

For 8 hundred weight of Corse potts	2	8	0
For 28 salt fishis	0	14	0
For tinn ware	1	7	0
For 1½ hundred weight of weake and bed cords	6	1	4
For 1 bunch of Cards salt peeter and tobacco	1	16	6
For hempseed of Musterdseed Corkes and oates	1	4	0

For a saddle bridle Cutting knife and bord empty Caskes wier Riddle and Nales	1	4	6
For Goods in the Garrett	6	11	8

The Grocer Chamber

For Rasons Corse Suger Corrons	11	15	8
For pruans Rasons Brimstone	0	15	0
For Suger	2	4	0
For Redwood and Logwood	0	15	0
For traine oyle and Salad oyle	1	17	0
For 3 Lead Cesternes and Empty Casks	0	12	0
For 1 Groce of faw Cards	3	0	0
For 14 Groce of fine Corkes	0	18	8

The Candle house

A Copper and Grate	9	0	0
The troff	1	0	0
For tubbs	0	10	0
For Mould bords and Rodds	1	4	0
For knifes and odd things	0	10	0
For 10 hundredweight of fine tallow (at 34s)	17	0	0
For 6 hundredweight of Corse tallow	6	10	0
For another Copper and odd things	3	10	0

The Shopp

For 14 hundredweight of Salt	7	0	0
For 7 dozen lbs. of Candles (at 4s 6d)	1	11	6
For 18 bed cords and 9 pair bellows	1	4	0
For 7 lbs of Ordinary Indigo	0	3	6
For 2 Lardge Chafeing dishis	0	3	6
For 4 Smale Chafeing dishis	0	5	0
For 2 dozen and a half of Clamps	0	15	6
For 2 dozen of Gimlitts	0	1	6

Mors goods in the Shopp

For brushis	2	0	0
For tinn ware	1	4	0
For 14 lbs of pack thrid	0	10	6
For seeds at hangs upp	0	8	0
For house Locks and other Lockes	0	13	4
For 18 lbs of Weake (at 8d)	0	12	0
For 1 bunch of Cards and hammers	0	9	6
For potts and Glassis	0	6	0
For Cords and Links	0	5	2
For 2 hand saws and Smoothing Irons	0	3	0
For door bands Shairs and Clouts	1	10	0
For Viniger and Casks and Sand	0	12	0
For 3 stones of hopps	1	10	0
For 6 bslomes and flagg broomes	0	14	6

For Syths and Iron ware	1	1	6
For 7 Candle Stickes	0	2	4
For Goods in ye uppermost Shelfe	2	4	5
For Goods in ye Next Shelfe	3	2	4
For 12 pair of Snekes and Cattchis	0	5	6
For T Jonts	0	8	0
For parcel of HL Jonts	0	10	0
For duftails	0	18	0
For Clasps and handles	0	3	0
For parcel of Locks	2	6	6
For parcel of brass Cocks	0	12	0
For Inkle file	2	9	0
For H Jonts	0	15	0
For parcel of buttons and incle	2	12	0
For 3 peices of buckerome	1	16	0
For fustaine	0	14	0
For Canvis	0	10	0
Parcel Caddose Laces tapes Black thrid Coller white and fine thrid	4	10	0
For Goolonie 2 Dozen of Gawk pins	2	3	0
Parcel odd things	0	18	0
For 5 Groce of Caddose and parcel odd things	2	4	0
For Nales and parcel of odd things	3	4	6
For parcel of tobacco and 6 Stone of Shott	1	3	0

The Celler

3 boxis of tobacco and parcel middlin tobacco	16	16	6
For brandy Ale and Caskes	2	10	0
For herings and potts	0	12	0
For scoles and weights	2	11	10
For a New Long beame and Scoles and weights	1	10	0

The Country Shop

For deals Syths Latts Potts and beezams	1	17	0
For 2 dozen of Scuttles tarr and pitch	0	11	0
For Redwood Logwood Salt Locks bands	0	12	0
For Goods uppon ye high Shelfe	0	2	0

More Goods in ye Country Shopp

For wool Cards brushis Jonts tinnware	0	11	0
For Inkle Caddose Laces and Nales in the bing	1	0	0
For thrid pinns Rozin Boale and allome	0	4	6
For Mace Clove Ginger Galls Sprigs and Smi Nails	0	8	0
For twisted thrid blew	0	1	6
For peper brimstone and tormerick	0	3	0
For Corons Rasons and Starch	0	4	6
For bone and treakle	0	3	0
For 4 Groce of Coat buttons	0	5	0

For 2 Groce of brest buttons	0	1	6
For a Counter Shelves and other odd things	1	0	0
For money taken since he died	22	9	2
Debts owing in the books	22	16	9
Debts desperate	19	18	7
	356	14	3
	(356	14	11)

50. Beezams – besom, a broom made from a bunch of twigs.
Birk – birch.
Bing – bin.
Boale – ochre used for marking sheep.
Brimstone – sulphur.
Bslones – besom.
Buckerome – buckram.
Clouts – piece of cloth or leather to use as a patch; swaddling clothes; handkerchief.
Deals – a plank usually of fir or pine measuring 6 feet by 9 inches by 3 inches.
Faw cards – teasels for raising the nap on cloth.
Flagg broomes – brooms made with rushes or birch twigs.
Gawk pins – large pins.
Goolonie – ribbons.
Half deals – see deals above, a half deal was 1.5 inches thick.
Jonts – joints – the T, HL and H refer the shapes of particular types of joint.
Latts – thin strips of wood.
Links – torch made of tow and pitch.
Mould bord and rodds – moulds for candle making.
Raft house – timber store.
Rudd – red ochre used for cosmetics and the marking of sheep.
Salad oyle – olive oil.
Salt peeter – saltpetre, potassium nitrate.
Scafle – pole.
Serdge – candles but possibly in this context a mis-spelling for 'searce' or a sieve.
Shairs – shears.
Smi nales – smith's nails, smiddie is a form of 'smithy'.
Sneke – a latch.
Spanish white – finely powdered chalk used as a pigment or for its cleansing properties.
Sprigs – a slender mail with no head.
Tormerick – a pungent East Indian root used for making a yellow dye.
Traine oyle – oil made from boiled blubber of whale.
Weake – wick.
Wool cards – instruments with iron teeth to comb fibres of wool.

51. Mr. William Norris **D. & C. Wills 27/8**

(Steward of the Choiristers and Singing Master) The Close 12.9.1702

	£	s	d
His own wearing apparrell and money in Pockett	3	0	0
In ye Roome cald ye Hall			
An ovall Table and nine Chairs	0	14	0
A Grate and fender on ye fire hearth	0	4	0
Twenty three prints great and small	1	0	0
Curtain and ye Rod	0	1	0
The Parlour			
The two peices of hangings etc	0	18	0
Six Cane Chairs and one arm'd Chair	1	4	0
Six Cushions	0	6	0
A Squabb	0	6	0
Two Cover'd Stooles	0	3	0
An Iron Grate fire shovell and Tongs	0	6	0
An Ovall Table of firr	0	3	0
Two glass Sconces and small Pictures ore the Chimney peice	0	8	0
The Toys	0	2	0
The Best Chamber			
A feather Bed, Bolster 2 pillows blanketts Quilt Curtains and valence	5	0	0
Hangings 3 window Curtains	0	14	0
A Chest of drawers	1	0	0
Glass Table, stands etc	2	0	0
A little Table and Six Cane Chairs	1	2	0
A fire grate fender Tongs and Shovell	0	5	0
Earthen Ware and Toys on ye Chimney	0	6	8
For ye Peices of painting	0	10	0
Two Silver Salvers 2 Tankards one Cupp, one porringer 6 Salts and 12 Spoons etc. weighing 113 ounces at 5s per ounce	28	5	0
One dozen and two Table Cloaths	0	14	0
Twenty Damask Napkins	1	0	0
Two dozen of old Diaper	0	12	0
Two dozen of Huckaback	0	16	0
Two dozen of Linn napkins	0	8	0
Two old Towells 6d Monteth and Bason of Earthenware 1s	0	1	6

The Green Chamber

	£	s	d
A feather bed bolster Pillows blanketts, Curtains etc.	2	10	0
Hangings 10s Chest of Drawers £1	1	10	0
Six old Leathern Chairs	0	6	0
A firegrate, Tongs and Shovell	0	3	0
A Glass 5s prints and pictures 3s	0	8	0
For his books	0	15	0
For other odd things in ye said Room	0	2	0
Three pair of old sheets and pillow bears	0	5	0
Six pair of Coarse sheets and four coarse Table Cloaths	0	14	0
In ye Boy's Garrett			
Three small feather beds etc.	1	15	0
The Best garrett			
A feathered, bed Cloaths Curtains and hangings	0	2	0
An old Table and Six chairs	0	3	8
Two Iron doggs	0	2	0
In ye School Rome			
An Harpsicord and frame	3	0	0
Anthem books Ruled paper etc.	1	15	0
In ye Mayds roome			
A feather bed bolster etc.	0	15	0
In the Kitchen			
The Pewter and Brass	4	0	0
Firegrate, Iron, Shovell etc	0	13	4
A Jack 10s	0	10	0
Dresser Pewter Case Tables forms Hen pen and Chairs	0	10	0
One Mum Cask 2 half hogsheads and three small vessells	0	10	0
8 dozen of bottles	0	12	0
Two washing Tubbs	0	2	0
A Marble Table	0	6	8
A Garden Rowler	0	2	6
Sevrall other odd things	0	3	0
Owing from Mr. Thomas Alinson organist of ye Church of Lincoln	6	0	0
	80	2	8
	(79	4	4)

51. **Monteth** – a vessel notched at the brim to let drinking glasses hang in cold water so that the bowl of the drinking glass might be cooled.
Mum – a kind of beer originally brewed in Brunswick.

52. James Osburne **L.C.C. Admon. 1702/50**
(Linen Draper) St. Peter Arches 9.10.1702

	£	s	d
His Purse and apparell	2	10	0
Shop Goods			
10 Peices of Blackamore Linen at 20s per peice	10	0	0
2 Peices of Dowlas at £1 8s per peice	2	16	0
168 Ells of Osenbridge at 7½d per ell	5	5	0
38 Ells Ditto at 7d per ell	1	2	2
141 yardes of hukaback at 8½d per yarde	4	19	10½
15 yardes Ditto at 15d per yarde	0	18	9
30 yardes Diaper at 9d per yarde	1	2	6
2 Diaper tabell cloths at 3s	0	6	0
32 Ells of Boreslap at 10d per ell	2	1	8
4 Peices of Ell wide Garlick at 26s per peice	5	4	0
2 Peices of Jermaine at 18s per peice	1	16	0
54 Ells ditto at 16d per ell	3	12	0
35 yardes of Irish Linen at 9d per yarde	1	6	3
13 yardes of Calicoe at 9d per yarde	0	9	9
1 peice of Jermaine at	1	10	0
169 yardes of blew linen at 10d per yarde	7	0	10
159 yardes of blew Osenbridge at 7d per yarde	4	12	0
13 yardes of blew Calicoe at 14d per yarde	0	15	2
3 peices and a remnant of tickin at	1	8	0
5 peices of Scotch cloth 51 yardes ½ at 13d per yarde	2	15	0
5 peices Ditto 49 yardes at 11d per yarde	2	5	4½
4 peices of tickin at 10s per peice	2	0	0
60 Ells and ½ holland at 2s 9d per Ell	8	6	9½
59 Ells and ½ holland at 2s 2d per Ell	6	8	11
22 Ells of holland at 5s per Ell	5	10	0
25 Ells of holland at 4s per Ell	5	0	0
39 Ells of holland at 2s 6d per Ell	4	17	6
18 Ells of holland at 2s 10d per Ell	2	11	0
7 yardes of blew linen in remnants at 7d per yarde	0	4	1
107 yardes of blew linen at 6d per yarde	2	13	6
5½ yardes of blew linen at 12d per yarde	0	5	6
72 yardes of blew linen at 10d per yarde	3	0	0
16 yardes of blew Scotch cloth at 11d per yarde	0	14	8
7 yardes of blew Scotch cloth at 8d per yarde	0	4	8
16½ yardes of blew Calicoe in remnants at 6d per yarde	0	8	3
1 peice of blew Calicoe at	0	16	0
6 peices of Camerick at 12s per peice	3	12	0
2 peices Ditto at 7s 6d per peice	0	15	0
3 peices Ditto at 16s per peice	2	8	0

28 Ells of Holland at 4s 6d per Ell	6	6	0
15 Ells Ditto at 20d per Ell	1	5	10
86 Ells Ditto at 10d per Ell	12	3	8
10 Ells Ditto at 18d per Ell	0	15	0
16½ Ells Ditto at 2s per Ell	1	13	0
10 Ells Ditto at 22d per Ell	0	18	4
10 Ells Ditto at 3s per Ell	1	10	0
6 Ells Ditto at 2s 4d	0	14	0
6 Ells Ditto at 1s 6d per Ell	0	9	0
10 Ells Ditto at 2s 6d per Ell	1	5	0
2 Peices of course Osenbridge at	2	6	1
6 Ells of Holland at 3s 3d per Ell	0	19	6
9½ Ells Ditto at 4s per Ell	1	18	0
6 Ells Ditto at 20d per Ell	0	10	0
7 Ells Ditto at 18d per Ell	0	10	6
9 Ells Ditto at 2s 6d per Ell	1	2	6
4 yardes of Scotch cloth at 10d per yarde	0	3	4
20 Ells of white Osenbridge at 8½d	0	14	2
17 yardes of Printed Calicoe at 12d a yarde	0	17	0
5 yardes Ditto at 9d per yarde	0	3	9
32 yardes Ditto at 12d a yarde	1	12	0
3 Ells of Checkerd linen at 8d per Ell	0	2	0
18 yardes Printed Calicoe at 10d per yarde	0	15	0
14 yardes Ditto at 8d per yarde	0	9	4
11 yardes Ditto at 10d per yarde	0	9	2
4½ yardes at 6d per yarde	0	2	3
16 yardes at 6d per yarde	0	8	0
6 yardes at 12d per yarde	0	6	0
9 yardes at 4d per yarde	0	3	0
7 yardes at 5d per yarde	0	2	11
3½ yardes at 8d per yarde	0	2	4
4 yardes at 6d per yarde	0	2	0
7 remnants of course cloth value	1	12	4½
7 remnants of printed calicoe value	0	12	8½
18 yardes printed Calicoe at 12d per yarde	0	18	0
9½ yardes Ditto at 12d per yarde	0	9	6
18 yardes of Printed Dimothy at 7d per yarde	0	19	6
6½ yardes of hukaback at 2s per yarde	0	13	0
5 Ells of Dowlas at 11d per Ell	0	4	7
4 Ells Ditto at 12d per Ell	0	4	0
10 yardes of Blackamore Linen at 12d per yarde	0	10	0
7 Ells of Holland at 2s 2d per Ell	0	15	2
1 Peice of Dimothy at 17	0	17	0
1 Peice Ditto at 12	0	12	0
1 Peice Ditto at 14	0	14	0
1 Peice Ditto at 12	0	12	0
10 yardes Ditto at 10d per yarde	0	8	4
14 yardes Ditto at 8d per yarde	0	9	4
1 peice Ditto at 13s	0	13	0

14 yardes Ditto at 8d per yarde	0	9	4
1 peice Ditto at 10s	0	10	0
14 yardes Ditto at 8d per yarde	0	9	4
1 Peice at 10s	0	10	0
19½ yardes Dimothy at 10d per yarde	0	16	3
23½ yardes of Scotch cloth at 10d per yarde	0	19	7
5 dozen English rumalls at 9s per dozen	2	5	0
23 yardes white Calicoe at 12d per yarde	1	3	0
6 yardes narrow holland at 18d per yarde	0	9	0
6 yardes Ditto at 11d per yard	0	5	6
6½ yardes Blackamore at 13d per yarde	0	7	0½
6 Ditto at 10d per yarde	0	5	0
40 yardes of cullerd linen at 6d per yarde	1	0	0
17 yardes of blackamore at 8d per yarde	0	11	4
3½ yardes Ditto at 6d per yarde	0	1	9
12 neckcloths at 10d	0	10	0
5½ yardes of blackamore at 12d per yarde	0	5	6
4½ yardes of Callicoe at 10d per yarde	0	3	9
8½ yardes of Ditto at 9d per yarde	0	6	4½
9 Ells of Jermaine at 18d per Ell	0	13	6
Some ould Peices of Calicoe value	0	2	6
2 Peices of Callicoe at 9s per peice	0	18	0
12 yardes ditto at 9d per yarde	0	9	0
1 peice of Genting at	0	6	0
3½ yardes of Ditto at 12d per yarde	0	3	6
29 yardes Ditto at 10d per yarde	1	4	2
31 Ells of Jermaine at 15d per Ell	1	18	9
3½ Ells Ditto at 10d per Ell	0	2	11
4 yards Genting at 6d per yarde	0	2	0
68 yardes of Stript Scotch cloth at 7d per yard	1	19	8
3 yardes of Dimothy at 6d per yard	0	1	6
2 peices of Stript muslin	3	0	0
36½ yardes of Stript muslin at 2s per yarde	3	13	0
15 yardes Ditto at 16d per yarde	1	0	0
6 yardes Ditto at 7d per yarde being Damaged by mice	0	3	6
43½ yardes Ditto at 2s per yarde	4	7	0
1 Peice Ditto at	1	15	0
17 yardes Ditto at 3s per yarde	2	11	0
11 yardes Ditto at 18d per yarde	0	16	6
1 Peice Ditto at	1	8	0
2 Peices Ditto at	2	16	0
18 yards Ditto at 16d per yarde	1	4	0
1 Peice 13 yardes at 12d per yarde	0	13	0
18½ yardes Ditto at 10d per yarde	0	15	5
9 yardes Ditto at 3s per yarde	1	7	0
18½ yardes of Cameriks at 18d per yare	1	7	9
5 yardes Ditto at 12d per yarde	0	5	0

9½ yardes Ditto Stript at 3s per yarde	1	8	6
10 yardes Ditto at 22d per yarde	0	18	4
16½ Ells of Allkemore holland at 2s per Ell	1	13	0
1 peice Jermaine at	1	8	0
6 Ells Ditto at 18d per Ell	0	9	0
10 Ells Ditto at 12d per Ell	0	10	0
1 peice of Garlick at	0	17	0
2 Peices of Osenbridge at 10s per peice	1	0	0
9 Ells Ditto at 6d per Ell	0	4	6
10 yardes course packing at 4d per yarde	0	3	4
16 yardes of Irish Cloth at 10d per yarde	0	13	4
24 yardes of hukaback at 6d per yarde	0	12	0
3 peices of Dimothy at	1	17	0
9 Ells Ditto at 15d per Ell	0	11	3
2 yardes Scotch cloth at 9d per yarde	0	1	6
20 yardes of narrow blew linen at 5d per yarde	0	8	4
39½ yardes of Cullerd linen at 6d per yarde	0	19	9
18 black hoods at 3s 6d and 9 at 3s	4	10	0
15 white hoods at £1 10s and 14 Ganse hoods at 6d	1	17	0
Some Silk tipitts and round Scarves value	0	18	4
6 tipitts at 12d	0	6	0
43 Ells of narrow black allamode at 2s 6d per Ell	5	7	6
8 Ells Ditto at 2s per Ell	0	16	0
A percell of caps and Some neckcloths value	0	15	6
A percell of bookes	2	12	0
A percell of thred and tape and fringes value	2	0	0
81 yardes of blew Scotch cloth at 12d	4	1	0
1 peice of blew linen 27 yardes at 7d	0	15	9
64 yardes of Scotch cloth at 9d a yarde	2	8	0
A percell of lace value	1	15	0
A percell of women's Girdles and purses and hare cuffs	0	10	0
4 Wastcotes at 5s	1	0	0
25 yardes of Stuff at 6d and 16 yardes at 9d per yarde	1	4	6
16 yardes of Printed Stuff at 9d per yarde	0	12	0
26 yardes of Printed Stuff at 6d per yarde	0	13	0
A Percell of Gloves to value	2	0	0
66 yardes of course Canvis at 4d per yarde	1	2	0
Some remnants of Callicoe and other odd things	0	5	0
A percell of Scotch halfe pennys in value	0	7	6
The Shelves and Counters and boxes in ye Shop	1	10	0

In the first low roome

1 fier grate with fier Shufle and tongues 7 Chares 2 tabells and other odd things there to value	1	5	0

In the Kittchin

	£	s	d
10 Pewter dishes and a bason 1 brass pott and a pan and an Ould Dresser and some trenchers	3	5	0

In the little Parler

1 ovill tabell 6 Chares and some bottles an ould bed stead an ould chare and 5 beesoms some pitt coale a washing tub and an ould barrell	2	18	4

In the Garden Chamber

1 bedstead with an ould tickin Stuft with Straw and a little trundle bed stead to value	0	12	0

In the middle Chamber

1 bedstead with hangings and a little fether bed and 6 Chares	2	15	0

In the best Chamber

1 bedstead with matt and cord a fetherbed and 2 pillows	2	15	0
4 paire window Curtins and an ould bed stead with ye beding 1 little tabell 1 stoole 2 boxes	1	14	0
1 Gray Mare bridle and Sadell	3	10	0

In the debt book

In bonds and book debts which there is noe likelyhood of ever getting	485	5	2
In other Debts good and bad	98	16	10
	864	15	10½
	(865	15	10½)
In addition			
Goods assigned to a bill of sale	141	18	1
And another	318	8	10

52. **Alkemore** – a red dyed linen.
Blackamore – a black dyed linen.
Cammerick – cambric.
Dimothy – Dimity, a stout cotton with raised patterns and figures.
Ganse – fancy, embroidered tapes used to edge hoods.
Garlic – a linen, originally from Pomeranian Silesia.
Genting – a fine linen cloth.
Jermaine – wool cloth of kind originally made in Germany.
Packing – cloth for wrapping or padding.
Rumalls – romall, handkerchief, often used as a scarf.
Scotch cloth – a coarse woollen.
Scotch half pennies – possibly used as trade tokens.
Tipitt – scarf, cape, trailing part of headdress.

53. Godfrey Hanson **Prob. Inv. 197/44**

Miller St. Michaels Mount 2.10.1703

	£	s	d
In purse and Apparrell	1	0	0
One large Oake Table and three Stoles with a little furr Table 8 bass Chayres one bad wanded Chayre all in the house	0	10	0
One Warming pan	0	2	0
One Paress Cubbard with some Earthenware all in the house with one Class Case	0	3	6
In the Buttery			
One Grate with fyre Shovell and tongs 2 kettle pans and 2 little panns one large great pann one brass pott 4 little pewter dishes 3 Candlesticks one large pewer flaggon with all other materialls thereunto belonging	1	10	0
In the Wash House			
One washing Tubb with some small other things thereunto belonging	0	3	4
The Linnens			
Three payre of sheetes with Three payre of billow bears one Table Cloth large and a little Tabble Cloth Eight napkins	1	10	0
In the Little Chamber			
Two bedds and bedding with 2 feather bedds all thereunto belonging 2 Chests one Screene with one bass Chayre	3	1	6
In the Large Chamber			
One bedstead and featherbed and all thereunto belonging to the bedd one little stoole one Trunke six bass Chayres Coloured one wanded Chayre one press Cubbard	3	5	0
In the Garrett			
One quarter of wheat Rye and barley and halfe a quarter	1	0	0
One strike shepp with some other things	0	5	0
One bedstead	0	2	0
One Spining Wheele	0	1	6
One large mill Rope and Small Ropes	0	5	0
One payre of Cart Wheeles with a Leather and Sales with some other things thereunto belonging all in the Washhouse	0	10	0

	£	s	d
One Mill standing and being udard the Comon comonly called or knowne by the name of ye Spring Mill in the City of Lincolne upon Lease	38	0	0
	53	8	0
	(51	8	10)

53. **Billow bears** – pillow coverings.
Paress – press.

54. William Pell **L.C.C. Admon. 1706/92**

Victuler 6.7.1706

	£	s	d
Purse and apparrell	10	0	0
In debts good and bad	10	0	0
In the Hall			
One large oake table and one oake ovall table	0	16	0
Two armed Chairs four bass chairs and some ordinary pictures	0	16	0
In the Kitchin			
Fourteen pewter dishes large and small	1	17	0
Eighteen pewter plates	0	12	0
One pewter flagon one pewter Quart four pewter pints four pewter porringers two pewter Chamber potts and some other pewter things of small value	0	12	6
Three brass panns two brass Kettles and one small brass pott and one small Copper Cann	1	5	0
One brass warming pann and four brass Candlesticks	0	9	0
Some small muggs and other earthen waire	0	2	0
One Andiron Grate and froggs a paire of tongs a horse gallow balke and hooks	0	15	0
One Jack and weights two spitts two iron Candlesticks and one smoothing iron	0	16	0
One paire of bellows Saltbox trenchers and trencher Hecks one wooden pye plate one Candlebox and grater	0	3	6
In books	0	7	0
One small looking Glasse and some other small glasses	0	2	0
Two tables two stools and eight ordinary Chairs	0	10	0

In the Brewhouse

One Copper and the grates	7	0	0
One mashing tubb one gathering tubb one underbeck one guile tubb and one Soe	3	0	0
One pewter Cooler	0	15	0
In the little Buttery			
One tinn dripping pann one tinn pasty pann a Lanthorne and some other householdstuff	0	10	0
In the Cellars			
One hogshed and Seven half hogsheds of ale and Caske	10	10	0
Some other small Caskes and ale	2	0	0
In the best Parlour			
One good bed with all its furniture	7	0	0
One Chest of drawers one oake ovall table one other little table a small box and eight bass Chairs	1	7	0
One small looking glass one glass-case severall figures and pictures	0	8	0
One iron grate with brass bosses	0	5	0
In the parlour Chamber			
One bed with all its furniture seven ordinary chairs and one draw bed	3	5	0
In the malt Chamber			
In malt	3	0	0
In the house Chamber			
One bed with the furniture one Chest six ordinary chairs and a small table	3	0	0
In the next roome			
One Chaff bed	0	6	0
In the Coal house			
In wood and Coals	4	0	0
In the upper room			
One pair of Querns	0	10	0
In Linnen ten paire of sheets fine and course	3	0	0
Eight paire of pillow-beers three dozen of Napkins and some other Linnen	2	10	0
	80	17	0

55. John Hobman **Prob. Inv. 200/34**

(Butcher) 2.1.1707

	£	s	d
Purse and Apparill	1	0	0
In the house			
Five Score and twelve pound of pewter	3	10	8
One Warmeing pann 2 Copper Cans 3 Candle sticks one Scummer and 2 bras ladles	0	7	0
One Dresser and pewter Case and a little Cuberd	0	10	0
Thre Tables and twelve Chares	0	10	0
One Press 2 Glasscases with Earthern ware in them	0	6	0
One fire Iren one Gallowbalke 2 Endirons 3 Reckon hookes 2 pare of tongues one horse 3 Candlesticks with other Small Irons	1	0	0
One Gunn and a Screene	0	4	0
In the Kitching			
Three Brass pots and one little morter	0	10	0
Two Brass pans 4 Scellets and 2 pots	0	10	0
4 barills 8s : 3 tinn Driping pans one Iron Driping pan one Cullinder one Chafing dish	0	12	0
Earthern ware 2s : 3 dussen of trenchers, one trencher Hacke 2 leather flackets	0	5	0
Two water Kitts one wash tub two trays one Soe and one pann with other Meterialls	1	0	0
In the Shop			
Two Clevers 2 blockes Scailes and Weights two Chists and hookes and other meterialls	1	0	0
In the Chamber over the house			
One Bedstead Curton and Vallands matt and Coords Matriss fether beed boulster 5 blanckets and rugg	3	0	0
Two Chists of drawers 9 Chares one stoole and hanging Shelves one Iron graite fire Shovell and tongues with other meterialls	2	10	0
Six Pillow Bears 11 Sheets 2 Window Curtons	1	18	0
Fowr Table Clothes 3 Dussen of Napkins 5 pare of Corse Sheets	2	8	0

In the Chamber over the Shopp

One bedstead mat Coard and Curtons fetherbeed one boulster 4 pillows 3 blanckets one Rugg and one pare of Sheets	2	10	0
One Bedstead mor one fether bed one boulster 2 pillows one pare of Sheets 2 blanckets one Rugg and one pare of Sheets two blanckets 2 Coverlids mat Coord and matteris	1	13	4
One Bedstead fetherbeed one boulster one Pillow one blancket and one Sheet 2 Cuverlids Matt Coord and Matris	1	10	0
Six Chares one Stoole one table 3 boxes 2 Cushons with other things	0	10	0

In the Garrat

One bedstead and Chaft bed 2 blanckets one Coverlid and one pare of Sheets	0	10	0
Two wheeles one Chare 2 Stooles 2 boxes one Chist one Sidsadle one pillion Seate With other meterialls	0	13	4

In the Slouter House

Two Sheepe Skins 2 blockes 2 neate Roopes one neate tree, one felling ax with other Meterialls	1	0	0
One mare and one Gelding 3 Sadles and 3 bridles	3	10	0
One Small Searstern and Cooles	0	13	4
Despret Deets in the Booke	5	0	0
	38	10	8

55. **Neate roopes** – ropes for tethering or hoisting carcases of cattle.
Neate tree – tethering frame.

56. William Faux **L.C.C. Admon. 1708/52**

Alderman (Mercer and Maltster) 10.5.1708

	£	s	d
Purse and apparell	44	6	0
89 ounces of Plate 5s per ounce	22	5	0
136 yards of Druget 18d per yard	10	4	0
168 yards of Shalloon 14d per yard	9	16	0
49 yards of Shag 3s per yard	7	7	0
1 piece of Sagathee 30s 1 piece of Black Damask	2	13	0

	£	s	d
1 piece Blew Damask 20s 2 pieces Cullered Damask 18s	2	16	0
3 pieces Cantaloon Stufs 20s 1 piece Stuf 8s	3	8	0
137 yards Cantaloon Stuf 4d per yard	2	5	8
13 pieces Stuf 13s per piece 1 piece Stript Camblet 30s per piece	9	19	0
162 yards Antherite 12d per yard 60 yards Damask 8d per yard	10	2	0
1 piece Scarlet and White Ditto 26s 430 yards Stuf 6d per yard	12	1	0
92 yards half silks 51 yards Black Damask 12d	4	9	4
135 yards Stuf 7d per yard 22 yards Stuf 6d per yard	4	9	9
96 yards Silk Crape 8d per yard	3	4	0
225 yards Stuf 6d per yard 32 yards Stuf 5d per yard	6	5	10
21 yards Callin	1	1	0
14 yards White Crape 8d per yard 2½ yards Black Shag 3s per yard		16	10
A Remnant Girth Web 2s 6d 8 yards Stript Searge 12d a yard		10	6
39 yards Drugets in Remnants 10d per yard	1	12	6
67 yards Lineing Silks 12d per yard 79 yards Wadding 4d per yard	4	13	4
154 yards Stuf in Remnants 4d per yard	2	11	4
6½ yards Black Flannel 18d per yard 1 piece Dimothy 18s	1	7	9
5 yards Dimothy 9d per yard 2 pieces fustian 15s per piece	1	13	9
69 yards Thickset fustian 8d per yard	2	6	0
14 yards Ticking 12d per yard 19 yards Printed Calico 18d per yard	2	2	6
82 yards Buckeram 8d per yard 38 yards Dyed Lyn 8d per yard	4	0	0
26 yards white Ossinbridge 6d per yard		13	0
2 petticotes 2s 6d per piece 7 yards Callico 12d per yard		12	0
7 yards Canvis 18d per yard 2½ yards Canvis 6d per yard		11	9
2½ Dozen Shamy Skins 5s 10 Large Ditto 9d per piece	1	0	0
2 Cullered Ditto 15d per piece		2	6
37 Lustring 3s 6d per yard	6	9	6
9½ lb Cullered Thred 2s per lb 14 lb Black and Brown 20d per lb	2	2	4
3½ lb Cullered Thred 14d per lb 6 pieces holland Tape 9d per piece		8	7
1 piece Narrow Ditto 6d 2 Dozen Wash Balls 12d per dozen		2	6

Item	£	s	d
1½ Dozen Balls 6d per dozen 14 quire Beste paper 6d per quire		7	9
1 Ream paper 7s 17 quire Ditto 4d per quire		12	8
12 quire Guills Ditto 3d per quire 2 lbs Number Thred 3s per lb		9	0
1 gross 9 Dozen Mettle Coate Buttons 4s per gross		7	0
1 gross Ditto 3s 4 Dozen brest Ditto 1½d per dozen		8	0
1 Dozen pins 8s 3 pieces White filliting 8d per piece		10	0
1½ lbs Nuns Thred 4s per lb 21½ lbs Mohair 5s per lb	5	13	6
Cullered Sewing and Sticking Silke 4 lbs 8s per lb	1	12	0
Light Ditto 3 lb 2 ounces 12s per lb	1	17	6
6 pair Mens Thred Hose 2s per pair 6 pair Womens Hose 16d per pair	1	0	0
1 pair fine Ditto 2s 1 pair fine Scarlet hose 5s		7	0
3 pair Rowling hose 2s 4d 4 pair Shorte Ditto 2d		13	8
1 pair White hose 2s 8d 3¾ ounces Silver Thread 3s per ounce		13	11
2¾ ounces Gold Thred 4s per ounce 2 ounces Gold Lace 3s 6d per ounce		18	0
6 ounces Silver Lace and Cord 3s per ounce		18	0
1½ gross Silver and gold Buttons 10s per gross		15	0
5 Silk Handkercheifs 20d		15	0
5 pieces ferrit 4s 6d per piece 2 pieces Narrow Ditto 3s per piece		8	6
2 pieces Ribon 5s per piece 1½ pieces Love Ribon 5s per piece		17	6
1 gross Caddas 6s per gross 4 pieces Galloon 3s per piece		18	0
3 pieces Stay Braids 8d per piece 3 pieces Stay Cord 8d per piece		4	0
10 pair White Lamb Gloves 10d per pair		8	4
9 pair Ditto 10d per pair 10 pair Ditto 5d per pair		13	8
9 pair Ditto 9d per pair 2 pair Norway Doe 15d per pair		9	3
5 pair Ditto Mens 8d per pair 9 pair Mens Wash 7d per pair		8	7
12 pair Mens White Lamb 6d per pair		6	0
2 Dozen 4 pair Womens Sad Sheep 6d per pair		14	0
8 pair Womens Wash 8d per pair		5	4
7 pair Womens Dyd Shamy 12d 4 pair Wash Mittins 8d		9	8
7 pair Womens White Lamb 6d per pair		3	6

3 pair Wash Lamb 8d per pair 7 pair Girles Ditto 3d per pair		3	9
3 pair Ditto att 4d per pair 1 pair gloves 12d		2	0
9 pair Wash Mittins 4d per pair		3	0
9 pair Womens Kidd 12d per pair 9 pair Gloves 3d per pair		11	3
30 yards Hatband Crape 12d	1	10	0
4 yards Black Taby 2s 6d per yard		10	0
5 yards More … Taby 4s per yard 1 petticote Lace 3s	1	3	0
1 piece Silk Laceing 3s 2½ Dozen Silk Laces 3s per dozen		10	6
4 gross Coate Buttons 3s per gross 4 gross brests Ditto 12d per gross		16	0
3 gross gimp Coates 12d 3 gross brests Ditto 6d per gross		4	6
2 gross White Thred Buttons 10d per gross		1	8
2½ gross haire Coate Buttons 12d per gross 1 gross brest 6d		3	0
20 yards Matting 2d per yard 1 lb Sken Silk 10s		13	4
3 pieces filliting 8d per piece 4 pieces Inckle 6d per piece		4	0
5½ lbs packthred 8d per lb 4lbs Shop Thred 4d per lb		5	0
Shott and Powder 12d Laces 12d		2	0
Black Ribon		1	0
1lb Sinimon 6s 1lb Mace 16s	1	2	0
1lb 6ozs Nutts at 8s per lb 6lbs Black peper 12d		17	0
4lbs white peper 2s per lb and 2lbs Jemaco peper 2s 6d		10	6
5lbs blak ginger 6d per lb 9lbs white ginger 8d per lb		8	6
8½lbs Black ginger 4d per lb		2	10
4½lbs Cariway Seeds 2d per lb 7lb annyseeds 5d per lb		3	8
4½lbs Indico 15d per lb 4lb Stone Blew 6d per lb		7	7
112 lbs Suger	2	10	0
12lbs Suger 6d per lb 40 lbs Pruans 3d per lb		16	0
29½ lbs Tobacco 14d per lb	1	14	0
21 lbs Tobacco 9d per lb		15	9
68 lbs Tobacco 9d per lb	2	11	0
18 lbs Loaf Suger att 6d Scales and Weights 10s		19	0

In ye Parlour

Seaven Cain Chairs		17	6
A Little Table		1	0
A Large Looking Glass	1	5	0

	£	s	d
5 Picktures		7	6
A Stove fire Shovel Tonges and fender		5	0
Earthern Ware and glasses in a Closet		1	6
In ye Hall			
A Case of Pistols and a Sword		6	0
6 bass Chairs		2	6
A Table		4	6
2 Dozen of pewter plates		16	0
2 Dishes and 2 Salvers 7s a pewter Cistern 2s		9	0
A Coffee Mill with other Small things		2	6
Knifes forkes and Baskets		5	0
In ye Cellar			
4 half hogsheads		8	0
9 Dozen Bottles 15d per Dozen		11	3
A Salting Tub 2 Wooden horses etc		2	0
In ye Kitchen			
1 pair Brass Candlesticks and pair Iron Ones		2	0
A warming pan 3s a Lead Cestern 25s	1	8	0
A Small Copper 12s an Old fire grate 3s		15	0
A Little Kettle pot and Sawce pan		2	0
2 Washing Tubs 2 Kitts and other things		4	0
A frying pan		4	0
A Coffee pot Copper can and Mugs		4	0
In ye Chamber Over ye Hall			
One Bedstead with Curtains and Twilt 2 Blankets and featherbed	4	0	0
6 Dutch Matted Chairs		9	0
A Glass Table and Stands		12	0
Ye hangings of ye Room		8	0
2 pair Window Curtains		5	0
2 Sconces and pictures On ye Stair Case		2	0
In ye Chamber Over ye Shop			
One Bedstead with Curtains and Twilt	1	5	0
2 pair Window Curtains		5	0
A Scrutor 15s a Chest of Drawers 2s		17	0
A Close press 5s a Close Stool 4s a Table 12d		10	0
In ye Stable			
A horse Saddle and bridle	3	4	6
Empty Casks and Lumber in ye Ware house and Stable		10	0
In ye Malt Killn			
46 quarters Malt	46	0	0
A hair Cloth and Screel	1	1	6

40 Strike of Coke		13	4
Good debts	295	11	0
The House Tenements and Gardens	400	0	0
	1000	10	0
Bad debts	211	0	0

56. **Annyseeds** - anniseeds.
Antherite - antherire, a kind of poplin.
Black ginger - unscraped root of East Indian ginger.
Buckeram - buckram.
Callim - collimencoe, a glossy woollen stuff.
Cantaloons - woollen stuff from West Country.
Flannel - open woollen stuff of loose texture.
Fustian - coarse cloth with linen warp and cotton weft.
Guills - quills.
Nuns thread - fine, white, sewing thread.
Rowl hose - stockings the tops of which can be rolled up or down the legs.
Scrutor - escritoir.
Shag - a worsted with velvet nap on one side.
Sinimon - cinnamon, a spice.
Shen silk - thread silk.
Stay braid - band of woven linen or other material ornamenting or padding underbodice.
Wadding - cotton lining material.
Wash balls - a ball of soap.

57. William Warriner — Prob. Inv. 203/381

Cordwinder St. Martins 1712

	£	s	d
Purse and Aparrill	5	0	0
In ye House			
One ovill table one other table 6 Chaires	0	16	0
One warming pan 2 Brass Candle Sticks 2 Iron Candlesticks one paire of bellows 1 Salt Box A Candle Box one Smoothing Iron with some small pictures	0	10	0
In ye Parler			
One Bed will all furniture	4	0	0
In ye Kitching			
One Kettle Pot 2 bras pots 2 bras pans one Skellet	0	13	0
One table 2 washing tubs 2 barrills a Searge a tems and a sive a water Kit with other od things	0	11	6

In ye Butterry

Three peuter Dishes one Dussin of plates a frying pan with other od things	0	10	0

In ye first chamber

One bed with all furniture	2	10	0
One table one Chest 2 trunks and 2 boxes	0	10	0

In ye Second Chamber

One small Bed with other od Things	0	10	0

In ye Shopp

Ten paire of Boots for men one paire for boys	2	18	0
Mens Shoes 3 Dussin and one paire	6	15	0
Womens Shoes 3 Dussin and 6 paires	4	4	0
Boys and Girls Shoes one Dussin and 10 paire	1	13	0
Childrens Shoes one Dussin one paire	0	13	0
Mens Lasts 4 Dussin womens 3 Dussin Boys and Girls Lasts 2 Dussin	0	18	0
Four pieces of Skins	0	6	6
A Grose of Heeles	0	11	0
One paire of Boot trees 2 paire of Shoetrees a frier a hammer and two Seates	0	6	0
Three paire of Offills Drest	1	16	0
One wrought Downhide one piece of Back	1	0	0
	36	11	0

57. **Boot tree** – block on which a boot is shaped.
Down hide – skin of a young beast with little hair.
Frier – vessel used for frying fish.
Last – the wooden model of a foot on which shoes were shaped.
Offill – odds and ends of wood, iron or leather; waste wood for kindling.
Seate – a piece of leather sewn to the shoe as foundation for a heel.
Shoe tree – block on which a shoe is shaped.

58. Charles Newcomen — L.C.C. Admon. 1714/65

Woollen Draper (...).1713

Goods in ye Shop

	£	s	d
24 yards of fine gray Cloth att 10s 6d per yard	12	12	0
15 yards Ditto att 13s 6d per yard	10	2	6
9 yards Light Drab att 12s per yard	5	18	0
13 yards Ditto att 11s per yard	7	3	0
13 yards Ditto att 8s 6d per yard	5	10	6

6 yards Snuff Couler'd Ditto att 11s per yard	3	6	0
7 yards Sad Cullered Ditto att 8s per yard	2	16	0
10 yards Ditto att 9s per yard	4	10	0
10 yards Ditto att 7s 6d per yard	3	15	0
12 yards Ditto att 8s per yard	4	16	0
12 yards fine Ditto att 13s per yard	7	16	0
14 yards Cyniment Cullered Ditto att 11s per yard	7	14	0
7 yards Ditto att 12s per yard	4	4	0
6 yards Ditto att 7s 6d per yard	2	5	0
7 yards Light Ditto att 10s per yard	3	10	0
4 yards Ditto att 9s per yard	1	16	0
7 yards Snuff Cullered Ditto att 8s per yard	2	16	0
5 yards Drab Ditto att 8s per yard	2	0	0
4 yards Ditto att 8s per yard	1	12	0
4 yards Ditto att 6s per yard	1	4	0
5 yards Sad Cullered Ditto att 11s per yard	2	15	0
6 yards Ditto att 7s per yard	2	2	0
4 yards Ditto att 7s per yard	1	8	0
3 yards Ditto att 10s per yard	1	10	0
36 yards Ditto in Remnants att 7s per yard	12	12	0
14 yards broad Cloth att 5s 6d per yard	3	17	0
3 yards more Ditto att 5s 6d per yard	0	16	6
11 yards Ditto att 5s per yard	2	15	0
14 yards Ditto att 7s per yard	4	18	0
13 yards fine Ditto att 10s per yard	6	10	0
11 yards Ditto att 8s per yard	4	8	0
9 yards Ditto att 12s per yard	5	8	0
12 yards Drab Ditto att 7s 6d per yard	4	10	0
6 yards Ditto att 7s per yard	2	2	0
10 yards Ditto at 7s 6d per yard	3	15	0
11 yards Ditto att 4s 4d per yard	2	4	0
2 yards half gray Ditto att 7s per yard	0	17	6
6 yards Green Ditto att 5s 6d per yard	1	13	0
20 yards Light Blew att 6s per yard	6	0	0
14 yards Ditto at 6s per yard	4	4	0
17 yards Ditto in Remnants at 4s per yard	3	8	0
20 yards broad black Cloth att 7s per yard	7	0	0
12 Ditto att 8s 6d per yard	5	2	0
9 yards Ditto att 10s per yard	4	10	0
11 yards Ditto fine att 12s per yard	6	12	0
5 yards Ditto att 10s per yard	2	10	0
15 yards Ditto fine att 12s per yard	9	0	0
8 yards Ditto att 5s 6d per yard	2	4	0
7 yards Ditto att 7s 4d per yard	2	9	0
5 yards Ditto att 8s per yard	2	0	0

6 yards Ditto in 2 Remnants att 6s 6d per yard	1	19	0
9 yards Queens Cloth 7s 4d per yard	3	3	0
23 yards Devonshire plaine att 3s 4d per yard	3	16	8
22 yards Ditto att 4s 4d per yard	4	8	0
11 yards Ditto att 3s per yard	1	13	0
15 yards Ditto att 3s 6d per yard	2	12	6
12 yards Ditto att 3s 6d per yard	2	2	0
10 yards Ditto att 3s 6d per yard	1	15	0
9 yards Ditto att 4s per yard	1	16	0
14 yards Ditto att 4s 4d per yard	2	16	0
30 yards Ditto in Remnants att 3s 4d per yard	4	10	0
21 yards Devonshire Kersey att 4s per yard	4	4	0
7 yards Ditto att 4s 6d per yard	1	11	6
29 yards Ditto in small Remnants att 2s 6d per yard	3	12	6
9 yards Darke Gray att 3s per yard	1	7	0
18 yards York Shire Kersey att 2s 8d per yard	2	8	0
18 yards Ditto att 2s 6d per yard	2	4	0
10 yards Ditto att 2s per yard	1	0	0
15 yards Ditto att 2s 6d per yard	1	17	6
19 yards Ditto att 2s 8d per yard	2	10	8
15 yards Ditto att 20d per yard	1	5	0
17 yards Ditto att 22d per yard	1	11	2
9 yards Ditto att 20d per yard	0	15	0
10 yards Ditto att 2s 6d per yard	1	6	8
8 yards Ditto att 16d per yard	0	10	8
8 yards Ditto att 20d per yard	0	13	4
10 yards Ditto att 2s per yard	1	0	0
23 yards Ditto att 2s 4d per yard	2	6	0
20 yards Ditto att 2s per yard	2	0	0
40 yards Ditto in Small Remnants att 2d per yard	2	0	10
3 yards broad Cloth att 8s per yard	1	4	0
66 yards broad Cloths in very small Remnants att 2s 6d per yard	8	15	0
42 yards of half thick Kersey att 12d per yard	2	2	0
30 yards of Swann Skinn att 18d per yard	2	5	0
30 yards of white flannell att 8d per yard	1	0	0
18 yards Ditto att 12d per yard	0	18	0
30 yards Ditto att 10d per yard	1	5	0
37 yards black Ditto att 13d per yard	2	0	1
14 yards Ditto att 16d per yard	0	18	8
17 yards Ditto att 10d per yard	0	14	2
10 yards blew plane att 10d per yard	0	8	4
9 yards white flannell att 14d per yard	0	10	8
13 yards of Yallow plaine att 12d per yard	0	13	0
20 yards of Base att 10d per yard	0	16	8
11 yards Cotten att 6d per yard	0	5	6

	£	s	d
For Counters and Shelves in ye shop 40s	2	0	0
Debts in the Booke	100	0	0

Goods in the House

Purse and apparrell	10	0	0

Goods in ye Hall

Three tables	0	10	0
13 bass botton Chaires att 8d	0	8	8
For Gunn and some other things	0	8	0
A Screen 8s	0	8	0
14 pewter Dishes 2 Dozeen and 10 plates 2 Salvers and 2 Rings weight 7 Stone 5 pound	3	0	1
A brass pann 10lb att 6d per pound	0	5	0
A brass pann 7lb att 6d per pound	0	3	6
A kettle pott 9lb att 6d per pound	0	4	6
A pott 5lb att 6d per pound	0	2	6
1 Saws pann	0	1	0

Goods in ye Kitchen

A warming pann and stew pann	0	5	0
4 brass Candlesticks a Chafeing dish and Copper Cann	0	5	0
For a Jack	0	10	0
A Land Iron end Irons and a horse	0	10	0
Fire shovell tongues 3 spitts and some other things	0	8	0
A Dresser pewter Case Table trencher heck	0	10	0
6 Chaires a pair of Bellows and some other things	0	2	0

In the Pantrey

1 Napkin press	0	5	0
A Lead and Salting tubb	0	5	0
A Tinn Beyler	0	1	0

In the Celler

2 Emty hogsheads and 5 half	0	16	0
2 horses 1 bing and a Cupboard	0	2	6
Coake and Billitting	0	15	0

In the Dineing roome

1 Large Looking glass	1	10	0
12 Cane Chaires att 2s 6d	1	10	0
A Stove fire shovell and tongues	1	0	0
A Deske and Table	0	15	0
For Toys on ye Chimney peice	0	10	0

10 Picktures	0	10	0
Hangings of the Room	0	15	0
In the Best Chamber			
For Curtains and beadstead and feather bed in ye best rooms	8	0	0
2 Looking glases	1	10	0
A Table and Dressing boxes	0	10	0
8 Cane Chaires att 4s	1	12	0
1 Easey Chaire	0	15	0
A Stove fire Shovell and Tongues	0	15	0
For Picktures and Toys	0	8	0
Window Curtains and hangings	0	18	0
In ye other Chamber			
1 feather bed and hangings	3	0	0
1 Case of Drawers	1	0	0
9 Bass Chaires	0	9	0
For Irons in the Chimney	0	5	0
In the Nursery Chamber			
A feather bed hangings and Window Curtains	3	0	0
A little Canopy Bed	0	10	0
An old Case of Drawers	0	5	0
Awanded Chair and 2 others	0	3	0
In ye Garrett			
For a bed and beadstead and other old things	1	0	0
A Serge and 2 Temses	0	2	0
In the other Garrett			
A bed and hangings	1	10	0
A Jappand Liestren punch bowl 2 Candlesticks and a Sett of Casters	2	0	0
2 Dozen of Damask Napkins	1	4	0
1 Damask Table Cloth	0	10	0
2 Dozen Coarse Napkins 6d	0	12	0
6 pair Sheets att 4s	1	4	0
6 pillow bears	0	6	0
1 Silver Tankard with 26 Ounces and half 1 Silver Cupp a Mugg and Salt and 10 Spoons	16	12	6
For hay 20s	1	0	0
	468	10	4
	(480	13	4)

58. Base – coarse woollen with loose texture and long nap.
Beyler – vessel for boiling water.
Broadcloth – best quality woollen cloth.
Cotten – fibre used to make candlewick.

Cyniment - yellowish brown.
Devonshire plaine - West Country flannel.
Drab - thick woollen cloth.
Japand - an imitation of oriental lacquering.
Liestren - ?
Queens Cloth - unidentified textile.
Swanskin - good quality thick flannel.

59. Elizabeth Gryme — L.C.C. Admon. 1714/37

Widow St. Martins 28.6.1714

	£	s	d
Purse and Apparrell	3	0	0
Bills and Bonds	15	0	0
In the Room where she died			
One bad feather Bed Bedstead and Beding	0	10	4
Two Chests	0	4	0
Six Boxes	0	2	0
All Hussements and old Rubbish	1	0	0
	19	16	4

60. Margret Lees — Prob. Inv. 204/153

St. Switterns 20.7.1714

	£	s	d
Apparrell	0	6	0
In ye house			
One table Six chairs and a livery cupboard	0	2	0
A Kettle pot and pans and some small Irons	0	5	0
And a little old Lumber	0	1	2
In ye Chamber			
One bed hangings and bedstead one pillow one bolster one blankett and one Coverlid	0	15	0
One Chest and 2 old Trunks	0	1	6
In ye Garrett			
Ye Table and frame	0	2	0
	1	12	8

APPENDIX I

The population of Lincoln 1642–1721

None of the six censuses made of Lincoln between 1642 and 1721 attempted to count each individual. The Protestation of 1642, the Hearth Tax of 1662, the Compton Census of 1676 and the three episcopal visitations between 1705 and 1721 attempted to count adult men, hearths, adult communicants and families respectively. Converting each of these elements to a global figure for the city's population presents an array of difficulties. A sub-literature has grown up based on each of these sources whereby demographers attempt to wring absolute population figures from sources which are flawed or partial or both. Every one of the censuses was the product of administrators or clerics who would not have found quantification as natural as we do today in an age of questionnaire and statistical returns. Despite the problems of attaining confidence in the absolute population figures derived from such sources they require consideration because they provide good evidence for trends in population as well as indicating in general terms the number of people inhabiting the city.

The first of these censuses, the Protestation of March 1642, was a declaration of loyalty to the King made by all males over the age of eighteen years.[1] Those who were absent or neglected to make their protestation were also listed and included in the Lincoln total. If it is assumed that there were as many women as men aged over eighteen years in the city and that those adult men and women comprised 65% of the population then there were 3,480 inhabitants in the city in 1642.

The Hearth Taxes were levied in the reign of Charles II. Payments were based on the number of hearths in each household but an unknown proportion of the population was exempted because of poverty.[2] An apparently good listing of the city's hearths exists for 1662.[3] The uncertainities as to the number of exempted poor and the difficulties of converting hearths to people in an urban environment makes this listing of small value in estimating population though the return is useful in any attempt to visualise the disposition and style of buildings in the city.

In 1676 Archbishop Compton required that each parish in his southern province of Canterbury should provide a return giving the number of adult Anglican communicants and of those who dissented from the Church of England. At this time some 31.2% of the population was below the age of sixteen years and would not by custom have taken communion.[4] Granted this assumption and adding 150 to provide a replacement for St. Margaret's missing return the population of Lincoln would have been 3,711.[5]

[1] W. F. Webster (ed.) *Protestation Returns 1641/2 Lincolnshire* (Nottingham, 1984) pp. 38–43.
[2] C. Husbands 'Hearth Tax Exemption Figures and the Assessment of Poverty in the Seventeenth Century Economy' in Alldridge *op.cit.* pp. 45–52.
[3] L.A.O. Lincoln City Q.S. 1/1, ff. 115–124.
[4] E. A. Wrigley and R. S. Schofield, *The Population History of England 1541–1871* (London, 1981) p. 570.
[5] *Lincolnshire Notes and Queries Vol. XVI* (Horncastle, 1921) pp. 43–44.

Between 1705/6 and 1721 two bishops of Lincoln, Wake and Gibson, required their clergy to make returns of the number of families in their parishes. Three such returns exist, in part, for 1705/6, 1715/18 and 1721.[6] The returns for 1705/6 and 1715/18 show a significant rise in population, an increase that is confirmed by study of the parish registers of the period. If sixty families are allocated to St. Peter Arches for 1718 there would appear to have been 960 families in Lincoln. Estimating family size, particularly in towns, presents an array of difficulties and the fact that just two vicars or curates were responsible for enumerating seven of the city parishes are arguments for caution in the interpretation of the episcopal visitations.[7] If a multiplier of 4.75 is used for each recorded family it would mean that Lincoln's population was about 4,560.

In so far as these disparate censuses can help towards a definition of Lincoln's population their evidence does suggest an increase from some 3,500 in 1661 to 4,500 in 1714.

[6] R. E. G. Cole (ed.) *Speculum Dioeceseos Lincolniensis 1705–1723* Part I (Lincoln, 1913) pp. 80–83.

[7] P. Laslett 'The history of the family' in P. Laslett (ed.) *Household and Family in Past Time* (Cambridge, 1972) pp. 46–49; cf. R. Wall 'Mean household size in England from printed sources' *ibid.* pp. 159–192, L.A.O. Gibson 5.

GLOSSARY

ALLAM, ALLOM, ALUM - a mineral salt used in dyeing and tanning
ALLAMODE, ALLMOOD - a thin, light, glossy, black silk
ANDIRON - a device for raising logs above hearth level
ANGELICO WATER - drink made fromm the herb angelica
APPLE IRON - implement for cooking apples over an open fire
ARMES - coat of arms of a person, family or corporation

BASS, BAST - plaited rush or straw
BEAM - transverse bar on a set of scales
BEASTCOUPE - a cart or waggon with closed sides
BED COUCH - a day bed
BEDSTEAD, BEDSTED - wooden framework of a bed
BELFERAY, BELLFERAY, BELLFORION, BELFREY - a shed used as a shelter for animals, carts and agricultural implements
BENIS WEIGHTS - see Venice weights
BILLETING, BILLETS - firewood
BINDEY, BINDING, BIRDY - scarf; cloth that secures raw edges of a fabric
BOILING IRON - a grid iron
BOLSTERER - bolster
BONE - whale bone
BOULES - bowls
BRANDRETH - grid iron; rail round opening of a well
BROAD CLOTH - the stoutest and best woollen cloth, a smooth, springy textile with short nap
BUCKET AND BAND - bucket and chain
BUCKRAM - fine linen or cotton fabric
BUCKS - buckskin
BUFFET, BUFFITT STOOL - stool, normally associated with a dining table
BUMBLE - woven bull rushes
BURNT SILVER - silver calcined for use as a drug or pigment
BUTTERY - storeroom for food and drink

CADDAS, CADDOSE - worsted tape used for garters
CALICO - a cotton textile originally East Indian but copied in Norwich from the 1690s
CALLIMANCOE, CALLIM - Flemish woollen stuff with glossy surface and satin twill
CAMBRIC - a fine French linen
CAMBLET, CAMLET - a mixed cloth of wool, hair and silk, much used in upholstery
CANNOPE, CANNAPRE BED - a half headed bed
CANVAS - unbleached cloth made from flax or hemp, used for clothing, cushions, sheets and tapestry
CARPET - a covering used for furniture such as cupboards or tables
CARRAL - a railed in space for children, a play pen
CARRAWAY, CARRIWAY SEEDS - small fruits used to flavour sweetmeats and as a carminative
CASTER - small vessel with perforated top to sprinkle sugar or pepper
CHAFFE, CHAFS, CHAFT BED - a mattress filled with husks of corn

CHAFER, CHAFEIN, CHAFEING, CHAFING DISH – a small container with hot charcoal or coal used to keep food and drink warm
CHAIR TABLE – a chair of which the back folds forwards to make a table resting on the arms of the chair
CHALDER – a chauldron; a dry measure of 4 quarters or 32 bushels
CHEESE PRESS – a compressing device used in the manufacture of cheese
CHENY, CHINY WARE – china
CHIMNEY PEICE – a hood like projection over the fire to catch smoke, often associated with a shelf or mantle
CHIST – chest
CINNAMON, SINIMON – an aromatic spice
CLEVER – cleaver
CLOSE BEATER – clothes beater
CLOSE BED – a box bed, one totally enclosed and entered by sliding doors or shutters
CLOSE PRESS – a cupboard for clothes
CLOSE STOOL – a commode
CLOVES – small bulbs which make up compound bulb of garlic, shallots, etc.
COAT – petticoat
COBIRON – a small version of an andiron, usually with hooks on the front to support spits
COCKS – pipes with taps in them
COIF, COIFE – a close fitting cap
COLLAR, COLLER – horse bridle or halter
COOLER – vessel used to cool wort in brewing process
COPEROSE, COPPERAS, COPPORAS, COPRAS – green sulphate of iron used for ink and dyes
CORDIVANT – leather from Cordova in Spain
CORPORATION LEASE – lease on property held from the Corporation of Lincoln City
COTTON – a wool cloth with a fuzzy nap
COUCH – a day bed
COUCH CHAIR – a backless sofa positioned against a wall
COUNTER – a board or table on which money was counted
COUNTERPAINE – an ornamental top covering for bedclothes
COUPE – a cart
COVERED CHAIR – a chair with padded seat and back
COVERLID – the uppermost covering of bedclothes, a counterpaine or quilt
CRAPE – a light Norfolk cloth
CREDDLE, CREDLE – a cradle
CREDLE IRON – a grating or framework of bars to support vessels near fire
CREEPER – small andirons
CYMNILL – kimnel or tub

DAMASK – twilled, linen fabric woven with patterns, much used for table linen
DEAN AND CHAPTER LEASE – lease of property owned by the Dean and Chapter of Lincoln Cathedral
DIAPER, DIPER, DYAPER – twilled linen cloth with geometric patterns
DIMITIE, DIMITY, DIMOTHY – stout cotton cloth woven with raised stripes
DOG, DOGG – an andiron
DOOR PEICE – curtain before a door
DOVETAIL JOINT – tenon joint in shape of a dove's tail to fit mortice of that shape
DOWLAS – a coarse linen
DRAW BED – an extending bed

DOWN BED – the soft under plumage of birds used to provide the most highly regarded filling for mattresses and pillows
DRAWERS, DRAURE – bolster case
DRAW TABLE – with hinged draw leaves at either end to double the surface
DRESSER – kitchen sideboard
DRESSERBOARD – table for preparing meat and other food
DRESSING BOX – a case for toilet accessories and jewellery with a small mirror inside
DRIPPING, DREEPIN PAN – a pan which collects fat from meat turning on a spit
DRUGGET, DRUGEST, DRUGGIST – a woollen stuff, a mixture of wool and silk or wool and linen
DUBLER – a dish or charger usually of pewter
DUCAP – plainly woven, stout, silk fabric
DUTCH CHAIR – a ladder back chair with a rush seat

EASEY CHAIR – a chair with wings and a sloping or hinged back
EAST DISH – a yeast dish
ELL, ELLN – a measure of length, 45 inches
END – remnants
ENDIRON, EDIRON – see andiron

FABRIC LEASE – lease of a Cathedral property rents of which were allocated to the upkeep of the Cathedral Fabric
FATTS – vats, tubs or casks
FERRET – a stout tape for garters and bindings
FIGURE – an image, statuette or patterned ornament
FILLITING – tape or a head band
FIRDALE, FIRDEAL, FURRDEAL – fir planks
FIRE FORK – for stirring logs on a hearth
FIRE IRON – a large trivet
FIRE IRONS – the set for wood fires included tongs, firefork and brush, for coal fires poker, tongs and shovel
FIRKIN, FIRKEIN – a small cask
FLACKET, FLASKETT – a small bottle or shallow basket
FLINT GLASSES – lead crystal glasses
FLITCH – side of bacon
FLOCK – wool refuse used for stuffing mattresses
FOLD UP BED – a folding bed usually for servants
FOLLOWERS – calves or foals
FOOTPACE – a mat or hearth stone
FORMER – tools which form articles, often the round piece of wood of less than the bore of a musket used to form a cartridge
FRAME, FRAM – legs and cross rails of a table
FRENCH BARLEY – Buckwheat, a coarse wheat used for animal fodder
FRENCH BEDSTEAD – a bed with simple wooden framework with hangings on rods which joined four corner posts
FROG – an oven fork or poker
FURR – furze for kindling a fire

GALBS, GALLS – excresence on trees used to make ink, tannin and in medicine and dyeing
GALLERY – landing or passage
GALLOON, GALLOMS, GALLOWNE, GOOLONIE – narrow woven strip, ribbon or braid of gold, silver or silk for trimming clothes

GALLOWBALKE, GALLYBAWKE – iron bar fixed across chimney on which hooks and cooking vessels were hung
GANTREY – a stand for barrels
GARTH, GIRTH, GIRTS WEB – belt or harness securing the saddle or pack on a horse
GATHERING TUB, GEATHERING TUB – mash tun in which malt is added to brew beer
GIMP, GIMPE, GYMPE – silk worsted or cotton twist with cord or wire running through it
GIRDLE – a belt
GRATE, GRAITE – framework of bars holding fuel which was usually coal
GREDIRON, GRIDIRON – an iron grate with short legs and a long handle used for broiling food over an open fire
GRINDLE STONE – a mill stone
GUILE TUB – brewing vat in which the wort is put to work after yeast has been added

HAIR CLOTH – the fabric usually associated with the straining or drying of malt
HALF HEADED BED – bed with a tester or sometimes a cloth canopy covering the top half of a bed
HANGING – used to describe wall fixed furnishings such as shelves, cupboards or candlesticks
HARDEN – coarse flaxen cloth
HARTSHOME – smelling salts
HEATER, HEETER – metal box with wooden handle which was heated by inserting hot metal strips into the box. It was used to keep smoothing irons hot
HECK – a rack for storage, often for trenchers
HEMPEN – made from hemp
HIGH BED – see French bedstead
HODGHEAD, HOGSHED, HOGGSHEAD, HOGSHEAD – barrel and measure of liquid usually of ale or beer at 54 gallons and of wine at 52.5 gallons
HOLLAND – a fine linen originally made in Holland
HORSE – a bench or plank on which vessels, often beer barrels, were stored: A framework on which clothes were dried
HOUSEHOLDMENTS, HUSHLEMENTS, HUSLEMENTS, HUSSEMENTS – minor and miscellaneous furnishings
HOVEL, HUSSEL – a frame for drying hay or peas sometimes with a thatched cover : an outhouse without sides
HUCKABACK – a coarse linen or cotton fabric with rough surface much used for towelling

INCKLE, INCLE, INKLE – linen tape
INDIGO, INDOCO, INGDIGOE – a blue dye
IRN – iron

JACK – machine with weights and cords that turns spits
JOYNE. JOYNT, JOYNID – applied to furniture, especially stools, with turned legs in the form of columns of balusters

KETTLE, KETTILL – open cooking pot; covered vessel used for boiling and brewing
KIDDERMINSTER – double cloth of two interwoven contrasting colours used for carpets and hangings made at Kidderminster
KIDDES, KIDS – faggots or bundles of fire wood
KILDERKIN, KILDERKINE, KILDREKIN – a cask to hold ale, beer or cider, usually some 18 gallons

KIMLIN - household tub used in salting
KINE, KYNE - a cow
KIT, KITTE - tub
KNOBS - ornamental bosses

LACE LOOP - lace with patterns of small net worked in it
LANDIRON - an andiron
LARDER - service room usually for storage
LARUM WATCH - an 'alarm' watch that rings at a fixed time
LAY METAL, LAY PEWTER - an allayed or alloyed mixture of tin and lead giving a kind of pewter
LEAD - leaden vat used for heating water in the brewing process
LEADING STRINGS - reins to help children learning to walk
LEATHER CHAIR - upholstered in leather
LEAVEN - eleven
LEAVEN, LEVEN, LEVIN, LEVINGE TUB - tub in which dough is fermented
LIVERY CUPBOARD, LIVARY, LIVERAY, LIVERIE, LIVERA, LIVERRAH - a small cupboard for storing food and drink
LOGWOOD - heartwood of an American tree used to give brown and red dyes
LOVE - a think silk stuff much used for mourning garments
LOW BED - either a couch or trundle bed
LUTESTRING - a glossy silk fabric

MACE - spice made from the dried outer covering of nutmeg
MASHTUB - brewing tub in which malt in added to a boiled mixture of malt and water
MATT AND CORD - the support for a mattress on a bedstead formed by cords fastened to the bed frame on which rested woven mats
MATTED CHAIR - rush bottomed chair
MEAL, MEALE - ground grain
MILCH - milk, usually used to describe a milking cow
MOEHAYRE, MOHAIR - an expensive watered silk material
MUSLIN - delicately woven cotton fabric

NATT - mat
NEATS - cattle

OCCIMY - metalic composition imitating the appearance of silver
ONGONS - onions
OSSENBRIDGE - a kind of linen originally made at Osnaburg

PACKING - stuffing
PANILL CLOTH - peice of cloth placed under saddle to prevent horse's back being galled
PANTREE - pantry
PANYERS - paniers
PAPER CHAMBER - room with paper hangings
PAPER WINDOW - window in which oiled paper is used instead of glass
PASTIE, PASTY, PATTY - pie
PATTERNS - wooden sole mounted on an iron ring which is secured to foot or shoe in order to keep clothes off street surface
PECK - measure of dry goods, quarter of a bushel or two gallons
PEELE - flat, long handled shovel with which bread or pies were thrust into a hot oven
PERTIAN - persian

PILLION, PYLION – saddle, pad or cushion for second person riding a horse
PILLOWBEAR, PILLOWBEERE, PILLOWBER, PYLLABEAR – pillow cover
PIT COAL – coal obtained from pits and thus described to distinguish it from charcoal
PLUSH – a kind of cloth with long nap used in rich garments such as footmen's liveries and in saddlery
POOLES – poles, stakes
PORRIGER, PORRINGER, POTTINGER – bowl shaped vessel in metal or earthenware
POSNET, POSNETT, POSSNITT – small metal pot with handle and three feet used for cooking
PRESS, PARESS – a large storage cupboard
PRESS BED – one designed to fold up in the shape of a cupboard
PULLEN – poultry
PUNCH BOWL – bowl in which the ingredients of punch are mixed

QUARTER – a measure of capacity of grain, usually 3 bushells
QUARTRAM – a quartern
QUERNE, QUEARNE – a handmill for grinding grain
QUIE, QUYE – heifer of up to three years or until it has calved
QUILT – top coverlet on a bed
QUIRE – 24 sheets of paper

RACK – storage rack for spits
RACKON HOOKS – chain and hooks or similar apparatus whereby cooking vessels were suspended over the fire
RAFFE – imported timber
RAILS – fence; side of a cart; bars on which to hang things, rails of a staircase
RANGE – an iron grate, usually a coal burner
REDWOOD, REEDWOOD – tropical wood used as a dye
REED WROUGHT CHAIR – rush bottomed and backed chair
RINGS – circular plates of pewter for table use; rings for horse harness
ROSIN – adhesive derived from trees
ROULER – roller
ROWLING HOSE – stockings the tops of which may be rolled up or down legs
RUG, RUGG – a counterpaine, thick woollen stuff
RUNNING HOOKS – see rackon hooks
RUSHIA CHAIR – a chair with leather upholstery
RUSHION, RUSSE LEATHER – a durable leather much used in upholstering chairs, the most prestigious in quality was originally imported from Russia
RUSHEY, RUSHY – made of rushes

SAD – a variety of meanings; usually dark or sober in colour; neutral in colour from the early 1700s; 'solid' when used in reference to metal ware
SADDLE, SATTLE, SETTLE – long wooden bench with arms and a high back
SAFE, SAFFE – a food cupboard with panels of woven hair to allow ventilation of contents
SAGATHA, SAGATHEE, SAGATHY – a cheap and light serge
SALAD OIL – olive oil
SALT – a salt cellar
SASH WINDOW SHUTTS – shutter used to secure or darken a window
SAUCEPAN, SAWSPAN – a small skillet with a long handle used for boiling sauces
SAWCER, SAWIS, SASER – small dish usually of metal to hold condiments or sauces
SCONCE – bracket candlestick fixed to wall with a screen to protect flame
SCOPE – shovel used for spreading loose materials such as barley and malt

SCREELE, SCREELL – a screen used for separating dust and chaff from grain
SCREEN, SCRINE, SKREENE – sieve for separating dust and chaff from grain; a folding, portable partition
SCUMER – see Skimmer
SCUTTLE – dish, platter, trencher
SEACOAL – mineral coal, usually from the Newcastle area
SEARGE – see Serge
SEARSE – a sieve or strainer
SEELED BED – bed with canopy
SEELED CHAIR – chair with canopy
SELLER OF BOTTLES – a case of bottles
SERGE – woollen textile with a twill or diagonal ribbed effect
SETS, SETTES – mould in which substances, for example liquorice, harden; fitting of hair beneath the ground seat of a saddle
SETTLE – see Saddle
SETTLE BED – bed which folds up in the form of a settle
SET WORK CHAIR – chair with tapestry or needlework upholstery
SHALLOON, SHALLOWNE – a light woollen fabric much used for linings
SHAMY SKINS – chamois wash leather
SHOPBOARD – a counter or table on which shop business was transacted or goods displayed
SIVE – sieve
SKELLETT, SKELLITE, SKELLIT – metal cooking utensil with three or four feet and a long handle
SKEP, SKIP – basket or hamper
SKIMMER, SKUMER – a ladle to remove the top liquid from a cooking vessel or an iron to take ash from a fire
SLICE – fire shovel particularly used to remove ashes from a baking oven
SMALL BEER – weak beer
SMOOTHING IRON – a flat iron
SNUFFER – an instrument for putting out candles
SOA, SOE – a large tub
SPANISH TABLE – a portable table that folds up
STAND – a base on which utensils such as casks can stand; item of furniture on which candlesticks and ornaments were placed
STANDARD – a standard measure such as a measuring rod or vessel
STANDING BED – a substantial bed with high head and foot-ends connected by a tester with cloth over it.
STIRRUPS – a footless stocking having a strap that passes under the foot
STOCK – a hive of bees
STONE BLEW – compound of indigo and starch used by laundresses
STOOPS – posts and pillars
STOUPE – flagon; gate post
STOVE – a grate or a footwarmer burning charcoal
STRIKE – a measure of half a bushel or a container for such a quantity
STUFF – lightweight woollen cloth or mixtures of worsted and silk, a speciality of Norwich in printed, dyed and patterned forms
SUTE – set of brasses
SWEETMEATS – confectionery such as sugared nuts, fruit flavoured sugar concoctions and pasties
SWEET POWDER – perfumed powder used as a cosmetic

TABBIE, TABY – a watered silk

TABLE BASKET – see Voider
TABLE CUBBERT, TABLE CUPBOARD – table with a cupboard in it
TAFFETA, TAFFITIE – silk ribbon with different colours for warp and weft; a fine plain woven silk
TALLOW – animal fat used for making candles, soap and in dressing leather
TANKER – tankard
TASTER – small, shallow cup, often silver, used for tasting wines
TEARCE, TEARSE – cask holding a third of a pipe of wine, some 42 gallons
TEE-TABLE – table with a tray type top
TEMES, TEMS, TEMSSES – a sieve
THRALL – stands for beer barrels
TICK, TICKING – the strong linen which provided covers for pillows, bolsters and mattresses
TRAIN OIL – made from whale blubber and used by clothiers and soap makers
TRENCHER, TRENCHERT, TRENSHER – wooden plate
TROY WEIGHTS – a system of weights used for precious metals
TRUCKLE, TRUCKELL, TRUNDEL, TRUNDLE – simple bedstead mounted on wheels so that it could be stored under the main bed in the room
TUMBRILL – counterpoise for raising a well bucket; cart with a backward tilting body for emptying load
TUNN – a measure of various commodities, 2,000 or 2,440lbs, eight chests of tobacco, two pipes of wine
TURF – block of peat
TURKEY WORK – tapestry worked upholstery, much used for chairs
TWILT, TWILST – bed covering to twill cloth

UDARD – under
UNDERBECK – vessel placed below mash tub to receive raw wort

VALLANCE, VALLANTS, VALLENCE, VALLENTS, VALLIANS – deep frill usually of bed furnishings either from top structure or from mattress level to floor
VARDER – see Voider
VAT – large cask or cistern
VENICE WEIGHTS – weights for a Roman beam
VIOLL – musical instrument with 5–7 strings played by a bow
VOLURE – velvet
VOIDER, VOYDER – basket or tray used for clearing the table after a meal

WAINE, WAYNE – large, open cart
WAINSCOTE – good quality, imported oak; chair or furniture with wood panelling
WANDED CHAIR – chair made of wickerwork or with wickerwork seat and back
WASHBALL – a ball of soap
WHEELE – a spinning wheel
WHISKET – basket
WINDOW FRAME – see Window Grate
WINDOW GRATE – framework of bar preventing entry
WORSTED – cloth made from long stapled wool

YARDWAND – a measuring rod

INDEX OF PERSONS AND PLACES

A name given in heavy type indictes that the inventory of this person is printed. Names of parishes and minor towns are in Lincolnshire unless otherwise stated. References to footnotes are indicated by the addition of the letter n.

INDEX OF SUBJECTS